RESEARCH IN LAW AND ECONOMICS

Volume 1 • 1979

BOARD OF REFEREES

RESEARCH IN LAW AND ECONOMICS

A Research Annual

Editor: RICHARD O. ZERBE, JR.
  SMT Program and Department of Economics
  University of Washington

VOLUME 1 • 1979

Ai JAI PRESS INC.
Greenwich, Connecticut

CONTENTS

FOREWORD

Research in Law and Economics addresses the rapidly growing area of economics and law, an area which began at the University of Chicago but which has broadened remarkably. A result of this growth is the need for the publication of articles longer than is usual for journals. *Research in Law and Economics* seeks to meet this need, not by limiting itself to longer articles but by its willingness to publish results of major research which are best presented at length. By combining this service with the commissioning of a substantial number of articles, my hope is to stimulate new work and an even greater interest in law and economics.

The range of articles is quite broad and is representative of the general scope of the book. Although some of the articles are mathematical, an attempt is made to present the results so that they are broadly accessible.

Two articles, one by Carroll and Gaston and one by White, address the question of occupational licensing which has recently generated great legal interest. Most of the economic analysis of licensing hinges on whether

vii

such licensing does in fact improve quality and whether the improvement in quality is worth the costs. Carroll and Gaston provide a rather imaginative measure of quality in the real estate market which answers in the negative the question about whether or not quality is increased. This answer of course obviates the need for the second question concerning cost, at least in the real estate market.

The typical economic view is that occupations themselves seek licensure. White shows that it is more complicated than this. Bureaucrats and crusaders play a major role in getting licensure, acting apparently as agents neither of consumers nor of the occupation. White also shows that licensing which seems reasonable when viewed as a short-term phenomenon may not be reasonable when a broader view is taken.

Jordan, with his usual care, exploits the regulatory insights available from a comparison of U.S. and Canadian airline regulation. The results of the comparison are generally consistent with a producer-protection cartel hypothesis. The regulatory similarities of Canadian and American airlines suggest, at the least, a common rationale. I would hope the considerable quantity of new data produced by Jordan will stimulate further work in this area.

Miller, in a useful piece, is able to show that the bothersome possibility of loss-equilibrium for airline markets is not very credible. This more rigorous analysis of the possibility of "destructive competition" is reassuring. Since this paper in draft form served to vitiate the airline's argument for capacity-limiting agreements before the CAB Board, its usefulness is both practical and scholarly.

Friedlaender and de Neufville attempt to explain from the perspective of political economy the type of regulatory inefficiencies noted by Jordan. They note that much of transportation policy seems explainable when the following are incorporated as part of the goals of policy makers: fairness, support of rural and agricultural interests, industry stability.

Kormendi's paper speaks to important recent work in the externality literature. A series of recent papers, the best known of which is probably by Groves and Ledyard (1977), provides an elegant tax solution to the free-rider, public goods problem. These taxes purport to solve this problem by making it profitable for everyone to tell the truth. Kormendi shows that (1) the question of what to do with the taxes collected, (2) the problem of finding a cost allocation, and (3) the problem of excluding undesirable projects essentially reintroduce the types of efficiency problem the tax was devised to eliminate. The fact that the size of the taxes may be large in relation to the net surplus increases the probability of inefficiency.

Clarkson and Tollison begin the somewhat novel task of considering government advertising. Galbraith uses the existence of advertising by the private sector for perhaps the strongest part of his argument that there is a production imbalance toward the private sector. The effort by Clarkson and Tollison tends to eliminate the basis for this argument by documenting the substantial government advertising. They go further and suggest that there is a link between advertising and monopoly in government.

Goldberg continues here his important work, viewing regulation as a set of administrative contracts. In this article he focuses on a particular "contractual" question, the conditions under which a service can be eliminated. By analyzing in detail the considerations relevant to this question, Goldberg raises further questions which economists are only beginning to examine concerning the definition of rights in a dynamic society.

Samuels and Mercuro are among the few writers who, like Goldberg, are examining these questions. In the first part of a two-part article, they consider the role of the compensation principle in society. In an extensive and erudite discussion, they show *inter alia res* that (1) by no means are losses compensated, (2) it is impossible that they should be, (3) the law seems conflicting, and (4) the protection of the institution of private property, not of particular property rights, is the function of the compensation principle. This sort of exercise in jurisprudence by economists serves to explain the legal system for both lawyers and economists.

Mann's article constitutes a challenge for economists to quantify the dynamic functional relationships in the regulatory environment. Mann demonstrates the necessity of developing these "variable linkages" before economists can provide policy prescriptions or even make predictions.

This point is illustrated in a concrete way by McNicol's paper. McNicol shows that traditional prescriptions for peak load pricing may be wrong when considered in the context of institutional behavior. Indeed, McNicol shows that when the behavior model is an A-J Model extended to account for periodic shifts in the level of demand and price discrimination, the traditional peak load prescription is in fact wrong. Clearly, Mann and McNicol in their separate papers establish the importance for regulatory policy of (1) determining what instruments actually are available to regulatory agencies, (2) determining agency behavior, and (3) taking into account both instruments and behavior in economic models.

Richard O. Zerbe, Jr.
Editor

STATE OCCUPATIONAL LICENSING PROVISIONS AND QUALITY OF SERVICE: THE REAL ESTATE BUSINESS

Sidney L. Carroll, UNIVERSITY OF TENNESSEE, KNOXVILLE

Robert J. Gaston, UNIVERSITY OF TENNESSEE, KNOXVILLE

Occupational licensing, imposed by states with the rationale of insuring a minimum of consumer safety, can also result in restricted numbers of occupational practitioners and higher prices. This restriction can also result in a possible lower quality level of services received by consumers. Some empirical evidence of the net effect of the two quality effects is the objective of this paper. This study, using average amount of time a house for sale is vacant and unsold as a measure of net quality of real estate agent service, finds an adverse effect of real estate broker licensing on the quality of consumer received services.

Research in Law and Economics, Vol. 1, pp. 1–13.
ISBN: 0–89232–028–1.

I INTRODUCTION

State occupational licensing of professions and other occupations is widespread in the United States. The universally cited rationale for licensing is that imperfect consumer knowledge (prohibitive information costs) compels the states to impose standards of performance on occupations through the issuance of licenses to operate only after proof of the attainment of certain criteria, such as educational levels, tests passed, prior occupational experience. Only through a licensing procedure, it is publicly argued, can a minimum quality of service be guaranteed the citizen.

While such desirable quality effects are certainly possible—though hard to measure—it is also true that licensing is a restrictive device which quantitatively can result in curtailed numbers of practitioners and increased rates of income for the licensees.

Restrictive licensing can also result in *declines* in the *quality* of received service in that there may be (1) self-substitution of inferior products and/or services; for example, home wiring with extension cords compared to properly done electrical work; (2) decreases in the average per capita service time rendered; for example, short, hurried, delayed office visits with a harried physician; (3) differential geographic availability as numbers are reduced *and* the remaining members of the profession can choose their locations with more discretion, such as doctor shortages in rural areas; and (4) increased waiting time for provision of a service where delay in service entails expense for the buyers; an illustration would be long delays in selling goods by brokers which cause elevated inventory costs.[1]

Economists have periodically investigated the quantitative effects of licensing provisions; that is, they have attempted with some successes to measure price increases and quantity decreases resulting from licensing restrictions; Benham (2), Friedman and Kuznets (4), Maurizi (5), and Moore (6). By contrast they have found measurement of the qualitative effects to be a much less tractable problem. This paper approaches the quality of service effects from two angles.

Section II is an investigation of the factors which can be isolated as having significant impacts on the state licensing board examination pass rates for real estate brokers. This is important because it is claimed by proponents of licensing examinations that restrictions such as prior experience and the exams themselves serve as a seine to eliminate less qualified applicants. Some economists have contended that the primary determinant of pass rates is the degree of restrictiveness on entry desired by licensing officials. The relative strength of these determinants of pass rates, then, are of interest to an evaluation of the efficacy of the licensing process as a quality control on those who *get* licensed.

Second and possibly of greater interest is the attempt in Section III to determine the effect of various restrictive devices on a proxy measure for quality of service received by customers of real estate brokers. Here it is well to remember that examination pass rates are but one in an extensive arsenal of weapons available to licensing boards in their efforts to control numbers and "qualities" of practitioners. Thus there are educational, residence, experience, test scores, sponsorship and many other possible hurdles which can be erected to increase the difficulty of obtaining a license. As for quality, it can only be gauged through proxies; the appropriate quality proxy or proxies must be chosen with a judicious eye to both common sense and data availability. There will never be the ideal proxy for quality of service, but this should not deter attempts to do the best one can.

Section IV goes further and recognizes that while pass rates and quality measures can fruitfully be discussed separately, they are in reality jointly determined. Thus a simultaneous equation system is formulated in that section in order to recognize this interdependence. Section V then sums up.

II PASS RATES ON LICENSING TESTS

Ideally in occupational licensing "... the test is the objective standard that separates the competent practitioner from the one who may not be trusted to function properly and safely," according to Shimberg (8), p. 193. Although there are multitudinous difficulties in comparing interstate test results, one can make some general statements as to the efficacy of tests as true quality screening instruments. For instance, the higher the educational requirements the higher the pass rate; or, pass rates should be positively related to experience requirements.

If, on the other hand, pass rates are manipulated up or down as a restrictiveness tool, one would expect pass rates to vary consistently in response to economic factors. Specifically, in the long run, licensure boards would be seen decreasing pass rates of broker applicants in order to protect relatively high incomes from being eroded by new entrants into the occupation. That is, high incomes would swell the numbers of applicants and pass rates would be reduced to keep numbers down.[2] Further, there might even be some simple per capita stock depressant on the pass rate, unrelated to the income variable.

To test the theses stated above, which are by no means mutually exclusive, the simple basic structural form used is

$$X_1 = a + bX_2 + cX_3 + dX_4 + eX_5 \tag{1}$$

where the variable definitions are[3]

X_1 : licensure examination *pass rate for broker applicants*, 1970;
X_2 : *education* classification: a binary variable which takes the value of 1
    if the licensure board required any schooling, whether professional

Table 1. Ordinary Least Square Estimates of Brokers' Pass Rates Regressed
on Education, Experience, Agents' Incomes and Number of Real Estate
Agent Licenses.

X_1	Intercept	X_2 Education	X_3 Experience	Median earnings all earners	Total licenses in effect per capita
Brokers'	1.426***	0.158***	26.731	−0.079***	−7.112
pass rates	(0.233)	(0.053)	(58.484)	(0.022)	(12.785)
	t = 6.119	t = 2.971	t = 0.457	t = −3.684	t = −0.556

Note: Number of observations: 37 $R^2 = .386$ $F = 5.024$***
***Significant at the 1% level
Source: For detail on these and other data see the Appendix.

or general, prior to being eligible to take the broker licensing examination in 1970, and takes a value of 0 if not;

X_3 : experience classification: a binary variable which takes the value
1000 (for scale purposes) if the licensure board required of the broker
applicant any amount of apprenticeship or experience in the occupation or in a related occupation in 1970, and equals 0 if not;

X_4 : the median earnings of all persons (all earners) who reported to the
U.S. Census Bureau that their occupations were "real estate agent"
in 1969;[4]

X_5 : per capita total licenses in effect.

Table 1 gives the results. Both views of licensing tests seem to have some
validity. Pass rates do vary positively and significantly with education so
that, to the extent that the ability to leap educational hurdles indicates
higher "quality" potential practitioners, the tests do reflect it. Experience,
however, while receiving a positive sign shows no significant effect. As for
the restrictiveness variables, median income is quite highly negatively
significant while the stock variable has the anticipated sign but is not significant. To conclude, pass rate investigation seems to reveal both the "quality"
control and income protection (restrictiveness) roles of licensing strongly
at work.[5]

III THE QUALITY OF REAL ESTATE
SERVICES RECEIVED

Even conceptualizing quantitative proxies for the average level of quality of
service received by the public from occupational groups is difficult. Often
the proxies which first suggest themselves turn out to be various forms of
supply or price information. It is same with many "measures" of real estate
quality; such as commissions, incomes, and density of agents in the popu-

lation. Some obvious candidates for a quality proxy measure are simply not available; such as self-sold vs. realtor-sold residences.

There is at least one important element in the service rendered to the customers by real estate agents that profoundly affects consumers' perceptions of the "worth" of that service. That element is the quickness of the sale. After a point in time, the longer one's property remains unsold the less gratified one becomes.[6] Evidence is available cross-sectionally on the duration of vacant-for-sale housing by state. It is further broken down into rural and urban property within states. Specifically, the Census of Housing gives the number and median value of single-family dwellings vacant and for sale for (1) less than two months, (2) two to six months and (3) more than six months in 1970.

Some econometric experimentation with "fitting" the variables showed the best of these measures to be the third one. Further, six months' vacancy seems likely to be long enough to have avoided "too quick" a sale. So the dependent variable representing the quality of real estate housing is the proportion of all vacant housing units which have been on the market for more than six months in 1970. With these quality considerations in mind, six more variables are introduced.

X_6 : the *proportion of vacant housing units located in urban areas*, which stayed on the market for more than six months during 1970;

X_7 : the *proportion of vacant housing units located in rural areas*, which stayed on the market for more than six months during 1970;

X_8 : the *median value* of vacant housing units located in *urban* areas in 1970, \$10,000's;

X_9 : the *median value* of vacant housing units located in *rural* areas in 1970, \$10,000's;

X_{10} : the *proportion of all vacant housing units* which were on the market for more than six months during 1970;

X_{11} : the weighted *median value of all* vacant housing units in 1970, \$10,000's.

A first approach to a quality equation[7] is

$$X_{10} = a + bX_1 + cX_5 + dX_2 + eX_3 + fX_{11} + gX_{11}^2 \qquad (2)$$

X_1 (brokers' pass rates), X_2 (education), X_3 (experience), and X_5 (total licenses per capita) represent policy choice variables by the state licensing authorities. As such, if stricter licensing hurts quality, one expects $b < 0$; $c < 0$; $d > 0$; $e > 0$; or verbally, quality of service will be lower (vacancies higher) the lower the pass rate, the less people are licensed (per capita) in a state, the higher the educational standards and the more experience required for a license. If stricter licensing helps quality of service, just the reverse signs are anticipated. Variables X_{11} and X_{11}^2 represent the reasoning that

Table 2. Ordinary Least Squares Estimations of the Vacancy Ratio for All Houses on Brokers' Pass Rates, Total Licenses in Effect, Education, Experience and Median Value of All Vacant Houses.

X_{10}	Intercept.	X_1 Brokers' pass rates	X_5 Licenses per capita	X_2 Education	X_3 Experience	X_{11} Median value all houses	X_{11}^2 Median value all houses; squared
Vacancy Ratio All =	0.805*** (0.094) t = 8.526	−0.062 (0.081) t = −0.761	−12.526* (6.727) t = −1.862	0.021 (0.028) t = 0.765	12.262 (30.225) t = 0.406	−0.356*** (0.091) t = −3.901	0.060** (0.022) t = 2.734

Note: $R^2 = .621$ F = 8.199***
***Significant at the 1% level
**Significant at the 5% level
*Significant at the 10% level
Source: For detail on these and other data see the Appendix.

6

Table 3. Seemingly Unrelated Regressions of the Percentages of Vacant Houses in *Urban and Rural Areas*, Vacant 6 Months or Longer, on Brokers' Pass Rates, Total Licenses in Effect, Education, Experience and Median Value of Vacant Houses, Urban and Rural.

	Intercept	X_1 Brokers' pass rates	X_5 Licenses per capita	X_2 Education	X_3 Experience	X_8 Median value urban	X_8^2 Median value urban; squared	X_9 Median value rural	X_9^2 Median value rural; squared
X_6; Vacancy Ratio, Urban =	0.711*** (0.098) t = 7.225	−0.106 (0.067) t = −1.577	−8.636* (4.966) t = −1.739	0.013 (0.022) t = 0.570	0.764 (0.023) t = 0.033	−0.243*** (0.073) t = −3.331	0.029* (0.015) t = 1.97		
X_7; Vacancy Ratio, Rural =	0.920*** (0.062) t = 14.869	−0.115 (0.0691) t = −1.664	−8.514 (5.936) t = −1.434	0.0227 (0.0252) t = 0.902	27.786 (27.266) t = 1.019			−0.430*** (0.065) t = −6.606	0.090*** (0.019) t = 4.841

Note: Number of observations = 37
***Significant at the 1% level
*Significant at the 10% level
Source: For detail on these and other data see the Appendix.

7

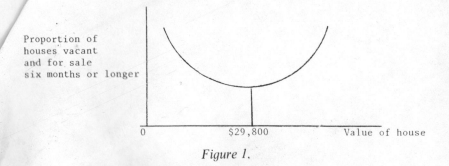

Proportion of
houses vacant
and for sale
six months or longer

0          $29,800   Value of house

Figure 1.

rapidity of housing sales declines as the market becomes smaller (thinner) at both ends of the housing value continuum. In other words, turnover time between owners decreases from low housing values down to a minimum and then increases again as the value of housing rises. This is depicted in the figure below. Here the smallest percentage of houses vacant and for sale six months or longer is reached for houses valued at approximately $29,800.[8] Therefore, one expects, regardless of licensing effect, $f < 0, g > 0$.

Table 2 gives results for this regression. All four signs agree with the adverse effects hypotheses, while the effect of X_5 (total licenses per capita) is significant at the 10 percent level and the intercept; X_{11} and X_{11}^2 (median value of all vacant housing) are significant at the one percent level.[9] In Table 3 the samples are divided into urban and rural sets and the same structure runs as a seemingly unrelated regression system. There are no surprises here, but brokers' pass rates seem to edge up in importance. The results are robust with respect to signs.

IV PASS RATES AND QUALITY AS A SYSTEM

If one has kept a careful econometric eye out on Sections II and III, it has become clear that if Eq. (1) is correct then Eq. (2) and others like it (such as those reported in Table 3) are misspecified because brokers' test pass rates, X_1, included as an exogenous variable in Eq. (2), should be treated as endogenous as is done in Eq. (1). To attempt to rectify this shortcoming the following three equation recursive system has been formulated.

$$X_6 = f(X_1, X_5, X_2, X_3, X_8) \tag{3}$$

$$X_7 = g(X_1, X_5, X_2, X_3, X_9) \tag{4}$$

$$X_1 = h(X_5, X_4, X_2, X_3) \tag{5}$$

Each equation was linear in the variables, plus Eq. (3) and (4), respectively, included X_8^2 and X_9^2 as variables (linearly).[10]

Results of the three-stage least squares estimation are shown in Table 4.

Table 4. Three Stage Squares Estimates† of the Vacancy Ratio Urban and Rural, Brokers' Examination Pass Rate on Education, Experience, Median Value of Urban and Rural Houses, Median Earnings of Real Estate Agents, and Number of Licenses in Effect.

	Intercept	X_1 Brokers' pass rates	X_5 Licenses per capita	X_4 Median earnings all agents	X_2 Education	X_3 Experience	X_8 Median value urban	X_8^2 Median value urban; squared	X_9 Median value, rural	X_9^2 Median value rural; squared
Vacancy Ratio, Urban =	0.650*** (0.151) t = 4.302	−0.041 (0.140) t = −0.296	−9.275* (5.129) t = −1.808		0.005 (0.027) t = 0.183	−0.001 (0.023) t = −0.030	−0.229*** (0.079) t = −2.882	0.029* (0.015) t = 1.908		
Vacancy Ratio, Rural =	1.088*** (0.081) t = 13.421	−0.399*** (0.110) t = −3.62	−7.741 (6.351) t = −1.219		0.059* (0.029) t = 2.031	0.033 (0.029) t = 1.141			−0.424*** (0.066) t = −6.434	0.085*** (0.019) t = 4.482
Brokers' Pass rate =	1.291*** (0.194) t = 6.641		−5.878 (11.0464) t = −0.532	−0.067*** (0.018) t = −3.713	0.153*** (0.046) t = 3.341	0.026 (0.051) t = 0.507				

Note: Number of Observations = 37

* Significant at the 10% level

*** Significant at the 1% level

† Under certain circumstances ordinary least squares estimates would "be adequate," leading to consistent, unbiased and asymptotically efficient estimates. However, comparison of estimates results (instrumental ordinary least squares and three stage least squares) showed the latter to be more efficient because of considerable cross-talk between error terms in the equation; i.e, the variance-covariance matrix of the disturbance terms exhibited definite nonzero off-diagonal elements.

Source: For detail on these and other data see the Appendix.

All signs remain consistent with previous results. However, some interesting new findings are evident. The effect of the density variable (licenses per capita) becomes more pronounced in urban areas, while the education variable slides up in rural areas and pass rates are highly significant and negative there.[11] Without any claim to certitude it could be argued that stiffer educational requirements for licenses tend to erode rural real estate service quality much more than in urban areas.[12] On the other hand, constraints on per capita number of brokers tend to affect urban results.

V SUMMARY AND CONCLUSIONS

The effects of real estate broker licensing activities on test pass rates and on quality of real estate services received by the public seem to conform strikingly well to restrictive economic theoretic expectations. When pass rates and service quality (measured inversely by duration of vacancy before sale) are examined systematically, the following statements are supported: (1) in states where overall numbers of brokers per capita are low, *urban* service quality suffers; (2) where either pass rates are depressed by licensing authorities or where there are specified prior educational requirements, the result is lower quality service in *rural* areas; (3) test pass rates are enhanced by the imposition of educational minimum requirements and are lower when the brokers' incomes are higher.

In addition to the above statements which contain some statistical significance, the signs of all variables in every regression were those predicted by the view of licensing as restrictive and harmful to service in contradistinction to the licensing proponents' claims to benevolence.

These conclusions stated above are consistent with the statistical evidence based upon the empirical measures used. It must be clearly borne in mind that the actual statistical measures fall far short of ideal and are themselves open to alternative interpretations as discussed in various footnotes.

FOOTNOTES

The authors, listed alphabetically, are both at the University of Tennessee, Knoxville, and are, respectively, associate and assistant professors of economics.

This research was conducted with the support of National Science Foundation Grant No. APR75–16792. Any opinions, findings, conclusions or recommendations expressed in this publication are those of the authors and do not necessarily reflect the views of the National Science Foundation. We very much appreciate George Choksy's research assistance and the stimulating comments of an anonymous referee and the editor. However, if there are errors, none but the authors may be held responsible.

1. It is suggested that legislative underestimate of these feedback effects and others has resulted in overregulation; see Richard O. Zerbe and N. Urban (9).

2. Obviously causation can run both ways: such as low pass rates cause smaller

numbers, which elevate incomes—but this is a result over time rather than cross-sectionally. Other scenarios can be envisioned. For example, low incomes might lead to low pass rates in an attempt to raise incomes; or given brokerage fees and housing prices lower turnover results in lower brokers' incomes. These lower incomes could result in fewer examination applicants and a higher pass rate, thus producing a negative correlation between housing turnover and exam pass rates. However, in *equilibrium*, if pass rates are manipulated to control incomes in some states and not in others, high incomes and low pass rates will coincide. Untestable with available data but also possible is that higher incomes might be associated with harder examinations. Here we retain the simple restrictiveness hypothesis which is given some additional empirical support in A. Maurizi (5). Maurizi finds that increased excess demand for entry into an occupation is associated with low entrance examination pass rates for most occupations tested. The present authors, using 1970 data (compared to 1940 and 1950 data used by Maurizi), find the same relationship with strengthened results. See Carroll and Gaston (3). Elton Rayack (7) has found that pass rates for a variety of non-professional occupations are inversely correlated with the unemployment rate of the occupation. It is also possible that successful manipulation of pass rates or other licensing requirements resulting in excessive rents to licensees could induce its own long run constraints in the form of government intervention and/or competition from a close substitute. But there seems little or no consistent evidence to support this conjecture.

3. The actual data sample varies with each table but the basic set of data is a cross-section of U.S. state experience during 1970.

4. Unavailability of separate income data for broker and salesman prevent using the income of brokers only in the following estimates. Additional estimates were made using the incomes of only full-time brokers and salespersons and the results did not differ materially from those presented here for all earners. The variable "earnings of all earners" was retained for its conceptual consistency with the stock of licenses variable which includes both full and part-time earners.

5. A stepwise regression procedure reveals that agent's income is the largest contribution to R^2 accounting for 0.20 of the total, the education measure is of secondary "importance" but adding a substantial 0.17 to total R^2. Experience and total licenses in effect together add only a marginal 0.01. Increased income associated with low examination pass rates does not necessarily imply that monopoly rents are being received by all current suppliers after account is taken of increased entry costs paid by those who gain licenses after licensing or an increase in its restrictions. Indeed, as pointed out by Simon Rottenberg ("Economics of Occupational Licensing" in *Aspects of Labor Economics*, Universities-NBER, 1962), in equilibrium the return in all occupations is the same after entry restriction. Even though incomes are higher in the regulated occupation so are costs. It follows then that the elimination or relaxation of entry restrictions could impose a capital loss on those supplies not earning capital rents and such a move may not result in a rise in social efficiency (see G. Tullock, "The Transitional Gains Trap," *Bell Journal of Economics*, Vol. 6, No. 2, Autumn 1975).

6. Market liquidity, i.e., the speed and price of the sale, is a more desirable proxy but data on the spread between real estate asking price and actual sales price is not available. When only duration is considered the relationship is probably nonlinear since "too quick" a sale, sacrificing price, is non-optimum as well as "too long" a duration of waiting. See (1), pp. 27–53.

In general, we want to measure not just quality but quality per unit price when quality includes a measure of consumer risk reduction and where price includes search costs. A low housing turnover rate could be representative of higher quality per unit price if it is associated with lower brokerage fees. No systematic data is available cross-sectionally on real estate brokerage fees to our knowledge and we suspect that if it were it would be unlikely that low fees and low turnover would be coincident. Nevertheless, information on fees would strengthen our use of lower housing turnover rates as a proxy for lower quality service.

7. Ideally, a control measure is desired for the variance of quality of the location (e.g., taxes, public services, crime rate, air quality, etc.). Again, a satisfactory measure of this variable is unavailable and constructing one itself could constitute an entire research project.

8. This amount is derived from the equation estimated in Table 2.

9. These results are open to alternative hypotheses, for example, low numbers of brokers per capita could reflect that where houses are slow to turn over the demand for brokers is low. This reverse causation interpretation is further discussed in terms of brokers' incomes in footnote 2.

10. Unavailability of licenses in effect by the urban-rural breakdown means there is some misspecification in the system. However, the seemingly unrelated regressions run, without that variable, leave the other results essentially unchanged.

11. Licenses in effect are still not separated by urban or rural categories.

12. This result is not surprising since (1) as the number of brokers falls, locational preferences can be pursued more cheaply, and (2) as more education is required, the sense of "professionalism" and the desire of urban-suburban amenities are likely to increase in value to the successful licensees'. This certainly seems to be true in other occupations, most notably physicians.

APPENDIX

The variable definitions and sources are;

X_1: *Brokers' Pass Rate*; licensure examination pass rates for applicants for the broker's license, 1970; the source was the National Association of Real Estate License Law Officials, 505–6 Grant Building, Pittsburgh, Pennsylvania, 15219.

X_2: *Education*; a binary variable; $X_2 = 1$ if the licensure board required more than an 8th grade secondary education level of either the salesperson or broker applicants, or if the board required 30 or more hours of curriculum in a real estate school, for either the salesperson or broker applicants; $X_2 = 0$ otherwise. The source was a questionnaire called "State Licensing of Occupations and Professions" hereafter called Questionnaire, which was circulated by the University of Tennessee State Occupational Licensing Project.

X_3: *Experience*; a binary variable; $X_3 = 1000$ (for scale purposes) if the licensure board required of the broker's license applicant any amount of apprenticeship with a broker, or experience in the occupation or in a related occupation in 1970, $X_3 = 0$ otherwise. The source was the Questionnaire.

X_4: *Median Earnings, All Earners*; the median earnings of all persons who reported to the U.S. Census Bureau that their occupations were "real estate agent" in 1969; the source was the 1970 *U.S. Census of the Population*, tables 175–176.

X_5: *Licenses Per Capita*; the total number of real estate agent licenses per capita in effect in 1970; the source was the Questionnaire.

X_6: *Vacancy Ratio, Urban*; that proportion of vacant housing units located in urban areas, which stayed on the market for more than six months during 1970; the source was the 1970 *U.S. Census of Housing; Housing Characteristics for States, Cities, and Counties*, table 4.

X_7: *Vacancy Ratio. Rural*; that proportion of vacant housing units located in rural areas, which stayed on the market for more than six months during 1970; the source was the 1970 *U.S. Census of Housing; Housing Characteristics for States, C. es, and Counties,* table 4.

X_8: *Median Value, Urban*; the median value of vacant for sale housing units located in urban areas in 1970, in $10,000's; the source was the *1970 U.S. Census of Housing; Housing Characteristics for States, Cities, and Counties,* table 4.

X_9: *Median Value, Rural*; the median value of vacant for sale housing units located in rural areas in 1970, in $10,000's; the source was the *1970 U.S. Census of Housing; Characteristics for States, Cities, and Counties,* table 4.

X_{10}: *Vacancy Ratio, All*; that proportion of all vacant housing units which stayed on the market for more than 6 months during 1970; the source was the *1970 U.S. Census of Housing; Housing Characteristics for States, Cities, and Counties,* table 4.

X_{11}: *Median Value, All*; the weighted median value of all vacant for sale housing units in 1970, in $10,000's; the source was the *1970 U.S. Census of Housing; Housing Characteristics for States, Cities, and Counties,* table 4.

REFERENCES

1. Alchian, A. A. (1970) "Information Costs, Pricing and Resource Unemployment," in E. Phelps *et al.*, eds., *Macroeconomic Foundations of Employment and Inflation Theory,* New York, Norton, pp. 27–53.
2. Benham, Lee. (October 1972) "The Effect of Advertising on the Price of Eyeglasses," *Journal of Law and Economics,* Vol. 15: 337–352.
3. Carroll, Sidney L., and Gaston, Robert J. (1977) "Pass Rates as Barriers to Occupational Entry," unpublished paper, Department of Economics, University of Tennessee, Knoxville.
4. Friedman, M., and Kuznets, S. (1945) *Income From Independent Professional Practice,* New York, National Bureau of Economic Research.
5. Maurizi, A. (March 1974) "Occupational Licensing and the Public Interest," *Journal of Political Economy,* Vol. 82: 399.
6. Moore, T. G. (October 1961) "The Purpose of Licensing," *Journal of Law and Economics,* Vol. 4: 93–117.
7. Rayack, E. "An Economic Analysis of Occupational Licensure," unpublished manuscript, U.S. Department of Labor Grant No. 98–02–6851.
8. Shimberg, L. B., *et al.* (1972) *Occupational Licensing: Practices and Policies,* Washington, D.C., Public Affairs Press.
9. Zerbe, Richard O., and Urban, N. "Towards a Public Interest Theory of Regulation," forthcoming, National Bureau of Economic Research conference volume.

DYNAMIC ELEMENTS OF REGULATION: THE CASE OF OCCUPATIONAL LICENSURE

William D. White, UNIVERSITY OF ILLINOIS
AT CHICAGO CIRCLE

Attempts to analyze the "market" for regulation have focused mainly on the process by which regulation is introduced. The purpose of this paper is to suggest that once regulation is introduced, it may also have dynamic effects on its own supply and demand. For example, there may be "ratchet" effects which make it more difficult to remove regulation than to prevent it from being introduced to begin with. The introduction of regulation may also have "escalator" effects which create a demand for still more regulation. These effects are illustrated for the case of occupational licensure. The cases examined also indicate that the reasons for the origins of regulation may be more complex than existing theories indicate.

Research in Law and Economics, Vol. 1, pp. 15–33.
Copyright © 1979 by JAI Press, Inc.,
All rights of reproduction in any form reserved.
ISBN: 0–89232–028–1.

Economists have long been interested in the economic impact of regulation. Recently, there has also been a growing interest in the political economy of regulation and the process of institutional change by which regulations are introduced. Traditionally in neoclassical economics, the government has been treated as a benevolent, if sometimes misguided body which seeks to maximize social welfare.[1] In this type of model, the government imposes regulations because it believes, rightly or wrongly, that these regulations will increase allocative efficiency. More recently, economists have turned to economic models of political behavior like those developed Downs (6), and Buchanan and Tullock (4) to suggest an alternative approach.

In these models of political behavior, government behavior in democracies is determined by legislators who are basically political animals and seek to maximize their chances of re-election. They respond to political pressure by voters who are economic actors and seek to use their votes to maximize their economic welfare. Economists such as Davis and North (5), Stigler (16), and Posner (12) argue that the process of institutional change involved in the introduction of regulation can be analyzed in terms of investments in political and economic action for or against change by these economic actors. Whether or not a given type of regulation is introduced will depend on the amount of political pressure which different groups bring to bear on legislators, and not on any objective social welfare criteria. Stigler goes on to suggest that the introduction of regulation can be considered in a supply and demand framework where special interest groups have a demand for regulation and legislators supply it.

Two main types of questions are involved in analyzing what Stigler calls the supply and demand for regulation. First, what kind of conditions lead to the initial introduction of regulation? Second, how does the introduction of regulation affect the willingness of actors to make additional investments for or against regulation in the future?

Stigler, North, and others have focused their attention mainly on the first question and the conditions affecting the initial introduction of regulation. Specifically, they have sought to use economic analysis to explain why various types of regulation are introduced in some areas and not in others. They suggest two basic models of the introduction of regulation. First, there is what James Q. Wilson (19) calls the "public interest" model, in which regulation is introduced for the benefit of the general public at the behest of groups like consumers or their agents. Second, there is what Stigler (16) calls the "acquired" model of regulation. In this model, industries or occupations seek to acquire regulation (that is, get themselves regulated), for their own benefit rather than for the benefit of the public.

There has been little attempt to consider the second question and to analyze the dynamic consequences of regulation once it has been introduced. Descriptive studies of the history of regulation suggest that the dynamic effects of regulation may be quite important in determining its long-run impact on the economy. For example, in many industries, the introduction of regulation seems to spawn still more regulation.[2] At the same time, the resistance to "deregulation" in industries supposedly hostile to regulation has often been surprising.

The purpose of this paper is to examine the conditions under which regulation may be introduced and the dynamic effects of introducing regulation on its own demand and supply. The basic argument in this paper is that (1) regulation may have dynamic effects which make it easier to block the introduction of a given type of regulation than to remove it after it is introduced, and that (2) the introduction of regulation may create demands for additional regulation. These effects are illustrated in detail for the case of occupational licensure.

I SUPPLY AND DEMAND FOR REGULATION

We can begin our analysis by considering the kinds of factors which may affect the demand and supply of a given type of regulation in an industry. The actors, seeking to maximize their economic welfare, will invest in political action either in support of or opposition to a given type of regulation if they anticipate net gains from this type of investment. Investments in action for or against a given type of regulation may include political contributions, lobbying, advertising campaigns, and trading votes with other groups of actors.[3] The specific amount of action which actors are willing to undertake will depend on (1) their anticipations about the impact of regulation on their own welfare, (2) their anticipations about the impact of action for or against regulation on the probability that it will be introduced, and (3) the costs of taking action to these actors.

In supply and demand terms, actors will have a "demand" for a given type of regulation if they anticipate net gains from the introduction of this type of regulation (or net losses if it is removed). For any given group, the "supply price" of getting a given type of regulation introduced will be equal to the cost of the political action which the group must undertake in order to get this regulation approved by the legislature. Holding the actions of other groups who favor regulation fixed, the level of the supply price of regulation to a given group will depend on (1) the costs of action to the group and (2) the amount of action necessary to overcome opposition to this type of regulation from groups which anticipate net losses if it is introduced. The amount of action which these groups will be willing to take in opposition to regulation will in turn depend on (1) their action costs, (2) the size of the losses which they anticipate if regulation is introduced, and (3) their anticipations about each other's behavior.

Assuming that actors are rational, they will never be willing to invest more in action for or against a given type of regulation than the net gains or losses which they anticipate if this type of regulation is introduced. For the simple case in which there are only two groups, one which gains from regulation and one which loses, the maximum demand for regulation will be:

$$D_r = D_r(G) \tag{1}$$

where D_r is the demand for regulation and G is the present value of the anticipated net gains if regulation occurs. The maximum supply price of regulation will be:

$$S_r = S_r(P_A^+, A^-(P_A^-, L)) \tag{2}$$

where S_r is the supply price of getting regulation introduced, P_A^+ is the price of taking action to the group which favors regulation, and A^- is the amount of action taken in opposition to regulation, which in turn is a function of P_A^-, the price of action to the group which opposes regulation, and L, the size of the loss anticipated by this group if regulation is introduced.

In this analysis, the demand for regulation, D_r, will tend to increase with anticipated gains from regulation. The supply price of regulation, S_r, will tend to increase with the cost of action to actors who support regulation and the size of losses which actors anticipate if regulation is introduced. It will tend to decrease with the costs of action to actors who oppose regulation. Note that if costs of action to groups which support regulation are less than the costs of action to groups which oppose it, it is possible that S_r may be less than D_r even though anticipated losses from regulation, L, are greater than anticipated gains, G.

In general, action costs seem likely to be lower for small, well-organized groups with concentrated interests, such as firms or members of an occupation, than for large, disorganized groups with diffused interests, such as the consumers of many products. Groups such as firms or members of an occupation are also likely to have more accurate anticipations about the impact of regulations on their industry than consumers. Based on this analysis, Stigler (16), Wilson (19), and others argue that groups with concentrated interests are likely to be much more active in supporting or opposing regulation than groups such as consumers. As a result, they suggest that the "acquired" model of regulation, where firms or members of an occupation seek to get themselves regulated for their own purposes, may be much more useful in explaining the introduction of regulation in many areas of the economy than the "public interest" model.

The amount of regulation which is actually introduced in any given situation will depend on strategic considerations as well as gains and losses and action costs. Both D_r and S_r are upper bounds on the amount which groups may be willing to invest in political action. In the case above, the group which favors regulation will never be willing to invest more than G in support of regulation. The maximum amount of action this group will be willing to undertake will be G/P_A^+. The maximum amount of action which the group opposing regulation will be willing to undertake will be L/P_A^-, and the maximum supply price of regulation will be $P_A^+ (L/P_A^-)$.

In practice, groups may often invest less than these maximum amounts because of their anticipations about each other's behavior. For example, if actors begin to bargain with each other, game theoretic situations may develop in which the exact outcome is difficult to predict purely on the basis of information about economic variables. It is also possible that individual actors or groups of actors may be free riders and may not invest in action at all if they anticipate that regulation will or will not occur anyway as a result of the actions of other actors. However, despite these problems, examining changes in variables such as action costs and anticipated gains and losses from regulation can still provide a useful basis for considering the supply and demand for regulation under different economic conditions.

We can illustrate the possible impact of changes in anticipated gains and losses and the costs of action to actors graphically using Figure 1 for the

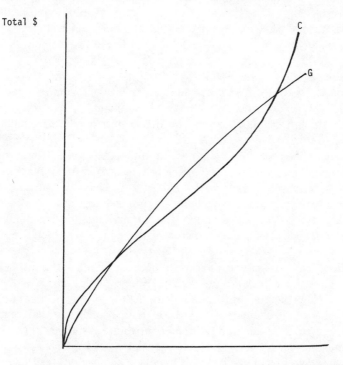

Figure 1. Impact of changes and costs of action in two-group case.

two-group case. Let the G curve in Figure 1 be the total gains G in equation (1) associated with any given level of regulation R. Let the C curve in Figure 1 be S_r, the maximum supply cost associated with obtaining any given level of regulation in Eq. (2). Assuming that actors simply make investments in action equal to their maximum anticipated gains or losses from any given level of regulation, the total gain curve in Figure 1 is analogous to a total revenue curve in the theory of the firm from the standpoint of the group which anticipates gains from regulation. The C curve is analogous to a total cost curve. The net gain or loss from investing in introducing a given amount of regulation for this group is the difference between the total gain curve and the total cost curve. Net gains (or profits) from investing in action in support of regulation for the group will be maximized when the positive difference between the gain curve and the cost curve is at a maximum. Assuming that actors are profit maximizers, the equilibrium level of regulation will occur at this point.

If actors begin to bargain with each other, the actual supply price of regulation may be less than C, but it will never exceed C unless actors are irrational. Note that, if bargaining occurs, the equilibrium level of regulation which results may be different from the nonbargaining equilibrium. For example, actors who are against regulation might offer to reduce their opposition to zero if actors who favor regulation reduce the amount of regulation which they are requesting from the legislature.

Changes in the parameters of the model may shift gain curves and cost curves either up or down and the equilibrium level of regulation may change accordingly. For example, an increase in anticipated gains from regulation will tend to shift the gains curve upward. A decrease in anticipated gains will tend to shift it downward. On the cost side, the supply cost of regulation can change either because of changes in anticipated losses from regulation or because of changes in the costs of action to actors. An increase in anticipated losses from regulation will tend to shift the cost curve upward, while a decrease in anticipated losses will tend to shift it downward.

An increase in the cost of action to actors who support regulation or a decrease in the cost of action to actors who oppose it will tend to shift the cost curve upward. A decrease in the costs of action to actors who support regulation or an increase in the cost of action to actors who oppose it will tend to shift the cost curve downward. For example, the development of consumer lobbies may reduce the cost of action to this group and make it less expensive for them to push through consumer-oriented regulation. Regulations on lobbying and political contributions may increase the costs of political action to small but well-financed special interest groups, while "Sunshine" laws may make it more difficult to arrange political "deals."

The introduction of a given type of regulation itself can also change anticipated gains and losses associated with this form of regulation and the costs of action to various groups of actors. As a result, both the supply price and the demand for a given type of regulation may change once it is introduced.

II OCCUPATIONAL LICENSURE

We can use occupational licensure to illustrate in detail the way in which this analysis can be applied to a specific type of regulation. We begin this discussion by looking at the impact of this type of regulation and then consider why licensure may be introduced and the kind of dynamic effects which it may have on its own supply and demand.

Occupational licensure laws limit the performance of certain tasks to a given occupation and impose constraints on entry into this occupation.[4] Examples of licensed occupations include physicians, lawyers, nurses, and a large variety of allied health occupations. Examples of entry constraints include entry fees, examinations, and education and experience requirements.

We can illustrate the impact of an increase in entry constraints on wages and employment in a licensed occupation using Figure 2. Suppose initially

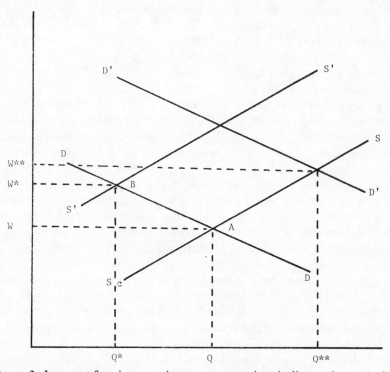

Figure 2. Impact of an increase in entry constraints in licensed occupation.

that the demand curve for personnel in an occupation is DD and the supply curve is SS. In Figure 2 equilibrium will occur at point A. The number of personnel employed in the occupation will be Q and the wage rate will be W. Now suppose that licensure constraints on entry are increased and that workers in the occupation are required to pay a higher entry fee or meet additional education requirements. Higher entry requirements will tend to increase the supply price of labor in the occupation and shift the supply curve upward. For example, suppose that the supply curve shifts from SS to S'S' in Figure 2. Assume for simplicity that entry constraints have no effect on quality and that the demand curve remains fixed at DD. A new equilibrium will now occur at point B. Wages will increase from W to W* and employment will decrease from Q to Q*. Workers in the occupation will now be paid more, but less of them will be employed and consumers will consume less services.

Allowing quality to vary, the impact of licensure on prices and quantities will also depend on the quality elasticity of demand. Suppose that licensure does increase the quality of output. If final demand is quality elastic, consumers will demand more output. For example, better quality medical services may lead consumers to buy more services from physicians at any given price. The demand curve DD will shift upward, for example to D'D', and both the wage rate and the quantity of labor which is purchased will increase. However, it is also possible that demand may be quality inelastic. For example, suppose that, prior to licensure, consumers usually consulted two physicians before undergoing a given type of operation. After licensure, they may consult only one. As a result, demand may decrease and the demand curve may shift downward. In this case, the impact of licensure on prices will be indeterminate and will depend on the relative price and quality elasticities of demand and supply curves. In general, it seems unlikely that this kind of perverse quality effect is very common, but it should not be ruled out automatically.

The speed which wages and employment adjust to changes in entry requirements and the effects of these changes on workers already in the occupation will depend on the way in which new requirements are introduced. If requirements are imposed on all the workers in an occupation immediately, adjustment will be relatively rapid and existing workers will be forced either to meet these requirements or leave the occupation. However, in practice licensure laws usually include "grandfather" clauses which exempt workers already in the occupation. In this case, new requirements apply only to new entrants. Wages will not begin to rise until existing workers start to leave the occupation and it is necessary to bid wage rates to attract new entrants.

As a result of grandfather clauses, there may be significant lags before the adjustment process is completed and the labor market reaches a new equilibrium. The length of these lags in any given occupation will depend on attrition rates in the occupation, the size of increases in entry costs to new entrants, and the demand for the services of personnel in the occupation. Holding changes in entry costs fixed, lags are likely to be shorter in occupations with high attrition rates than in occupations with low attrition rates, since it will be necessary to replace grandfathered workers more rapidly in the first case than in the second. Increases in demand will tend to speed up the adjustment process, since there would be a demand for additional workers even if all of the existing workers remain in the industry, while decreases in demand will tend to slow the adjustment process. Lags will also tend to increase with the size of increases in entry costs.

Given this discussion of the impact of licensure, what can we say about the introduction of this kind of regulation? The main models of the introduction of licensure in the literature focus on two groups, consumers and members of the occupation.[5] The basic question in these studies is whether licensure is introduced for the benefit of consumers (the public interest model), or for the benefit of the occupation (the acquired model).

The welfare impact of increases in licensure constraints on the general public can be analyzed using consumer surplus analysis. In the absence of quality effects, consumers will always lose from licensure. Returning to Figure 2, suppose that entry constraints simply take the form of a tax on entry payable to the government. If there are no quality effects from licensure, the demand curve will remain unchanged at DD. Higher taxes on entry will result in a deadweight loss equal to the triangle ABC. If, instead of a tax, entry requirements involve investments of time and resources in activities such as education, there will be an additional welfare loss equal to the cost of resources used up in meeting these requirements.

Based on this analysis, consumers will not support licensure unless it improves the quality of output. However, simply because quality increases does not mean that there will be a net gain for consumers. Consumers will not gain unless licensure reduces the costs of quality adjusted output. This may happen if licensure solves problems due to imperfect information or other forms of market failure. Taking into account quality changes, let SS in Figure 2 be the supply curve for quality adjusted services and let DD be the demand curve for quality adjusted services.

If licensure decreases the cost of quality adjusted services (that is, quality increases more than offset cost increases), the supply curve will shift downward, for example, from S'S' to SS, and consumers will be better off. If licensure increases the cost of quality adjusted services, the supply curve will move in the opposite direction, for example, from SS to S'S'. In this case, even though quality has improved, consumers will be worse off than before.

Members of an occupation will support licensure if they believe it will increase their net wage from the occupation.[6] The impact of licensure laws on the net wages of workers already in the occupation will depend on the effect of licensure on equilibrium wages in the occupation and whether or not there are grandfather clauses included in these laws. The impact of licensure on the equilibrium wage will always be non-negative unless there are perverse quality effects. If there are no grandfather clauses, workers already in an occupation will lose from increases in entry requirements if their net wage decreases after they meet these requirements or they are forced to move to other occupations in which wages are lower net of change over costs. If there are grandfather clauses, workers already in the occupation will receive short-run quasi-rents as wages are bid up in the occupation to attract new entrants and this may create an incentive for them to seek licensure. Note, however, that there will not be any gains from licensure for new entrants; in equilibrium, increases in wages will just offset increases in entry costs.

Since consumers and members of the occupation can both potentially gain from licensure, it is possible that they may both actively support it at the same time. However, even in this case, there is likely to be a good deal of conflict between the two groups over the specific type of law which is introduced. Consumers may wish to avoid grandfather clauses in order to realize quality gains from increasing entry constraints immediately. From their standpoint, these clauses may be viewed as a bribe to reduce resistance to licensure from members of the occupation, although they may also favor grandfather clauses for equity reasons. At the same time, members of the occupation may favor increasing entry constraints in order to gain quasi-rents even though this does not result in significant increases in the quality of services.

Overall, Stigler (16) and Moore (10) argue that attempts to introduce licensure are more likely to be led by occupations (the acquired model) than by consumers (the public interest model) for two reasons. First, in general action costs are likely to be lower for members of occupations than for consumers. Gains and losses from licensures will tend to be more concentrated for occupations, while they are also likely to be organized for other purposes and usually have more information than consumers. Because of lower action costs, occupations are likely to undertake larger investments in political action for or against licensure than consumers, even though their total gains or losses from licensure may be lower than the total gains or losses of consumers.

Second, the kind of situations in which consumers are most likely to gain from licensure also tend to be the kind of situations where they are least likely to engage in actively supporting it. Consumers are likely to gain most from licensure when they purchase small quantities of complex services on an irregular basis. But under these conditions, the benefits from licensure will tend to be highly diffused and action costs will tend to be very high; even identifying consumers may be a major problem. As a result, they are not likely to invest much in political action in support of licensure even if they anticipate gains. If purchases are more concentrated and they buy services on a more regular basis, action costs may be lower. But the anticipated gains from licensure are also likely to be much lower and consumers are more likely to oppose licensure than to support it.

III DYNAMICS OF LICENSURE

Whatever the motives for introducing licensure initially, this kind of regulation may have important dynamic effects on its own supply and demand once it is introduced. Two main types of effects are considered here. First, there may be "ratchet" effects which make it more difficult to remove licensure laws than to block them initially. Second, there may be "escalator" effects which result in demands for additional regulation once licensure is introduced.

Ratchet effects may occur in several ways. First, the impact of introducing and removing licensure laws on members of an occupation may be asymmetric because of grandfather clauses. As we have seen, grandfather clauses may permit workers already in the occupation to gain from licensure. But they also mean that wages will not rise to their new equilibrium level immediately, since new workers who must meet higher entry requirements will not begin to enter the occupation until old workers begin to leave and must be replaced.

There is no equivalent to grandfather clauses for removing licensure laws. If entry constraints are removed, new workers with lower qualifications can enter the occupation right away. Wages will fall immediately and everyone in the occupation will lose, whether or not they originally benefited from grandfather clauses or entered the occupation after entry constraints were introduced. As a result, the present value of these immediate losses to members of the occupation from removing licensure is likely to be greater than the present value of gains from introducing it. In this case, as Tullock (17) notes for several other types of regulation, members of the occupation may be willing to invest much more to retain licensure laws than to get them introduced.

Second, licensure may reduce the costs of action to workers in the occupation. Entry requirements tend to eliminate marginal members of an occupation and create a more homogeneous group which is easier to organize. At the same time, licensure may make it easier for workers to identify each other. At a minimum, government records usually provide occupations with an updated mailing list of everyone in the occupation whether they belong to professional associations or not.

Lower action costs may also produce an escalator effect. Since it now costs less to take action in support of licensure, groups may seek to increase constraints even more once licensure laws are introduced. Escalator effects may be reinforced if members of an occupation initially underestimated the impact of licensure and become more aware of possible benefits after it is introduced. Licensure may also create vested interest groups in schools that train licensed personnel and in government agencies that may be willing to make large investments to maintain and expand this type of regulation once it is introduced.

From the standpoint of consumers, dynamic effect may offset any initial benefits which they gain from licensure in two ways. First, ratchet effects may make it much more difficult for consumers to remove this type of regulation than to introduce it. As a result, licensure laws may remain in effect long after they have outlived their usefulness to consumers even though there may have been good reasons for introducing them originally. Second, licensure constraints may well be optimal from the standpoint of consumers when they are initially introduced. But escalator effects may lead to increases in these constraints which do not provide any additional net benefits to consumers.

If groups anticipate the dynamic impacts of licensure, this analysis suggests that several kinds of dynamic strategies may develop. On one hand, members of an occupation may deliberately set their initial targets very low, expecting larger gains in the future. This may make them willing to accept compromises which on the surface do not appear very favorable. For example, they may be willing initially to accept certification, where workers are simply certified by the government and no one is required to employ certified personnel, instead of licensure, if they believe certification will provide a basis for obtaining licensure later.

On the other hand, groups which stand to lose from licensure may be willing to invest heavily in blocking licensure from the start, even though initial losses from licensure appear small. If groups who oppose licensure believe that it is inevitable, they may try to introduce some form of "colonial" licensure in which they, rather than the group itself, administer licensure standards.

IV EMPIRICAL EVIDENCE

Empirical studies on the impact of licensure suggests that the economic effects of this kind of regulation can be substantial. For example, a study by White (18) of the impact of licensure of clinical laboratory personnel suggests that licensure may increase the wages of these personnel by as much as 20 percent. A study by Benham and Benham (2) suggests that licensure of optometrists may increase the cost of eyeglasses by as much as 40 percent, while a cross-section study by Holen (9) suggests that licensure may significantly reduce geographic mobility in some occupations.

There are no detailed empirical studies on lags involved in specific licensure laws because of grandfather clauses. White's study (18) of clinical laboratory personnel suggests that laws for this group which have been in effect more than ten years have had a major impact on wages and employment of these personnel, while laws passed within the last five years do not appear to have had any impact at all. However, it is not clear how general this finding is. The two groups of laws are not strictly comparable, so differences in impact may be due to difference in the types of constraints imposed by these laws, rather than lags due to grandfather clauses.

Members of licensed occupations frequently stress the impact of licensure on the quality of services in their occupations. But these statements are usually based on qualitative evidence. Quantitative studies on the impact of licensure are very limited and can be difficult to interpret because of problems in defining outputs. For example, a study by Healy (8) of clinical laboratory personnel suggests that licensure has no impact on the accuracy of laboratory tests. However, advocates of licensure argue that kinds of measures which were used may not be appropriate and suggest that other kinds of variables may be more important.

Empirical evidence on the introduction of licensure tends to be consistent with the kinds of economic models of licensure discussed in the previous sections. But experiences with licensure also suggest that the dynamics of licensure may be a good deal more complex than the simple "public interest" or "acquired" models imply. Other groups of actors need to be taken into account, especially government bureaucrats. We can illustrate this by looking at the experiences of several health occupations.

Some health occupations seem to fit a simple "acquired" escalator model of licensure quite well. For example, registered nurses have become licensed largely as a result of a drive organized by professional groups in this occupation during the period between 1900 and 1920. Afterward, the same groups built on these laws to upgrade standards for their occupation. They also used these laws to develop a system of "colonial" licensure for practical nurses in the period following World War II.[7]

In other occupations, the picture is more complicated and government bureaucrats often play a key role. For example, a study by Brown (3) suggests that the state health department was largely responsible for getting X-ray technicians licensed in New York State in the early 1960s. Studies by Brown (3) and White (18) also suggest similar conclusions for clinical laboratory personnel. Brown investigated the introduction of licensure for laboratory personnel in New York City. White looked into attempts to introduce licensure for these personnel in two states—California, which has one of the oldest, most stringent laws in the country, and Massachusetts, where attempts to introduce licensure have repeatedly failed.

According to Brown, licensure was introduced in New York City in 1963 as a result of the efforts of the City Bureau of Laboratories. Most of the pressure for licensure seems to have been generated by the bureau itself. The bureau became interested in licensure after officials began to discover major quality problems in the city while conducting proficiency studies. Bureau officials used these studies to publicize problems with quality control in laboratories and to generate public support for licensure. However, there is no evidence of an independent public campaign for this type of regulation. Laboratory personnel do not seem to have been very enthusiastic about licensure either. Their main concern seems to have been to make sure that laws included grandfather clauses which would allow them to avoid making additional investments in training. However, now that licensure has been introduced, it seems likely that they would oppose any effort to remove it.

In California, state officials seem to have deliberately tried to generate escalator effects involving laboratory personnel. Licensure was introduced in California in 1937. According to White's study (18) there is no evidence of strong pressure for licensure from either consumers or laboratory personnel. Instead, licensure appears to have been introduced mainly as a result of the efforts of the director of the state public health laboratories, Dr. Wilfred Kellogg. Kellogg first became involved in efforts to regulate laboratory personnel in 1917 when he discovered problems with quality control in state public health laboratories. The 1937 law came at the end of a life-long career in public health work and Kellogg retired shortly after the law was passed. Kellogg's basic philosophy was that the only way the quality of tests could be improved was to improve the quality of the personnel performing them and to allow only highly skilled workers to do tests. Far from being pressured by laboratory personnel, he encouraged them to develop their own professional organization and to engage in political lobbying in support of licensure.

Before 1937, the efforts of laboratory personnel were feeble at best. However, after the introduction of licensure they developed a strong statewide professional organization for skilled personnel and began to make substantial investments in political action in support of this type of regulation. As a result, there was a gradual change in the relative importance of the state health department and these personnel began to assume more of a leadership role.

After World War II, laboratory personnel in California became strong advocates of upgrading entry standards for their own group and worked hard to put pressure on the legislature. They also sought to encourage the introduction of licensure in other states and did not hesitate to point out the possible economic benefits of this type of regulation to their fellow workers in other areas.

The development of a strong professional organization for laboratory personnel also seems to have had important ratchet effects. During the later 1960s there was a major attempt to dilute California laws and to increase the range of tasks which could be performed by low-level personnel in laboratories. This attempt was led by laboratory directors who wished to take advantage of new automated equipment which could be operated by less skilled workers. The state health department seems to have remained largely in the background during this struggle. Nevertheless, skilled personnel were still able to ward off this attack and preserve the existing system of licensure basically intact. However, given current conditions, it is doubtful that they would ever have been able to introduce this kind of system had it not been already in existence.

In Massachusetts, the public department has been interested in regulating clinical laboratories since the 1930s. However, the basic philosophy of the department has been to work with laboratory directors rather than with laboratory personnel. Support for licensure has come mainly from laboratory personnel, led by a few devoted members of the laboratory workers' professional organization. State officials have either remained neutral or opposed licensure bills introduced by laboratory personnel and these bills have repeatedly failed.

V CONCLUSIONS

Existing empirical studies on the impact of licensure suggest that this kind of regulation can have a significant effect on economic variables like price and wages. These effects may create a strong incentive for occupations to seek licensure. The impact of licensure laws on the quality of services provided by licensed occupations is unclear and additional research is urgently needed in this area.

The case studies of the introduction of licensure considered in this paper suggest three main conclusions. First, laboratory personnel do not seem to have been very successful in acquiring licensure on their own. Instead, bureaucrats appear to have played a pivotal role in the introduction of licensure for these personnel. In California and New York City, bureaucrats introduced it. In Massachusetts, they helped block it. However, laboratory personnel seem to have played a major role in maintaining licensure laws and increasing entry standards once laws were introduced. This suggests that, at least in this case, the acquired model of regulation may be more useful in explaining ratchet and escalator effects than the initial introduction of this type of regulation.

Second, the important role of bureaucrats tends to support the public interest model of regulation to the extent that bureaucrats act purely as agents of the public. But in practice, their actual motives are not completely clear. Brown (3) and White (18) both suggest that professional orientation, interest in expanding agency operations, and concern for public welfare were all important considerations. However, one thing that is clear from these studies is that bureaucrats cannot be treated simply as agents of consumers. While they may be ultimately responsible to voters, they have many of the characteristics of independent interest groups in the private sector. Like private interest groups, they are perfectly capable of trying to introduce regulation for their own advancement.

Ignoring the private interests of bureaucrats may tend to misleading conclusions. While bureaucrats may act partly as agents of the general public, the public interest model does not completely explain their behavior. Since they may also seek to "acquire" regulation for their own ends, we need to expand existing models to take these personnel into account. We also need a theory of bureaucratic behavior to explain their actions.

Third, these case studies suggest that we need better models of group behavior in order to understand the way in which interest groups operate. In California and Massachusetts, individual crusaders—or what Downs (7) calls "zealots"—often played key roles in attempts to introduce licensure [White (18)]. Wilfred Kellogg is just one example. Others include leaders of laboratory professional organizations and other government agencies. Often the motives of these individuals are unclear. Economic factors alone do not explain their behavior; Kellogg was on the verge of retirement when he pushed through licensure in California. This kind of behavior suggests that it may be important to look at the way in which interest groups become organized and the kind of incentive systems these groups use in order to understand their behavior. Even though the group as a whole may be motivated mainly by economic considerations, noneconomic factors may be very important in determining the way in which leaders behave and the kind of objectives which they select. As a result, group dynamics may play an important role in determining the overall level of regulation.

From a public policy standpoint, the analysis in this paper suggests that it is important to question the motives of government bureaucrats who wish to introduce regulation as well as the motives of private interest groups. This analysis also suggests that as a result of ratchet and escalator effects, it is important to look at the long-run consequences of regulation as well as the immediate effects. Regulations which may seem like a very reasonable way to deal with a short-run problem on the basis of their immediate effects may seem much less reasonable if ratchet effects make them difficult to remove once the problem is over. Likewise, regulations which seem quite reasonable if constraints are maintained at their original levels may seem much less reasonable if the introduction of these constraints results in escalator effects which raise constraints above optimal levels in the long run.

In some cases, long-run dynamic effects may be so strong that it may seem better to do without regulation completely, despite short-run benefits. But in general, such Draconian solutions are not likely to be satisfactory. Rather, the problem for policy makers is to find ways to minimize unwanted dynamic effects. The individual case studies considered in this paper suggest that we still have a good deal to learn about the way in which dynamic effects actually occur, especially in cases where government agencies and individual crusaders are involved. However, several lines of approach seem potentially fruitful. One way to reduce ratchet effects may be to build in automatic expiration dates into legislation so that regulations must be periodically reintroduced in order to survive. At a minimum, this at least forces public debate over these laws at regular intervals and puts the burden of doing something about them on groups who support them, rather than on groups who oppose them. Another way to reduce ratchet effects may be to develop more gradual methods of "deregulating" industries and to explicitly recognize the losses imposed by deregulation on various groups and offer to compensate these groups. Escalator effects may be reduced by making it more difficult to increase regulatory constraints without explicitly introducing new legislation. This would make it more costly to increase regulation, although, unfortunately, only at the price of reducing the flexibility of many regulatory agencies. Since government agencies themselves may have strong vested interests in regulation, it may also be important to separate evaluation and enforcement. At a minimum, policy makers should not assume that simply because a proposal originates in the public sector, it is in the public interest.

Obviously, the appropriateness of these various types of measures varies with the goals of policy makers and the type of regulation involved. Measures which may be appropriate for licensure may not seem appropriate for environmental protection laws. But in any case, this analysis suggests that policy makers should be aware of the potential dynamic effects of regulations, as well as their immediate impact on the economy, and take these effects into account in shaping regulatory policy. Otherwise they are likely to underestimate the full impact of regulation and arrive at misleading conclusions about the usefulness of particular types of legislation.

FOOTNOTES

This paper is based on my doctoral dissertation, White (18). Support for this research was provided by U.S. Department of Labor Doctoral Dissertation Grant 91–25–73–31 and the Robert Wood Johnson Foundation. The views expressed in this paper are those of the author and do not necessarily reflect the position of these organizations. I am grateful to Martin Feldstein, Joe Persky, Brian Wright, and Dick Zerbe for their comments on earlier drafts of this paper. Any mistakes are, of course, my own.

1. See Baumol (1) for a general discussion of theories of the state.

2. For example, see Phillips (11).

3. The economic value of votes to economic actors may be measured in terms of the opportunity cost involved in not using these votes for other purposes. For example, a group of voters may have to forgo supporting subsidies for themselves in order to push through a given type of regulation.

4. This analysis assumes that there are no quotas on entry into the licensed occupation. However, in many occupations like medicine, entry is not completely free. For an analysis of the effects of entry quotas see Rottenberg (13).

5. See Moore (10), Rottenberg (13), and Stigler (16).

6. Note that even if the nominal wage rate remains unchanged, licensure may still increase the effective wage rate by reducing search costs involved in locating employment.

7. See Shimberg (14) and Shryock (15) for a discussion of licensure of practical nurses.

REFERENCES

1. Baumol, William J. (1965) *Welfare Economics and the Theory of the State*, Cambridge, Mass., Harvard University Press.

2. Benham, Lee, and Benham, Alexandra. (October 1975) "Regulating through the Professions: A Perspective on Information Control," *Journal of Law and Economics*, Vol. 18: 421–448.

3. Brown, Carol. (1971) "The Development of Occupations in Health Technology," Ph.D. Dissertation, Department of Political Science, Columbia University, National Technical Information Service Publication No. PE–197 690.

4. Buchanan, James, and Tullock, Gordon (1962) *The Calculus of Consent: Logical Foundations of Constitutional Democracy*, Ann Arbor, University of Michigan Press.

5. Davis, Lance, and North, Douglass. (1971) *Institutional Change and American Economic Growth*, London, Cambridge University Press.

6. Downs, Anthony. (1975) *An Economic Theory of Democracy*, New York, Harper & Row.

7. ———. (1967) *Inside Bureaucracy*, Boston, Little, Brown.

8. Healy, Katheryn. (1973) "The Effect of Licensure on Clinical Laboratory Effectiveness (with Specific Reference to Effect of Quality of Output)," Ph.D. Dissertation, Department of Public Health, University of California at Los Angeles.

9. Holen, Arlene S. (October 1975) "Effects of Professional Licensing Arrangements on Interstate Mobility and Resource Allocation," *Journal of Political Economy*, Vol. 73: 492–499.

10. Moore, Thomas G. (October 1961) "The Purpose of Licensing," *Journal of Law and Economics*, Vol. 4: 93–117.

11. Phillips, Almarin, ed. (1975) *Promoting Competition in Regulated Markets*, Washington, D.C., The Brookings Institution.

12. Posner, Richard. (Autumn 1974) "Theories of Economic Regulation," *Bell Journal of Economics*, Vol. 4: 335–358.

13. Rottenberg, Simon. (1962) "The Economics of Occupational Licensing," *Aspects of Labor Economics*, New York, National Bureau of Economic Research Conference Volume.

14. Shimberg, Benjamin; Esser, Barbara, and Kruger, Daniel. (1972) *Occupational*

Licensing and Public Policy, Final Report to the Manpower Administration, U.S. Department of Labor, Princeton, N.J., Educational Testing Service.
15. Shryock, Richard. (1959) *The History of Nursing: An Interpretation of the Social and Medical Factors Involved*, Baltimore, Johns Hopkins University Press.
16. Stigler, George. (Spring 1971) "The Theory of Economic Regulation," *Bell Journal of Economics and Management Science*, Vol. 2: 1–21.
17. Tullock, Gordon. (Autumn 1975) "The Transitional Gains Trap," *The Bell Journal of Economics*, Vol. 6: 671–678.
18. White, William D. (1975) *Occupational Licensure and the Labor Market for Clinical Laboratory Personnel 1900–1973*, Ph.D. Dissertation, Department of Economics, Harvard University.
19. Wilson, James Q. (1974) "The Politics of Regulation," in James W. McKie (ed.), *Social Responsibility and the Business Predicament*, Washington, D.C., Brookings Institution.

AIRLINE PERFORMANCE UNDER REGULATION: CANADA VS. THE UNITED STATES

William A. Jordan, YORK UNIVERSITY, TORONTO

The economic performances of the federally regulated airlines of Canada and the United States have been markedly similar while differing substantially from those of the less-regulated California and Texas intrastate carriers. Federally regulated fares in short-haul city pairs frequently have been over 90 percent higher than the intrastate carriers' fares. High fares, however, have not provided large profits because such things as the underutilization of aircraft and generally lower employee productivity have resulted in appreciably higher operating costs. These performance differences are consistent with the implications of the producer-protection hypothesis regarding the actual effects of regulation.

Research in Law and Economics, Vol. 1, pp. 35–79.
ISBN: 0–89232–028–1.

A fundamental question regarding government regulation is the extent to which it actually changes the performance of firms in a regulated industry. Following the enactment of regulatory legislation, it is desirable to provide feedback to policy makers regarding the actual effects of their collective decision so that they might modify the legislation (if the actual effects depart appreciably from those intended) or be more precise in designing subsequent legislation pertaining to other industries.

Even though many may agree that it is desirable to have fully relevant information regarding the effects of legislation, controlled experiments are not a common characteristic of the political process. Thus it is often difficult to obtain direct evidence with which to measure industry performance under regulation. The regulation of Canadian airlines suffers from this problem. When Parliament gave the Board of Transport Commissioners regulatory power over commercial air service in 1938, it was careful to include all parts of the industry under the act.[1] Thus, the Board's jurisdiction ranged from scheduled airlines down to the smallest contract carriers and flying clubs regardless of whether they operated extraprovincially or intra-provincially. The Board exercised extensive power over aviation until its failure to award a route to Trans-Canada Airlines (now Air Canada) resulted in its aviation authority being transferred to the Air Transport Board (ATB) in 1944.[2] The ATB was made responsible to the Minister of Transport and was required to comply with cabinet decisions regarding Crown airline routes. The ATB existed until 1967 when it became the Air Transport Committee (ATC) of the Canadian Transport Commission (CTC).[3]

The U.S. Congress was less thorough than the Canadian Parliament in establishing airline regulation back in that year of 1938. The Civil Aeronautics Act of 1938 gave the Civil Aeronautics Board (CAB) regulatory authority over only interstate, overseas, and foreign common carriage by air.[4] Thus, private carriage for hire, common carriage within the boundaries of a single state, flying schools, and other small commercial air activities were not made subject to economic regulation by the CAB. Furthermore, in 1952 the CAB chose to exempt from regulation interstate common carriers operating small aircraft.[5] This diversity of airline regulation in the United States has provided some basis for measuring the effects of regulation on airline performance in that country; see Jordan (22). It also provides a way to estimate the effects of regulation on Canadian airlines. Specifically, if the performances of the larger regulated airlines in Canada and the United States are similar, but differ appreciably from that of the relatively un-regulated airlines in the United States, it may be concluded that regulatory effects are comparable in the two countries. This means that the performance of the regulated Canadian carriers may then be compared with that of the relatively unregulated U.S. carriers to measure the effects of regulation in Canada. This is the approach used in this article with the CAB-regulated airlines providing the linkage between the regulated Canadian airlines and the relatively unregulated U.S. carriers.

There are differences between Canada and the United States, just as there are differences between various regions within each country. These differences, however, do not appear to be important with regard to airline performance. The major airlines of each country (Air Canada and CP Air for Canada and the ten trunk carriers plus Pan American for the United States) provide services over large areas of North America and even share a number of transborder routes. Also, they connect North America with many of the same cities in Europe, Asia, South America, and the Caribbean, and they often operate identical aircraft types. Furthermore, the concentration of Canada's population and economic and transportation activities along its common border with the United States results in fewer differences between the dominant southern sections of Canada and the northern sections of the United States than are found between the two countries overall. If there were only small differences between the performance of the regulated airlines of both countries, on the one hand, and that of the relatively unregulated U.S. airlines, on the other, it might be inappropriate to disregard intercountry differences. But the performance differences are large and are consistent with recent theory regarding the actual effects of economic regulation. Therefore, there is good reason to believe that regulation is the major source of differences in airline performance and that intercountry factors can be largely ignored in this study.

I A THEORY OF REGULATION

During the past fifteen years a tremendous amount of research has been done concerning government regulation. Associated with this has been the proposal of several new theories regarding why regulation is implemented by governments and regarding the actual effects of regulation after it has been adopted (for whatever reasons); see Stigler (41), Posner (32 and 33), and Peltzman (31). One theory that predicts and explains a large part of the actual effects of CAB regulation is the producer-protection or cartel hypothesis [Jordan (24)]. In sum, it asserts that a primary result of regulating an industry that lacks monopoly power is to cartelize the industry, thereby resulting in a transfer of wealth from consumers to producers with possible subsequent transfers from producers to those suppliers of inputs who also have monopoly power, such as members of labor unions [Jordan (23), pp. 57, 62–63, 67–68]. The implications of this hypothesis are relatively straightforward. In comparison with situations where regulation does not exist, regulated airlines should have the following differences in performance:

1. Entry and Exit
   a. Entry of new firms should be effectively limited.

    b. Relatively fewer airlines should exist at any given time.

    c. Exit should be controlled and the market shares of departing carriers should be reallocated or transferred to one or more of the remaining carriers.

2. Prices

    a. Higher price levels (average revenues) should be achieved.

    b. A more varied price structure should exist, with greater use of price discrimination.

3. Costs

    a. The costs of reaching, policing, and enforcing cartel agreements should yield upward shifts in industry cost curves.

    b. Failure to assign production quotas to cartel members so as to equate marginal costs will increase average costs.

    c. Inputs supplied by monopolists should be higher priced.

    d. Decreasing the number of firms in an industry may result in existing firms experiencing decreasing returns to scale/size.

Comparisons of CAB-regulated airlines with relatively unregulated California and Texas intrastate airlines and with small airlines exempt from CAB regulation have provided evidence consistent with these implications. Under CAB regulation, airline entry has been restricted, the number of airlines in existence at any one time has been greatly reduced, merger has been the sole means of exit from the industry (thereby reallocating market shares), passenger fares have been appreciably higher, price discrimination has been more prevalent, and costs higher than in situations where regulation did not exist [Jordan (22 and 25)]. Similar evidence for Canadian airlines will be useful in measuring the effects of regulation in that country. In the limited space of this article, however, it will only be feasible to review the following factors, but they should be indicative of airline performance in general:

1. Fare policies and structures of regulated Canadian and U.S. carriers have many similarities and differ from those of relatively unregulated carriers.

2. Regulated fares are appreciably higher than relatively unregulated fares.

3. Productivity and economic efficiency are decreased by regulation.

II FARE POLICIES AND STRUCTURES

Since World War II, most fares of the major regulated airlines in both Canada and the United States have been changed across-the-board, that is, the fares for scheduled service between most or all city pairs in each jurisdiction have been increased or decreased by all carriers at the same time in accordance with changes in various policies, formulas and/or relationships which have been approved by the ATB/ATC or by the CAB; see Jordan (22), pp. 62–70.[6] In the United States there has been some difference of opinion regarding whether the dominant role in determining the size and timing of these across-the-board fare changes has been played by the airlines or by the CAB,[7] but in Canada fare changes consistently have been proposed by Air Canada and then approved by the ATB/ATC.[8]

The Appendix lists all of the significant across-the-board fare changes approved by the ATB/ATC and the CAB between 1946 and mid-1977.[9] In addition, it lists the fare changes made by California Central Airlines (CCA) and Pacific Southwest Airlines (PSA) within California between 1949 and mid-1977, as well as those of Southwest Airlines (SOU) within Texas from mid-1971 to mid-1977. Table 1 summarizes the number of increases and decreases implemented by these various airline groups during these years.

Obviously, there have been many more across-the-board fare changes among the U.S. interstate carriers than among the major Canadian carriers. During these years the CAB authorized over twice the number of changes authorized by the ATB/ATC. Despite this difference in relative activity, however, several important similarities between the fare policies of the two countries' regulatory commissions are apparent. First, the fare decreases authorized by either commission have been few and, in comparison with some of the fare decreases adopted by the California and Texas intrastate carriers, not particularly large.[10] Second, since 1953–1954, base first-class or coach fares have been established nationwide, with all other general and discount fares in the fare structure being derived from those base fares through the application of various percentage relationships. In contrast, the California and Texas intrastate carriers have had essentially no first-class fares and relatively few discount fares; see Jordan (22), pp. 144–157.[11]

Table 1. Number of Across-the-Board Fare Increases and Decreases Implemented by Canadian, U.S. Interstate, California and Texas Carriers Between 1946 and Mid-1977.

Type of Change	Number of Fare Changes			
	Canadian	*U.S.Interstate*	*California*	*Texas*
Increases	11	29	19	3
Increases and decreases	1	3	1	1
Decreases	2	2	4	2
Total	14	34	24	6

Source: Appendix.

A third important similarity is the way the airlines and the regulatory commissions in both countries came to establish simplistic "cost-related" coach fare formulas in 1969–1970. These formulas consist of some terminal charge for all one-way trips plus line-haul charges of so many cents per mile for one or more mileage blocks. The fixed terminal charge results in a fare taper in which the average fare-per-mile decreases with distance, and this taper is reinforced when two or more mileage blocks are established with lower rates for the more distant block(s). In these formulas, distance is the only recognized variable, thereby excluding other relevant cost factors such as aircraft size, suitability, configuration, utilization; traffic density; average load factor; route characteristics; regional price differences; and so forth. Again, this practice differs from that of the intrastate carriers who do not utilize such formulas and whose fares-per-mile are based only in part on distance.

It is important to understand that under these formulas a long-haul passenger, such as one flying 2,000 miles one way, does not simply pay a fare composed of the fixed terminal charge plus the same relatively low long-haul rate per mile for each of the 2,000 miles. Instead, as shown in Table 2, in both countries his coach fare is obtained by summing the terminal charge plus the charge derived from the high per-mile rate for the miles in the first block, plus the lower rate for miles in the second block, plus, in the United States, the remaining miles at the still lower rate in the third block. This means that even though average costs per mile for long-haul flights do tend

Table 2. Calculation of Coach Fares for a 2,000 mile City Pair
Using Canadian and U.S. Coach Fare Formulas
As of March 1, 1977.

Formula Item	Canadian		U.S. Interstate	
	Rate	Fare Component	Rate	Fare Component
Terminal charge	$27.82	$27.82	$16.05	$16.05
Line-haul charge				
First 500 miles	8.00¢ per mile	40.00	8.77¢ per mile	43.85
Next 1000 miles	" " "	80.00	6.69¢ " "	66.90
Over 1500 miles	7.39¢ " "	36.95	6.43¢ " "	32.15
Total Fare	—	$184.77[a]	—	$158.95[b]

[a]$185.00 when rounded to nearest whole dollar.

[b]$159.26 when modified to yield the nearest whole dollar ticket price after application of the 8% federal transportation tax.

Source: Calculated from information in Appendix.

to be less than for short-haul flights (other things being equal), the airlines charge each long-haul passenger as if he were a short-haul passenger for the first part of his one-way trip, then as a longer-haul passenger for the subsequent parts, rather than charging him the same low mileage rate for all miles flown. Thus, *if* the distance-related average costs underlying the formulas are correct, this method of applying the formulas tends to yield average revenues larger than average costs for long-haul passengers. In Canada this practice gave the major airlines $9.15 in extra revenues for every passenger trip over 1,500 miles in length as of March 1, 1977, and in the United States it yielded $14.30 extra per trip in excess of 1,500 miles.

In summary, while the U.S. interstate carriers have been much more active than the major Canadian carriers in changing fares, there have been important similarities between the federally regulated airlines of the two countries. These similarities are particularly evident in the emphasis on increasing fares, on establishing complex fare structures, and on adopting "cost-related" formulas to establish base fares, and they are highlighted by the different fare policies adopted by intrastate carriers operating within California and Texas. The similarities between the federally regulated airlines in the two countries and the differences between these airlines and those airlines operating in other jurisdictions are consistent with the assertion that similar regulation yields similar results.[12] More evidence on this matter will be considered in the following section on relative fare levels.

III RELATIVE FARE LEVELS

Airline fare policies and structures are important matters, but the level of fares is even more important. Just because the federally regulated airlines of the two countries have gradually adopted similar fare structures and formulas doesn't mean their fare levels are the same, nor does the fact that there have been more fare increases in the United States than in Canada mean that U.S. fares are necessarily higher.

It has been found that the coach fares of the relatively unregulated California intrastate carriers have been much lower than the fares that would have existed in major California city pairs had the CAB's jurisdiction extended within the state.[13] Indeed, as of 1965 California intrastate fares were 32 to 47 percent lower than comparable CAB-authorized fares, and there is good evidence that those differences were due to the effects of CAB regulation; see Jordan (22), pp. 110–113. If, on the one hand, the federally regulated Canadian and U.S. airlines have had similar fare levels, there is a basis for concluding that regulation has also served to increase the Canadian fare level. On the other hand, Canadian fares appreciably lower than regulated U.S. fares would challenge this conclusion.

Table 3. Lowest Widely-Available Fares per Mile
Canadian, U.S. Interstate, California and Texas Carriers
Selected City Pairs, Various Dates 1946 to Mid-1977.

Carrier Group and City Pair[a]	Mileage[b]	Fares per Mile (Canadian and U.S. ¢, as appropriate)						
		1/1/46[c]	1/1/50[d]	7/1/58[e]	7/1/66[f]	1/1/71[f]	7/1/75[g]	7/1/77[g]
Short Haul								
Canadian								
YUL–YOW	94	7.18¢	8.24¢	7.45¢	9.57¢	12.77¢	24.47¢	30.85¢
YUL–YQB	146	6.16[h]	7.09[h]	6.85[h]	8.90	10.96	19.86	21.92
YYZ–YOW	226	7.08	8.14	7.96	8.41	10.18	15.93	19.91
U.S. Interstate								
NYC–PHL	95	4.63	6.16	7.00	10.21	15.59	22.78	25.34
LAX–SAN	109	4.51[i]	6.19	6.61[j]	10.00[j]	14.44[j]	19.85[j]	23.79[j]
BOS–NYC	184	4.54	6.06	5.87	8.48	11.07	15.78	17.61
NYC–DCA	215	4.67	6.23	5.84	7.63	10.33	14.37	16.37
DAL–HOU	241	4.69	6.10	5.60	7.82	9.61	13.20	14.98
Calif. & Texas								
LAX–SAN	109	—	5.18	5.00	5.83	6.80	9.72	10.58
DAL–HOU	241	—	—	—	—	8.30[k]	9.61/ 5.76[l]	9.61/ 5.76[l]
Medium Haul								
Canadian								
YUL–YYZ	315	6.90	7.94	5.08	7.30	8.89	13.33	17.14
YYZ–YQB	455	6.76[m]	7.77[m]	7.47[m]	7.91[m]	7.91	11.43	14.07
U.S. Interstate								
LAX–SFO	340	4.63[i]	6.19	5.46[j]	6.97[j]	8.99[j]	12.36[j]	13.34[j]
BOS–DCA	399	4.61	6.15	5.34	6.67	8.35	11.46	12.99
SAN–SFO	449	4.61	6.19	5.28[j]	6.51[j]	8.04[j]	11.00[j]	12.37[j]
DAL–HAR	460	—	—	—	—	—	11.27[n]	12.68[n]
Calif. & Texas								
LAX–SFO	340	—	2.93	3.47	3.97[o]	4.49	6.02	7.07
SAN–SFO	449	—	3.47	3.84	4.42[o]	5.05	6.37	6.66
DAL–HAR	460	—	—	—	—	—	8.05/ 5.03[l]	8.05/ 5.03[l]
Long Haul								
Canadian								
YYZ–YWG	934	7.23	8.31	5.57	5.57	6.75	8.99	11.03
YUL–YVR	2,287	6.90	7.93	5.38	5.25	6.12	7.43	9.01
U.S. Interstate								
MSP–DCA	933	4.49	5.98	4.92	5.98	6.85	8.37	9.43
LAX–DCA	2,288	4.87	6.49	4.50	6.00	5.91	7.02	7.93

[a]The following is a list of the city codes used in this table:

Canadian:	YOW Ottawa	YUL Montreal	YWG Winnipeg
	YQB Quebec	YVR Vancouver	YYZ Toronto
U.S.:	BOS Boston	HOU Houston	PHL Philadelphia
	DAL Dallas	LAX Los Angeles	SAN San Diego
	DCA Washington	MSP Minneapolis	SFO San Francisco
	HAR Harlingen	NYC New York (La Guardia)	

[b]Airport-to-airport.

[c]All first-class fares per mile.

[d]First-class fares per mile for Canadian and U.S. interestate carriers. Coach fares per mile for California carriers.

[e]First-class fares per mile for YUL-YOW, YUL-YQB, YYZ-YOW, and YYZ-YQB. Coach fares per mile for all other city pairs.

[f]Coach fares per mile for Canadian carriers. Jet-coach fares per mile for U.S. interstate, California and Texas carriers.

[g]Jet-coach fares per mile for all carriers.

[h]Service provided by CP Air until November 1, 1955, at fares per mile lower than those adopted by Air Canada. These low fares were retained by AC until the 1/2/61 increase which introduced the cost-related coach fare taper.

[i]In 1946 fares for Los Angeles city pairs were derived from mileages to/from the Burbank Airport which was the main commercial airport at that time. Therefore these fares per mile are calculated using the following distances: BUR-SAN = 123 miles, BUR-SFO = 327 miles.

[j]Based on the coach fare calculated from the relevant CAB policy or formula in effect as specified in the Appendix using the current CAB mileages. This calculated fare per mile would have been in effect had the low-fare rivalry of the California intrastate carriers not caused the CAB-regulated airlines to reduce their coach fares to the same or similar levels.

[k]Effective June 18, 1971, the day Southwest Airlines inaugurated service.

[l]Weekday fares per mile/night and weekend fares per mile.

[m]Combination of local fares. AC and CP Air provided two-carrier service until November 1, 1955, when AC replaced CP Air on the YUL–YQB route thereby inaugurating single-carrier YYZ–YQB service. AC continued to use the combination of local fares in this city pair until the coach fare formula was adopted on 8/5/70.

[n]Common fared with Dallas-Brownsville (475 mi.), yielding a higher fare per mile.

[o]Extensive turboprop coach service also provided by PSA in the LAX–SFO and SAN–SFO city pairs at fares per mile of 3.36¢ and 3.96¢, respectively.

Sources: Same as specified in the Appendix; *Official Airline Guide* (28), various dates, 1948–77.

A. Regulated Airline Fare Levels

The Appendix shows that there have been many changes in fares since 1946, but a good grasp of the major similarities and differences in Canadian and U.S. fare levels can be obtained by comparing the fares for seven representative dates in the 31-year period to 1977. First-class service was essentially the only service available on the regulated airlines in the 1940s, so first-class fares will be used in the initial comparisons. Since, however, the lowest widely-available fares are the most relevant in overall demand analysis, coach fares will be used in the comparisons as they become available in the 1950s, and, in the United States, jet coach fares will be used as they are introduced since jet aircraft rapidly replaced propeller aircraft in the 1960s.[14] Finally, to provide a common denominator when comparing fares for different city pairs, it is necessary to express the fares in terms of cents per mile, just as one compares the prices of bushels and bags of apples in terms of cents per pound.

Table 3 presents the lowest widely-available fares per mile for seven Canadian city pairs and eleven U.S. interstate and intrastate city pairs for the seven representative dates. This selection covers a wide range of distances (essentially the full range for the California and Texas carriers) with similar distances given for each jurisdiction. Thus they are fully comparable in regard to the factor selected by the federal regulatory commissions as being the relevant variable affecting fare level. In order to facilitate comparisons, these fares per mile are plotted on seven figures, one for each date.

The January 1, 1946, fares per mile in Figure 1 depict the immediate postwar fare levels. Each country's essentially constant level at that time is obvious, and it can be seen that the Canadian carriers' first-class fares per mile were around 50 percent higher than those authorized by the CAB — about 7.0 cents per mile vs. 4.6 cents per mile.[15] Note that these comparisons are between Canadian and U.S. currencies without adjustment for exchange rate differences. Throughout these years the Canadian dollar fluctuated between about .91 and 1.03 U.S. dollars, with the exchange rate being officially fixed at .925 U.S. dollars from May 22, 1962, to May 31, 1970, and with the two currencies exchanging roughly at par for several years before and after that period.[16] The airlines do not adjust for exchange rate differences when the two currencies are within 5 percent of each other and

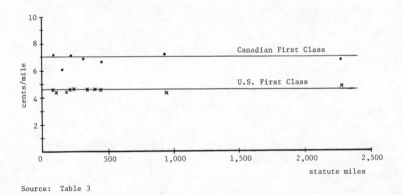

Source: Table 3

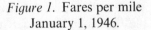

Figure 1. Fares per mile
January 1, 1946.

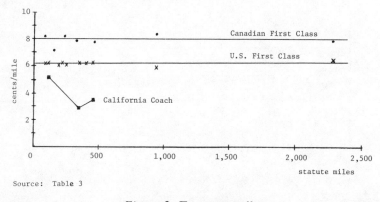

Source: Table 3

Figure 2. Fares per mile
January 1, 1950.

it seems undesirable to do so in this paper. The basic comparison here is between fares paid in Canadian dollars by Canadian residents for domestic Canadian services with fares paid in U.S. dollars by U.S. residents for domestic U.S. services. It is unlikely that passengers in either country believe their domestic airline fares change every time the exchange rate fluctuates. Of course, exchange rate changes do affect long-run Canadian airline costs since aircraft and many other inputs are purchased in the United States, but there is little in the fare data to indicate that exchange fluctuations have more than a minor effect on fare levels (compare Figs. 4, 5, 6, and 7). In any case, the basic conclusions of this paper will not be affected by exchange rate adjustments.

Figure 2 shows that the constant fare per mile was still utilized as of January 1, 1950, but that the three 10 percent increases authorized by the CAB in 1947–1948 resulted in a greater change than the single 15 percent increase in Canada. As a result, the average Canadian fare per mile of around 8.1 cents was only about 30 percent above the 6.2 cents per mile fare for U.S. interstate carriers. However, the Canadian fare increase was associated with the removal of the 15 percent wartime transportation tax while this tax was still assessed in the United States.[17] Therefore, the average difference in prices (fares plus tax) actually paid by travelers was reduced to about 15 percent.

Several important developments occurred between 1950 and mid-1958. First, the CAB authorized two $1 per one-way ticket fare increases which introduced a small distance taper whereby fares per mile for short-haul trips were higher than those for longer-haul trips. Second, coach service had been inaugurated in both countries and by this time coach fares were about 75 percent of first-class fares in the United States and 67 or 80 percent of first class in Canada.[18] Third, unlike the United States, the Canadian

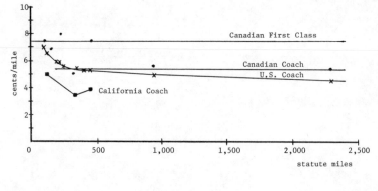

Source: Table 3

Figure 3. Fares per mile
July 1, 1958.

carriers lowered their fares on January 1, 1958. Another reason why mid-1958 is a good time to compare fares is that jet aircraft did not appear in domestic U.S. service until December 1958 and they would not appear in Canada until April 1960;[19] thus the fare comparison is not complicated by the U.S. jet surcharge.

The effects of the above developments can be seen in Figure 3. The fare taper made U.S. coach fares per mile about equal to those for Canadian first-class service at around 100 miles (and only first-class service was available in Canada in most short-haul city pairs), and about equal to the constant Canadian coach fares per mile at 400 miles. Canadian coach fares per mile ranged up to about 20 percent higher than U.S. coach fares per mile for distances over 2,000 miles, but the 10 percent U.S. transportation tax did much to eliminate these differences for longer-haul trips. Overall, by mid-1958 the available regulated fares per mile in the two countries were becoming quite similar.

During the next eight years the U.S. carriers inaugurated jet service with its surcharge in most city pairs, introduced two more across-the-board fare increases, and increased coach fares relative to first class. The Canadian carriers, meanwhile, embraced the fare taper, made coach the basic fare, and experienced a small amount of price rivalry in major transcontinental city pairs when CP Air delayed adopting Air Canada's April 1, 1962, fare increase until April 25, 1965.[20] Figure 4 shows the substantial similarity that had developed between the coach fare tapers of the two countries by July 1, 1966. Canadian coach fares per mile were fractionally lower than U.S. jet coach fares per mile up to about 175 miles and then over 500 miles, while being slightly higher in the intervening 175–500 mile range. Indeed, the now 5 percent U.S. transportation tax eliminated even the 175–500 mile

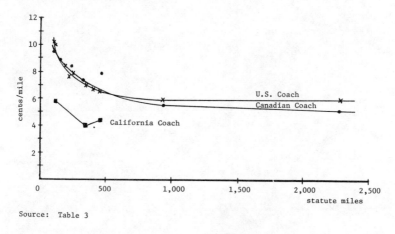

Source: Table 3

Figure 4. Fares per mile
July 1, 1966.

price differences while increasing the Canadian advantage in long-haul prices per mile.

Figure 5 shows that this substantial similarity was continued through 1970. During those four and a half years, the Canadian carriers implemented a 10 percent fare increase and then adopted their first explicit fare formula with a $10 terminal charge and a single line-haul charge of 5.7 cents per mile,

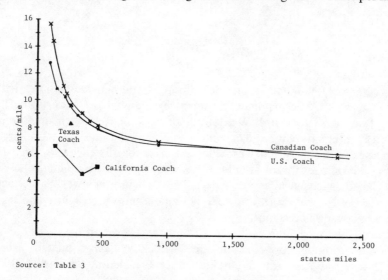

Source: Table 3

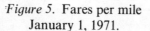

Figure 5. Fares per mile
January 1, 1971.

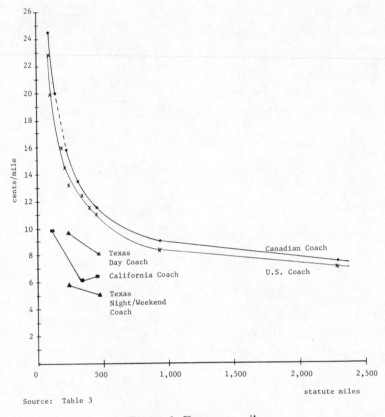

Source: Table 3

Figure 6. Fares per mile
July 1, 1975.

but with fares for short hauls (under about 200 miles) held down below the formula level.[21] The major development in the United States during this period was the October 1, 1969, adoption of an explicit jet-coach fare formula with a $9 terminal charge and 6.0 cents to 4.8 cents per mile line-haul charges. The fares from this formula provided the base for all other U.S. fares and increased average fares by about 6.35 percent.[22] Overall, by January 1, 1971, the Canadian coach fares per mile fell just slightly below U.S. jet-coach fares per mile for distances up to 1,000 miles, and were slightly above the U.S. level over that distance.

During the next four and a half years the Canadian carriers adjusted their fare formula upward four times while the CAB-regulated airlines implemented six across-the-board fare increases including the April 29, 1975, increases and decreases (for trips over 1,000 miles) resulting from the final decision in Phase 9 of the *Domestic Passenger Fare Investigation.* In addition, the U.S. carriers adopted security surcharges of 34 cents or 59 cents per ticket coupon. Figure 6 shows that by July 1, 1975, the federally regulated airlines in the two countries retained the similarity in fare levels, but that the Canadian carriers' fares per mile were consistently above those of the U.S. carriers.[23]

The most striking feature of these more recent fare formulas is the very large tapers they produce. Back in mid-1966 the early Canadian fare taper yielded a ratio of 1.8:1 for short-haul/long-haul fares per mile. By mid-1975 this ratio had increased to around 3.3:1. The fare per mile for a 94-mile city pair increased 156 percent from 9.57 cents in mid-1966 to 24.47 cents in mid-

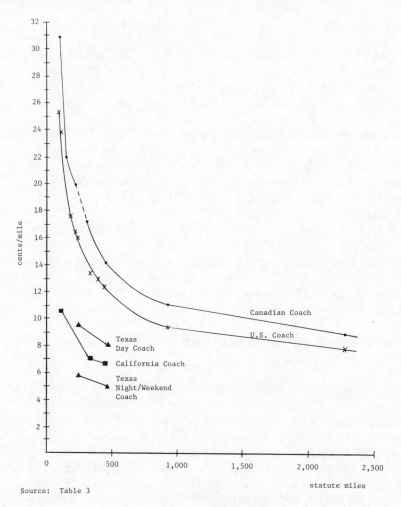

Source: Table 3

statute miles

Figure 7. Fares per mile
July 1, 1977.

1975, and the increase would have been larger had not the Minister of Transport requested some relief for city pairs less than 230 miles apart.[24] The increase in U.S. short-haul fares was almost as large, going from 10.21 cents per mile for a 95-mile city pair in mid-1966 to 22.78 cents in mid-1975, a 123 percent increase. The increases for the 2,287-mile city pairs were much less, 40 percent in Canada and only 17 percent in the United States. Thus, both carrier groups increased their fares per mile more in short-haul city pairs (where demand is relatively elastic) than in long-haul city pairs (where demand is less elastic). Hopefully the 1966 fare formulas did not yield the profit-maximizing fare tapers, for if they did, the 1975 formulas likely did not.[25]

Figure 7 depicts the fares per mile in effect as this article is being written in mid-1977. In the two years since mid-1975, Canadian fares have been increased three times and U.S. coach fares have been increased six times. As a result, Canadian fares per mile are now 21 to 26 percent above what they were two years ago,[26] and U.S. fares per mile have increased about 12.6 percent. Thus, while the Canadian and U.S. fares continue to share the same extreme distance taper, the Canadian fares per mile consistently range above those of the United States by 22 percent (94 miles) to 17 percent (934 miles) to 14 percent (2,288 miles). Clearly, the essential fare parity that Canada achieved in the 1960s and early 1970s is in the process of being lost even though the fare formulas still result in many similarities in the fares of the federally regulated airlines.

In summary, Table 3 and Figures 1–7 show that the fare levels of the federally regulated Canadian and U.S. airlines were remarkably similar during most of the 1960s and early 1970s. These similarities were in addition to those in fare policies and formulas which were sustained even when the fare levels departed from each other in the 1940s, 1950s, and the latter half of the 1970s. These similarities are emphasized by comparing, in the following section, the federally regulated fare levels with those of the relatively unregulated fares per mile of the California and Texas intrastate carriers.

B. Intrastate Carrier Fare Levels

Tucked away in the lower left-hand corners of Figures 2–7 are the fares per mile of the California and, later, Texas intrastate carriers. They are in this relative position for two reasons. First, since their operations are confined within the borders of single states, the cities they serve must all be fairly close to each other in contrast to those cities served by the federally regulated airlines which are dispersed throughout each country. Second, and most important, the fares per mile of the intrastate carriers consistently have been much lower than the fares of the federally regulated airlines. Clearly, there is a major difference between the fare levels of the intrastate carriers and those of the regulated airlines for comparable distances.

Table 4. Extent to Which Federally Regulated Fares per Mile Exceed
Comparable Intrastate Fares per Mile, Various Dates 1950 to Mid-1977.

Carrier Group and City Pair	Mileage	Percent in Excess					
		1/1/50	7/1/58	7/1/66	1/1/71	7/1/75	7/1/77
Federally Regulated over California							
Canadian							
YUL–YOW	94	59.1%	49.0%	64.2%	87.8%	151.7%	191.6%
YUL–YYZ	315	171.0	46.4	83.9[a]	98.0	121.4	142.4
YYZ–YQB	455	123.9	94.5	79.0[a]	56.6	79.4	111.3
U.S. Interstate							
LAX–SAN	109	19.5	32.2	71.5	112.4	104.2	124.9
LAX–SFO	340	111.3	57.3	75.6[a]	100.2	105.3	88.7
SAN–SFO	449	78.4	37.5	47.3[a]	59.2	72.7	85.7
Federally Regulated over Texas							
Canadian							
YYZ–YOW	226						
Weekday		—	—	—	—	65.8	107.2
Night/Weekend		—	—	—	—	176.6	245.7
YYZ–YQB	455						
Weekday		—	—	—	—	42.0	74.8
Night/Weekend		—	—	—	—	127.2	179.7
U.S. Interstate							
DAL–HOU	241						
Weekday		—	—	—	—	37.4	55.9
Night/Weekend		—	—	—	—	129.2	160.1
DAL–HAR	460						
Weekday		—	—	—	—	40.0	57.5
Night/Weekend		—	—	—	—	124.1	152.1

[a]Somewhat greater differences for propeller coach service.
Sources: Calculated from data given in Table 3.

Table 4 summarizes the percentages by which the fares per mile of the
federally regulated airlines have exceeded those of the California and Texas
intrastate carriers. Direct comparisons are made for the same U.S. city
pairs so the percentages are fully accurate in these cases. Similar comparisons
are made between Canadian city pairs and the nearest intrastate city pairs,
but in these cases the mileages are not exactly the same, so that small
inaccuracies result in 1966 and later years after the coach fare taper was
introduced in Canada. These inaccuracies, however, are inconsequential
relative to the large percentage differences that have existed between the
fares per mile. Also, it should be remembered that to date short-haul

Canadian fares have been held down below the formula fare levels.

Table 4 shows that the differences were least around 1958 when Canadian fares per mile were about 46 to 94 percent higher than those in California and when U.S. interstate carrier fares per mile were 32 to 57 percent higher. These differences have generally increased since then, until in mid-1977 the Canadian fares per mile ranged from 111 to 192 percent above those in California and the U.S. interstate differences ranged from 86 to 125 percent higher. Compared with recent Texas intrastate fares per mile, the Canadian carriers have charged 75 to 107 percent more for weekday service and an astronomical 180 to 246 percent more for night and weekend flights. During the last two years covered by this historical review, differences in excess of 100 percent have been the rule rather than the exception.

Another relevant point brought out by Figures 2–4 is that a distance taper was adopted within California before the federally regulated carriers adopted such a fare structure. The fares per mile for the shortest distance, Los Angeles–San Diego (109 miles), consistently have been much higher than for the next distance, Los Angeles–San Francisco (340 miles). But the fare structure clearly is influenced by more than just distance, because the even longer-haul city pair, San Diego-San Francisco (449 miles), has had fares per mile that, until recently, have fallen between those for the other two city pairs. One possible explanation for this is that while San Diego–San Francisco has the longest distance of the three, it also has had the smallest traffic volume.[27]

Figure 7 shows that his exception no longer exists. Perhaps traffic between San Diego and San Francisco is now large enough to yield full economies with regard to this factor. Another possible reason is that the California PUC has recently played a more active role in determining fare structure. Prior to January 4,1974, the San Diego–San Francisco fare was obtained simply by combining the two local fares (SAN-LAX plus LAX-SFO). This practice ended with the first interim fuel increase authorized by the PUC in late 1973.[28] Then, in January 1976, a subsequent PUC final opinion in another series of fuel-related fare increases resulted in the San Diego–San Francisco fare per mile falling below that for Los Angeles–San Francisco for the first time.[29] Could it be that making distance the dominant variable in determining fares per mile is a characteristic of active regulation?

A final perspective on the present differences between the fares of the federally regulated airlines and those of the intrastate carriers can be obtained by focusing on the terminal charges in the federally regulated fare formulas. As of March 1, 1977, this charge was $27.82 in Canada, while the CAB-approved terminal charge was $16.05. In essence, the fixed terminal charges imply it cost $27.82 or $16.05 in these two jurisdictions for a passenger to take a *sightseeing* trip on a regulated airline, that is, to obtain a seat reservation, to be ticketed, handled at the airport (including baggage handling),

boarded on a plane which taxis out, takes off, climbs, circles the airport and then lands and returns to the terminal, whereupon the passenger disembarks and collects his baggage. There is much intuitive appeal in the idea of a constant passenger cost regardless of distance traveled, but this notion ignores many relevant differences between the costs of handling various passengers, between operating costs at different airport, between costs of operating different aircraft, and so on. Just as one example, it assumes the same costs are incurred in handling an experienced business traveler on a one-day business trip with no baggage as are incurred in handling an elderly woman on her first winter trip to Florida.

Rather than getting involved in a detailed analysis of the complexities underlying the terminal charge, a possible weakness in it and the cost formulas in general can be indicated by comparing the alleged costs of the so-called sightseeing trip with actual experience in intrastate carrier operations. In California, PSA will do all the things involved in the sightseeing trip *plus* fly a passenger the 360 miles between Los Angeles and Sacramento for $24.95, about $3 less than the Canadian terminal charge. Similarly, it will fly a passenger the 159 miles between Fresno and San Francisco for $15.04, $1 less than the CAB-approved terminal charge.[30] In Texas, Southwest Airlines will fly passengers 241 miles between Dallas and Houston for $23.15 on weekdays and for $13.89 on evenings and weekends. Indeed, on evenings and weekends a passenger can fly 460 miles (Dallas-Harlingen) for $23.15.[31] Why can the intrastate carriers do so much more than a sightseeing flight for roughly the same cost? The following section of this paper will seek to provide some preliminary answers to this important question, and it will indicate that there is more to these apparent cost differences than simply the failure of the fare formulas to reflect the diversity in costs of airline operations.

C. Summary

The above analyses demonstrate that in broad terms the ATB/ATC-regulated, lowest, widely available fares of Air Canada and CP Air were very similar to the CAB-regulated fares in the United States in both level and structure during the 1960s and early 1970s. Recently, the Canadian fare level has risen somewhat above the U.S. level, but the fare structures have remained essentially the same. In contrast, really major differences have consistently existed between the federally regulated fare levels in both countries, on the one hand, and those of the intrastate carriers within California and Texas, on the other hand. Sustained fare differences in excess of 90 percent (and as high as 246 percent) are just too large to be dismissed as exceptional abberrations. Differences of this magnitude are fundamental and are consistent with the implications of the producer-protection (cartel) hypothesis of regulatory effects. Furthermore, the similarities in the fare structures and levels of the regulated airlines in Canada and the United States, and their common differences with those of the intrastate carriers, are also consistent with the hypothesis that long-term economic regulation has common effects on airline performance. Thus, it does seem reasonable to measure the effects of airline regulation in Canada by comparing Canadian airline performance with intrastate airline performance in California and Texas.

IV PRODUCTIVITY AND EFFICIENCY

If the fares per mile of the federally regulated airlines have been increased so much by regulation, why haven't these favored and protected airlines made consistently large profits? Of course, at various times since 1938, Air Canada, CP Air, and most of the U.S. trunk carriers have enjoyed substantial profits, but on the whole their profits have been less than spectacular and certainly lower than would be expected from their cartel market structure.[32] At the same time, despite their low fares per mile, the profits of the three intrastate carriers generally have been surprisingly good except for their earliest years of operation when high start-up costs and low market penetrations resulted in losses.[33]

The fundamental reason for the poor profit performance of the regulated airlines appears to be that regulation serves to increase costs as well as fares. Three major sources of these increased costs may be proposed: (1) the emphasis on service quality (rather than price) rivalry; (2) regulatory entry restrictions which require each of a relatively few airlines to provide a diversity of services instead of being able to specialize in an operationally homogeneous service pattern; and (3) the assistance that entry restrictions give monopolistic or oligopolistic input suppliers in capturing larger portions of the airlines' gains by increasing the prices airlines must pay for inputs, such as labor. Some effects of these three factors—carrier rivalry, decreased specialization, and increased input prices—will be examined below.

A. Carrier Rivalry

The fares charged by the federally regulated airlines have been fully controlled so that two or more carriers serving the same city pair rarely charge different fares. Therefore, in the absence of pooling or other explicit market allocation agreements, whenever two or more members of the cartel find themselves serving the same city pairs their efforts to obtain larger shares of traffic, revenue, and, hopefully, profits must take the form of improvements in service quality. Operationally, this has meant that each carrier in multicarrier city pairs has endeavored to operate more frequent flights with the fastest, most modern and comfortable aircraft while providing elaborate inflight services and superior ground services. Such service-quality rivalry has been especially prevalent in the United States where capacity agreements and other explicit allocation devices have been rare [Jordan (21)].[34] Less rivalry has existed within Canada between Air Canada and CP Air since CP Air's capacity share in the transcontinental city pairs has been strictly limited either to a specified number of daily flights or to a fixed percentage (25 percent from 1970 to 1977) of total available seat-miles operated by both carriers; see Jordan (21), pp. 200–202. However, these carriers still practice other forms of service-quality rivalry and face considerable rivalry on their transborder routes and on those international routes where pooling is not practiced.[35]

One important result of service-quality rivalry is the underutilization of aircraft. Service quality is improved by reducing the number of seats in each aircraft type (more leg room and less congestion), and by operating more flights in each city pair to increase passenger choice and decrease the likelihood that any one flight will be full and thus not available to the last-minute traveler. The first action serves to reduce the utilization of aircraft cabins; the second reduces the utilization of those fewer seats that are installed in each cabin (that is, increases the total number of available seats resulting in lower average load factors). The extent to which these actions have been encouraged by federal regulation can be estimated by comparing the practices of the federally regulated Canadian and U.S. airlines with those of the California and Texas carriers.

Two factors are relevant with regard to the numbers of seats installed in each aircraft—whether or not first-class service (and seats) is provided—and the density of coach seating. Even though decreasing in relative importance, the federally regulated airlines in both countries have continued to operate dual-configured aircraft with some low-density, first-class seating in addition to coach seats. In contrast, from 1949 to the present, no intrastate carrier has operated first-class service. Thus, on this basis alone, federally regulated airlines have had somewhat lower aircraft utilization (but higher service quality).

Differences in coach seating density are best determined by comparing the number of seats installed in identical aircraft types operated in all-coach configurations. It happens that the intrastate carriers generally managed to install more seats in their aircraft than did the CAB-regulated airlines operating the same aircraft types in all-coach service. Usually the differences were in the order of 5 to 10 percent, but in one case 24 percent more seats were installed by an intrastate carrier; and in a few other cases there were differences of only 1, 2, or 3 percent; see Jordan (22), pp. 199–201.

An indication of the effects of both factors is given in Table 5, which compares the seating densities of Air Canada and CP Air with those of the intrastate carriers for aircraft types operated by both carrier groups. The decreased utilization resulting from installing first-class seats can be seen

Table 5. Aircraft Seat Densities of Canadian and Intrastate Airlines, 1975.

Aircraft Type	Number of Seats Installed					
	Dual Configuration		All-Coach Configuration			
	Air Canada	CP Air	Air Canada	Air Calif.	PSA	Southwest
B–727–200	132	132	144	—	159	—
B–727–100	—	102	—	—	128	—
B–737–200	—	95	—	115	114	112
L–1011	257	—	—	—	297	—

Sources: Air California (2), p. 19; Air Canada (4), pp. 36–37; CP Air (16), p. 2; PSA (30) for 1975, p. 14; Southwest Airlines (34) for 1975, p. 7.

from Air Canada's configurations for the B-727-200. In 1975, its dual-configured aircraft had 12 first-class and 120 coach seats, compared with 144 seats in the all-coach configuration [Air Canada (4), p. 37]. Thus, installing 12 first-class seats resulted in the elimination of 24 coach seats. Furthermore, comparing Air Canada's all-coach version of the B-727-200 with that of PSA shows that the intrastate carrier installed 15 (10.4 percent) more seats in the identical aircraft type than the federally regulated carrier. Overall, the increases in seats in the intrastate carriers' all-coach aircraft over the number of seats in the dual-configured aircraft of Air Canada and CP Air were 20.4 percent (B-727-200), 25.5 percent (B-727-100), 18–21 percent (B-737-200), and 15.6 percent (L-1011).[36] Hardly inconsequential differences.

Even with more seats per aircraft, the intrastate carriers have often managed to fill an appreciably larger percentage of them than the federally regulated airlines. From 1954 through 1965, when there was open entry in California and when coach service was offered by the federally regulated Canadian and U.S. airlines, the average load factor for all California intrastate carriers was 71.2 percent compared with 59.1 percent for U.S. domestic coach service by the trunk carriers and 61.3 percent for the system-wide operations of the two major Canadian carriers [Jordan (22), pp. 200–203, and Dominion Bureau of Statistics (17)].[37] Some might argue that these differences were due to the high traffic densities in the three major California city pairs, but a detailed comparison of the scheduling practices of the regulated and unregulated carriers in those city pairs demonstrates that the successful intrastate carriers' higher load factors were due to management decisions. Specifically, the intrastate carriers adjusted their schedules to conform more closely with traffic fluctuations than did the regulated carriers [Jordan (22), pp. 203–209].

The above experience and data given in Table 6 demonstrate that it is possible for load factors of around 70 percent to be achieved by efficient

Table 6. Average System Load Factors–
Canadian, U.S. Interstate, California and Texas Carriers
1971–1976.

Year	Average System Load Factor					
	Air Canada	CP Air	Trunk & PAA	Air Calif.	PSA	Southwest
1971	54.9%	54.6%	48.7%	51.8%	54.7%	16.4%
1972	64.9	63.5	53.3	61.0	56.8	27.7
1973	66.7	62.7	52.4	66.7	58.1	50.1
1974	63.7	61.0	55.0	70.2	61.8	58.4
1975	58.0	59.3	53.8	70.1	61.6	62.5
1976	60.5	60.9	55.6	71.0	60.7	65.7

Sources: Air California (1) for 1972, p. 11, and for 1976, p. 21; CAB (10) for 1972, pp. 2, 7, 31, and for 1974, 1976, p. 2; PSA (30), p. 2; Southwest Airlines (34) for 1975, p. 9; and (35) for 1976, p. 1; Statistics Canada (40), p. 11.

airlines over extended periods of time, thereby resulting in high aircraft utilization. Table 6, however, also indicates that efficiency can be lost if one is not careful. The load factor performance of PSA deteriorated after the extension of more complete PUC regulation in September 1965. Load factor data are not available for PSA from 1966 through 1970,[38] but its average annual load factor decreased from 77.3 percent during 1963–1964 and 63.3 percent in 1965, to 54.7 percent in 1971 [Jordan (22), pp. 267–269]. This latter figure was about the same as Air Canada and CP Air for 1971, and was 6 percentage points above the unusually low load factors for the U.S. trunk carriers and PAA in 1971. It is not surprising to find that PSA's highest pretax profit as a percent of sales was earned in 1964 and that it experienced a substantial operating loss in 1975 [Jordan (22), p. 337, and PSA (29)]. Air California and Southwest Airlines also had low load factors in the early 1970s, but they were new airlines and their load factors increased steadily as they became more experienced and established.[39] Air California's average annual load factor has been above 70 percent since 1974, while Southwest's increasing load factor reached 65.7 percent in 1976 (including an impressive 79.4 percent load factor for its low-fare night and weekend service).[40] PSA's load factor has also increased since 1971, but it has yet to improve its position relative to the federally regulated Canadian and U.S. carriers.

In summary, it can be seen that the intrastate carriers have generally utilized their aircraft appreciably more than the federally regulated airlines. The 10 to 15 percentage-point differences in attainable average load factors, combined with the intrastate carriers' practice of installing 10 to 25 percent more seats in each aircraft, result in increased aircraft utilization of from 30 to 60 percent. To be conservative, the estimated increased aircraft utilization can be set at about 25 percent for Canada and 35 percent for the United States. Such increases in aircraft utilization mean that it should be possible for airlines in Canada to carry the same number of passengers with 20 percent fewer flights, while in the United States the reduction should be about 26 percent. Truly important differences in operating costs per passenger would be associated with such reductions, but it should be remembered that service quality would be somewhat lower under this form of operation. Aircraft types would be essentially the same, but there would be fewer flights, fewer empty seats, and no first-class service.

B. Decreased Specialization

In contrast to the federally regulated airlines, the intrastate carriers have been characterized by operational simplicity and homogeneity. Generally speaking, each carrier has operated only one or two aircraft types at any point in time, offered only one class of service, adopted simple fare structures and procedures, and operated between city pairs that provided traffic flows and stage lengths compatible with their chosen aircraft. During 1976, PSA served twelve airports while, prior to 1965, it never served more than five airports at one time. Similarly, in 1976 Air California served nine airports and Southwest served four.[41] To date, only one intrastate carrier has operated more than a dozen aircraft (PSA had 28 aircraft at the end of 1976), with three to ten aircraft encompassing the usual fleet sizes.[42] All this has allowed each employee to become intimately familiar with his work. Pilots, for example, spend large portions of their professional lives flying only one aircraft type between just a few airports. In the same way, the work of employees engaged in maintenance, engineering, scheduling, reservations, accounting, and so forth, is simplified, and managers can become intimately acquainted with the carrier's traffic and operational characteristics.

Contrast this with the federally regulated airlines in Canada and the United States. Worldwide, Air Canada served 64 airports in 1975 and CP Air served 36 [Air Canada (3) for 1975, CP Air (16)]. Air Canada's fleet of 119 aircraft was composed of ten different types, while CP Air's relatively small 29-unit fleet contained seven aircraft types [(3, 16), and AVMARK (6)]. Similarly, the smallest number of cities served by a U.S. trunk carrier in 1974 was 33 (National), while the largest number was 92 (United) [CAB (12), p. 1]. At the same time, the trunk fleets ranged from 54 aircraft (National) to 385 (United), with each carrier operating five to ten different types (12), pp. 127–128. The operational problems and complexities faced by these regulated airlines are much greater than those of the intrastate carriers.

Rough indications of the possible effects of specialization on airline productivity may be obtained by comparing the average output per employee of Air Canada, CP Air, total U.S. trunk carriers (including Pan American),

TWA, Northwest, Air California, PSA, and Southwest. TWA and Northwest were selected for comparison because they are the U.S. carriers most like Air Canada and CP Air in terms of system-wide geographic operating areas. Thus, to the extent geographic factors affect airline performance, such differences should be minimized by comparing Air Canada with TWA, and CP Air with Northwest.

The airline industry utilizes many measures of output per employee, four of which will be considered here. Scheduled revenue passenger-miles (RPM) and scheduled available seat-miles (ASM) per employee are two useful measures for those airlines emphasizing scheduled passenger service, with RPM being conceptually more relevant since the economic value of flying empty seats between various city pairs is low, and since a significant number of airline employees are actively engaged not in producing seat-miles but in attracting passengers to fill empty seats. Both of these measures, however, are biased against those carriers with relatively more cargo or nonscheduled charter operations, which is the case for the federally regulated airline in contrast to the intrastate carriers. All-service revenue ton-miles (RTM) per employee provides a more inclusive measure since it combines scheduled and nonscheduled passenger and cargo operations. Unfortunately, this measure is not available for the intrastate carriers. Finally, overall operating revenues per employee provides still another inclusive measure of output, but this one is biased against the intrastate carriers because their lower fares per mile require more physical output to yield a dollar of revenue. Taking all four of these output measures together, however, and making some allowances for the indicated biases does allow a useful overall estimate to be made of the relative efficiency of the various carriers or carrier groups.

Table 7 summarizes the above measures for 1962, 1968, and 1975—years selected to avoid the effects of most strikes and to cover three different operating eras. By 1962 the transition to jet aircraft was well underway; in 1968 narrow-bodied jet aircraft dominated operations; by 1975 wide-bodied jet aircraft were widely used. Turning first to a comparison of the federally regulated airlines in the two countries, we see that Air Canada's measures of output per employee were consistently below those of the trunk carriers & PAA, TWA, and Northwest for all years. The same was true for CP Air for 1968 and 1975, but not for 1962 when it did somewhat better than the trunks & PAA, and TWA, while being roughly comparable to Northwest in the RPM and ASM measures. Even though the averages for the trunks & PAA were consistently greater than Air Canada's output per employee, their advantage declined from about 32 percent in 1962 to around 22 percent in 1975. In contrast, CP Air lost its roughly 14 percent advantage over the trunks & PAA in 1962 and fell to around 10 percent below them by 1975. These figures indicate two things. First, given the larger size of Air Canada over CP Air, it appears that the combined Canadian carriers improved their

Table 7. Annual System Output Per Employee—Canadian, U.S. Interstate, California and Texas Carriers. 1962, 1968, and 1975.

Year and Item	Annual System Output per Employee[a]							
	Air Canada	CP Air	Trunk & PAA	TWA	Northwest	Air Calif.	PSA	Southwest
1962								
Sched. RPM	224,400	320,800	278,100	272,100	328,500	—	749,800	—
Sched. ASM	373,700	650,900	520,100	535,600	638,000	—	969,900	—
All Serv. RTM	25,700	36,000	35,500	34,400	45,100	—	n.a.	—
Overall Op. Rev.	$ 15,700	$ 22,800	$ 20,200	$ 19,400	$ 26,000	—	$ 31,600	—
1968								
Sched. RPM	337,200	382,100	417,000	389,400	480,700	478,700	728,700	—
Sched. ASM	583,400	760,500	786,100	784,300	954,800	866,900	n.a.	—
All Serv. RTM	43,800	48,300	62,600	57,100	91,100	n.a.	n.a.	—
Overall Op. Rev.	$ 23,300	$ 24,800	$ 26,900	$ 24,300	$ 36,700	$ 19,000	$ 33,800	—

1975

Sched. RPM	491,000	563,800	597,100	601,900	840,500[b]	792,600	856,400[c]	761,400
Sched. ASM	846,000	950,800	1,109,000	1,127,200	1,855,800[b]	1,130,300	1,390,500[c]	1,217,300
All Serv. RTM	67,800	73,200	81,400	81,800	132,600[b]	n.a.	n.a.	n.a.
Overall Op. Rev.	$ 46,500	$ 44,000	$ 53,100	$ 51,800	$ 72,300[b]	$ 53,800	$ 55,700[d]	$ 58,200

n.a. — not available.

[a]Total annual system output divided by number of employees. For U.S. trunk carriers, employee data are for the pay period nearest December 15 in 1962 and 1968, and the average number for December in 1975. For intrastate carriers, employee data are as of the end of each year or as of February 28 of the following year. Air Canada employee data are the average number for December of each year. CP Air data are the average annual number of employees in 1962 and 1968, and the average number for December in 1975. December and year-end employee levels are customarily below annual averages, but the differences are small. Annual and December averages are available for Air Canada and the annual averages exceeded the December averages by 1.7 percent in 1962 and 0.8 percent in 1968.

[b]Northwest partially suspended operations Aug. 4–11, 1975, due to a strike.

[c]Calculated using 2,364 airline-only employees.

[d]Commercial aviation revenues divided by 2,738 employees in commercial aviation activities.

Sources: Calculated from data in the following publications:

Air California (1) for 1968 and 1975; Air Canada (3) for 1975; CAB (9); (10) for 1975; (11) 1969 ed.; and "Total Number of Employees, December 1975 Quarter," (processed, n.d.); Dominion Bureau of Statistics (17) for 1962 and 1968; Jordan (22), pp. 267, 269, 337, 339; PSA (29) for 1970 and 1975; and (30) for 1975; Southwest Airlines (34) for 1975; Statistics Canada (40) for 1975.

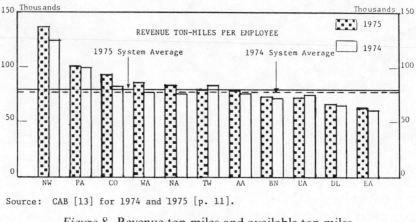

Source: CAB [13] for 1974 and 1975 [p. 11].

Figure 8. Revenue ton-miles and available ton-miles
per employee system trunks
calendar years 1975 and 1974.

position somewhat relative to the average for the major U.S. carriers, but
were still about 19 percent below the U.S. average. Second, as CP Air grew
in relative size and increased its restricted participation in the transcontinental route, its advantage in output per employee decreased and it
became closer to Air Canada in these measures, even though it did manage
to retain a small lead.[43]

Since TWA's employee productivity is close to the U.S. industry average,
Air Canada's position relative to TWA is similar to its position with regard
to the industry average, that is, somewhat inferior but improving. CP Air's
performance relative to Northwest is much different. Between 1962 and 1975,
Northwest increased its output per employee by substantial amounts and, as
shown in Figure 8, by 1975 it was by far the leading trunk carrier in terms
of RTM per employee. In 1962, Northwest's output per employee was about
10 percent greater than that of CP Air. In 1975 it was about 72 percent
greater. Thus, while CP Air's advantage relative to the industry was slowly
declining, that of Northwest, the U.S. carrier geographically most like CP
Air, was making substantial gains. This leads to the very tentative suggestion
that CP Air's weakening position in the industry may be unnecessary.

Given their small sizes and constrained, short-haul operations, one might
think that the California and Texas intrastate carriers would have low
employee productivity. Just the opposite is the case. PSA has consistently
exceeded the average for the trunks & PAA, and TWA by large amounts—43
to 169 percent for RPM per employee and 5 to 56 percent for operating
revenue per employee, the measure most biased against the low-fare intrastate
carriers.

Since 1968 was Air California's second year of operation, low employee productivity should be expected, but even in that year its RPM and ASM per employee exceeded the average of the trunks & PAA. Then, by 1975 Air California achieved the pattern of a successful intrastate carrier—RPM per employee 33 percent above that of the trunks & PAA, revenues per employee just slightly higher. This was also true for Southwest Airlines, with 1975 RPM per employee 27 percent greater than the trunks & PAA, and revenues 10 percent greater. There is nothing in these data to imply significant economies of scale in airline operations. Indeed, full economies of scale seem to be attainable when operating just four or five small jet aircraft (in 1975 Air California had seven and Southwest had five B-737-200s).[44] Data for 1976 show that these achievements were not temporary.

The only negative feature of the intrastate carriers' performances is that they did not achieve the increases in employee productivity experienced by the federally regulated airlines. PSA's RPM per employee increased only 14 percent from 1962 to 1975 compared with a 115 percent increase for the trunks & PAA. Similarly, PSA's revenues per employee went up by 76 percent while that for the trunks & PAA increased by 163 percent. The Canadian carriers also enjoyed much larger percentage increases than did PSA. Since Air California and Southwest did about as well, but did not surpass PSA in 1975, it may be that the geographic confines of these carriers have effectively limited their productivity. Also, the increased regulation under which these carriers are now operating may be limiting employee productivity.

In summary, it can be seen that over the years the small, homogeneous intrastate carriers generally have managed to obtain appreciably more output per employee than all but the most productive of the federally regulated airlines, even though the latter have had the advantage of long-haul routes and large aircraft. Of course, the federally regulated airlines provided higher quality service (including first class), staffed many conveniently located ticket offices, were engaged in extensive regulatory activities, and so forth, all of which would decrease employee output as measured in Table 7. In addition, their much larger and more diverse route structures added complexity to their operations. Combined, these latter factors appear to have decreased employee productivity in terms of fundamental output measures. Again, we can see why the successful intrastate carriers have been able to survive while charging fares appreciably lower than the federally regulated airlines, and why it may be necessary for the fares of Canadian airlines to be somewhat higher than those of the CAB-regulated U.S. carriers and much higher than the intrastate carriers' fares.

C. Increased Input Prices

By prohibiting the entry of new airlines, federal regulation may have also benefited airline employees. The employees of regulated airlines have known that they can obtain higher wages or more costly work rules without fear of having some new or existing airline enter and destroy their company and their jobs through price rivalry supported by lower labor costs. In addition, in the United States they have known that should their company fail it would be merged with another regulated airline, whereupon the CAB's labor-protective policies would result in their obtaining similar jobs in the merged company or receiving substantial termination payments.[45] Furthermore, where a union provides the only source of labor of a certain category for most of the industry (pilots, for example), or where labor can otherwise act industrywide, employees know that the airlines can transfer a large portion of above-market wage demands to airline customers simply by agreeing on price increases with their fellow carriers through regulatory procedures. The overall result of these factors should be higher wage levels among regulated airlines than among airlines without comparable regulatory protection.

The available evidence on this matter is not immediately consistent with the above implications of the hypothesis. As shown in Table 8, during 1973–1975 the average labor costs per employee for the CAB-regulated airlines were very similar and were all appreciably higher than those of the other airlines. Generally speaking, the average for the trunks & PAA was about 24 percent higher than Air Canada's average, and around 41 percent higher than CP Air's average; while being 45 to about 57 percent higher than Air California and Southwest, and 17 percent higher than PSA.[46] This implies

Table 8. Average Annual Labor Cost per Employee–
Canadian, U.S. Interstate, California and Texas Carriers
1973–1975.

Year	Annual Average Labor Cost Per Employee (Dollars)							
	Air Canada	CP Air[a]	Trunk & PAA	TWA	NWA	Air Calif.	PSA	South-west
1973	$13,981	$12,353	$17,554	$16,180[b]	$17,786	n.a.	$15,103	n.a.
1974	15,312	13,408	19,305	19,327	19,418	$13,300[d]	16,420	$11,982
1975	17,631	15,317	21,091	21,102	21,709[c]	n.a.	n.a.	13,834

n.a.—not available.
[a]Salaries and wages plus an estimated 7 percent for fringe benefits.
[b]TWA suspended operations Nov. 5-Dec. 20, 1973, due to a strike.
[c]NWA partially suspended operations Aug. 4–11, 1975, due to a strike.
[d]Estimated from data for the 11 months ended Nov. 30, 1974.

Sources: Air Canada (3) for 1973–1975, p. 4 or 5; CAB (13), pp. 25, 33; Clifford (15); Mitchell (27), p. 11; Southwest Airlines (35) for 1975, p. 6, and for 1976, pp. 5, 8; Statistics Canada (37), pp. 25, 31.

Table 9. Average Labor Cost per Unit of Output–
Canadian, U.S. Interstate, California and Texas Carriers
1973–1975.

Year	Average Labor Cost Per Unit of Output							
	Air Canada	CP Air[a]	Trunk & PAA	TWA	NWA	Air Calif.	PSA	South-west
Per 1,000 RPM								
1973	$ 28.41	$ 24.29	$ 31.53	$ 30.09[b]	$ 24.11	n.a.	$ 19.47	n.a.
1974	31.80	24.70	33.77	33.25	24.03	$ 15.31[d]	20.98	$ 18.54
1975	36.71	27.73	36.04	35.95	25.04[c]	n.a.	n.a.	17.06
Per $1,000 Operating Revenues								
1973	$390.80	$378.03	$436.33	$423.35[b]	$330.17	n.a.	$311.33	n.a.
1974	384.81	349.18	395.89	401.94	287.48	$239.52[d]	289.78	$230.07
1975	387.79	355.26	405.59	417.38	290.22[c]	n.a.	n.a.	223.41

n.a.—not available.
[a]Salaries and wages plus an estimated 7 percent for fringe benefits.
[b]TWA suspended operations Nov. 5–Dec. 20, 1973, due to a strike.
[c]NWA partially suspended operations August 4–11, 1975, due to a strike.
[d]Estimated from data for the 11 months ended Nov. 30, 1974.
Sources: Same as for Table 8.

that it is CAB regulation, not regulation in general, that results in high average labor costs.

There is another relevant factor, however, and that is employee productivity. The Canadian airlines have been consistently below the U.S. airlines in this regard and it seems reasonable for their wages to be affected by this lower productivity. To take account of this factor, Table 9 presents the available 1973–1975 average labor costs per 1,000 RPM (the measure biased against the federally regulated airlines) and per $1,000 in operating revenues (the measure biased against the intrastate carriers). Clearly, the lower employee productivity of the Canadian airlines did much to counter the advantage of their lower average wages. So, while their labor costs per unit of output were generally lower than those for the trunks & PAA for these years, they largely fell well within the lower end of the range established by Northwest. The California and Texas intrastate carriers, in comparison, were all below the Canadian and U.S. interstate carriers in this regard, which is consistent with the implications regarding the effects of federal regulation.

While the intrastate carriers all performed better than the federally regulated airlines in terms of labor cost per unit of output, there is a significant difference among the three carriers in that group. On the one hand, Air California and Southwest are similar, with labor cost per 1,000 RPM about half the average for the trunks & PAA and with labor cost per $1,000 operating revenues about 40 percent lower than the trunk & PAA average. On the other hand, PSA lies closer to the trunk carriers with average labor cost per $1,000 operating revenues almost the same as that for Northwest. Given the bias of this measure against the low-fare intrastate carriers, however, it seems fair to conclude that even PSA performed somewhat better in terms of lower employee labor costs per unit of output than the federally regulated airlines, but not as well as the smaller intrastate carriers.

One possible reason for PSA's relatively poor performance is its degree of unionization. PSA reports that most of its employees are unionized [PSA (30) for 1976, p. 15]. In contrast, just 52 percent of Southwest's employees are represented by unions and Air California only refers to its flight crews as being unionized [Air California (1) for 1976, p. 44; Southwest Airlines (35) for 1976, p. 4]. PSA was first unionized in early 1971 when its station personnel voted to be represented by the Teamsters Union.[47] Then, while initially voting against union representation, PSA's mechanics also joined the Teamsters and in November 1973 carried out the first strike in PSA's 24-year history [*Wall Street Journal* (44)]. It may be relevant that these actions followed the PUC's effective closure of entry into the major California city pairs by 1969 [Jordan (25), p. 466].

The only California intrastate carrier to be unionized during the period of open, unregulated entry prior to 1965 was California Central—the largest and most important of the California carriers from January 1949 until it was adjudged bankrupt in February 1955. Its pilots and mechanics were unionized, and the mechanics carried out a 37-day strike in July and early August 1953. It appears that this strike and the subsequent wage increase reduced California Central's ability to operate effectively against its low-fare rivals (including PSA). In January 1954, just six months after the strike, it initiated the voluntary bankruptcy proceeding that eventually resulted in its demise [Jordan (22), pp. 183–184].

Factors other than regulation doubtless influence airline labor costs. For example, both Air California and Southwest are young companies that may have relatively low seniority costs. Also, contracting out of various services (such as maintenance, reservations, ticketing, etc.) would serve to decrease labor cost per unit of output. Unfortunately, information available as this is being written does not provide a basis for determining the extent to which these differences may exist and, therefore, their impact on the above analysis. Obviously, there is much work to be done in this area and the above evidence in Table 9 can merely be taken as being consistent with the hypothesis, but not conclusive.

V CONCLUSION

One fundamental fact clearly emerges from the above analyses—there are indeed major differences between the performance of the Canadian and U.S. federally regulated airlines on the one hand, and the performance of the California and Texas intrastate carriers on the other. Furthermore, these large differences are consistent with implications of the producer-protection (cartel) hypothesis regarding the actual effects of regulation. The fare policies and structures of the federally regulated airlines have been similar, and their fare levels have been comparable and consistently much higher than those of the intrastate carriers. At the same time, their operating costs also have been appreciably higher than those of the intrastate carriers, with a prime source of those higher costs being the underutilization of aircraft through low seating densities and load factors. Employee productivity also appears to be lower among the federally regulated airlines, but the most effective of that group of carriers (Northwest) has utilized its employees as efficiently as the average successful intrastate carrier, so one cannot say that high employee productivity is limited to the intrastate carriers. The evidence is weak regarding higher input prices, but what evidence is available is consistent with the implications of the hypothesis.

Perhaps it is too simple to conclude that regulation automatically results in the performance that characterizes Air Canada, CP Air, and the CAB-regulated airlines. After all, effective regulation has existed within California since the end of 1965, and regulation there and in Texas has not prevented efficient, low-fare service. These are situations, however, where concurrent regulation by two commissions results in two cartels—a duopoly of sorts. CAB-regulated airlines also operate in both California and Texas, so price rivalry is not necessarily prohibited and the intrastate carriers do face possible extinction (rather than merger) should they fail. Under such circumstances, differences in performance should not be surprising. At the same time, we find PSA much weaker after twelve years of regulation than it was in 1965, while the much smaller Air California and Southwest Airlines are currently both very successful. Could it be that PSA has grown too large? Closed entry, which characterizes effective airline regulation, requires existing carriers to grow to accommodate traffic increases and new markets. The complexities associated with such expansion may well yield substantially increased costs.

Generally speaking, although the performance of the two major Canadian carriers has been similar to that of the CAB-regulated airlines in the United States, they have been among the less efficient of the federally regulated

airlines in North America. In terms of output per employee, they would rank
with Delta and Eastern at the low end of the scale (see Figure 8). Thus, it is
not surprising to find their fare levels seldom have been lower than those of
the CAB-regulated airlines and frequently have been somewhat higher.
However, the present differences in the fares of the regulated airlines in
these two countries seem small when the short-haul fares per mile generated
by their coach-fare formulas are compared with the fares per mile of the
intrastate carriers. The fact that the intrastate carriers have survived (and
even prospered) with relatively low fares fundamentally questions the
validity of the cost-related, coach-fare formulas of the regulated airlines
in both countries.

It seems clear that the performance of Canadian airlines can properly be
compared with those of the U.S. airlines and that the results of such comparisons can be used to measure and evaluate the performance of Air Canada
and CP Air. Whether or not their performance departs from what is desired
is something for the policy makers to decide.

APPENDIX

Summary of the Across-the-Board Passenger Fare Changes Authorized within Canada, the United States, California and Texas between 1946 and Mid-1977

Canada	United States	California and Texas*
1/ 1/46 First-class fares about 7.0¢/mi.	1/ 1/46 First-class fares about 4.6¢/mi.	
	4/ 1/47 10% increase in FC fares.	
	12/12/47 10% increase in FC fares.	
	9/ 1/48 10% increase in FC fares. 5% round-trip discount re-established, 10% pressurized aircraft surcharge removed.	
	11/ 4/48 Night-coach service inaugurated, 4.0¢/mi.[a]	1/ 2/49 CCA inaugurated coach service, 2.93¢/mi.[b]
1949[c] 15% increase in FC fares.		5/ 6/49 PSA inaugurated coach service, 5.18¢–2.93¢/mi. (partial distance taper).[b]
	12/27/49 Long-haul day-coach service inaugurated, 4.5¢/mi.[a]	
	11/15/50 Night-coach fares increased to 4.5¢/mi.	3/ 1/51 CCA/PSA increased lowest fare to 3.44¢/mi. (PSA as of 3/28).
	4/ 1/52 Night-coach fares decreased to 4.0¢/mi.	
	4/16/52 $1 increase per one-way ticket.	6/15/52 CCA increased lowest fare to 3.97¢/mi.
	10/ 5/53 Short-haul day-coach service authorized. Fare equal to 75% of first-class before dollar adjustment.[a]	8/25/53 CCA decreased lowest fare to 3.38¢/mi.
		1/15/54 PSA increased lowest fare to 3.97¢/mi.

Summary of the Across-the-Board Passenger Fare Changes Authorized within Canada, the United States, California and Texas between 1946 and Mid-1977

Canada	United States	California and Texas*
1954[c] Coach service inaugurated, fares = 80% of first-class.[a]		4/ 8/54 PSA decreased fares to 5.00¢–2.94¢/mi.
1/ 1/58 1–10% decrease. Coach fares = 67–80% of FC. All fares rounded to even $.	2/10/58 4% plus $1 increase per one-way ticket.	2/ 4/57 CCA decreased lowest fare to 2.94¢/mi. Terminated all service on 8/10/57.
	10/20/58 First-class round-trip discount canceled.	4/14/58 PSA increased lowest fare to 3.47¢/mi.
	12/10/58 $1–$10 jet surcharge.[d]	
	5/15/59 25¢–$2.50 coach meal charge.	
	7/ 1/60 2.5% plus $1 increase per one-way ticket.	
1/ 2/61 Increase—all fares based on a cost-related coach fare taper. FC = 140–50% of coach. FC round-trip discount canceled.	10/ 1/60 Increase in jet coach fares to 75% of first-class before dollar adjustments.[d]	12/12/60 PSA increased fares to 5.83¢–3.97¢/mi.
4/ 1/62 $1–$10 increase per one-way coach ticket. FC = 135% of coach ticket. CP Air adopted 4/25/65.	2/ 1/62 3% increase.	
4/28/68 10% increase, minimum $2 per one-way coach ticket. FC = 135% of coach.	2/ 1/68 Overall increase resulting from rounding fares up to whole $ in city pairs less than 750 miles, rounding down in pairs over 750 miles.	4/20/65 PSA lowest propeller fare decreased to 3.36¢/mi. Jet service inaugurated at existing fares (5.83¢ = 3.97¢/mi).

2/20/69 $3–$10 increase per one-way FC ticket, $2 for coach fares under 500 mi., $1 for 501–1800 miles.

10/ 1/69 Increase—all fares based on a cost-related coach fare formula: $9 plus 6¢/mi. first 500 mi., 5.6¢ next 500 mi., 5.2¢ next 500 mi., 5.0¢ next 500 mi., 4.8¢ over 2000 mi. FC = 125% of coach.

8/ 5/70 Increase/decrease (overall increase) based on a coach fare formula: $10 plus 5.6¢/mi.[e] FC = 135% of coach.

7/ 1/70 Fares rounded up to yield whole $ price after inclusion of 8% transportation tax.

3/ 6/71 Increase in coach formula: $12 plus 5.8¢/mi.[e] FC = 135% of coach.

5/ 7/71 6% increase over 10/1/69 fares.[f] FC = 125% of coach.

10/ 1/72 Decrease in coach formula over 1100 mi.:[h] $12 plus 5.8¢/mi. first 1100 mi., 5¢ next 400 mi., 4.5¢ over 1500 mi. FC = 135% of coach.

9/ 5/72 2.7% increase over 5/7/71 fares (8.9% increase over 10/1/69 fares). FC = 125% of coach.

4/ 1/73 34¢ security surcharge.

5/12/73 25¢ added to security surcharge.

8/ 2/69 PSA increased fares to 6.55¢–4.27¢/mi.

12/ 3/69 PSA increased fares to 6.77¢–4.41¢/mi.

12/16/70 PSA increased fares to 6.80¢–4.49¢/mi.

6/18/71 SOU inaugurated coach service in Texas, 7.68¢/mi.[bg] Night fare, 3.84¢/mi. added 11/21/71.[a]

7/ 6/72 SOU increased day fares to 9.98¢/mi.

10/30/72 SOU increased night fares to 4.99¢/mi. and made them applicable to all weekend flights.

2 1/73 SOU decreased weekday fares to 4.99¢/mi.

4/ 2/73 SOU reverted to 9.98¢ weekday and 4.99¢ night/weekend fares.

5/21/73 PSA 34¢ security surcharge.

9/ 5/73 PSA increased fares to 6.80¢–4.76¢/mi. plus 34¢ surcharge.

Summary of the Across-the-Board Passenger Fare Changes Authorized within Canada, the United States, California and Texas between 1946 and Mid-1977

Canada	United States	California and Texas*
		12/ 1/73 SOU increased fares to 10.76¢ weekday, 5.76¢ night/weekend.
		12/19/73 PSA added 12¢ to security surcharge.
	12/ 1/73 5% increase over 9/5/72 fares. FC = 125% of coach. Plus 59¢ surcharge.	1/ 4/74 PSA increased fares to 7.01¢–4.84¢/mi. plus 46¢ surcharge.
		2/ 1/74 PSA increased fares to 7.22¢–4.97¢/mi. plus 46¢ surcharge.
2/24/74 Increase in coach formula: $15 plus 6.1¢/mi. first 500 mi., 5.7¢ next 500 mi., 5.45¢ next 500 mi., 5.15¢ over 1500 mi.[e] FC = 145% of coach.		6 3/74 PSA increased fares to 8.92¢–5.31¢/mi. plus 46¢ surcharge.
		9/11/74 PSA increased fares to 9.26¢–5.51¢/mi. plus 46¢ surcharge.
7/21/74 Increase in coach formula: $16.43 + 6.68¢ + 6.24¢ + 5.97¢ + 5.64¢ (same mileage breaks as 2/24/74).[e] FC = 145% of coach.	4/16/74 6% increase over 12/1/73 fares. FC = 125% of coach. Plus 59¢ surcharge.	10/ 1/74 SOU decreased weekday fare to 9.61¢/mi.
	10/12/74 25¢ security surcharge deleted.	
	11/15/74 4% increase over 4/16/74 fares. FC = 125% of coach. Plus 34¢ security surcharge.	
5/27/75 Increase in coach formula: $21.43 + 6.68¢/mi. first 1500 mi., 6.18¢ over 1500 mi.[e] FC = 150% of coach.	4/29/75 Increase/decrease (under/over about 1000 mi.), from DPFI Phase 9 coach fare formula: $13.85 plus 7.79¢/mi. first 500 mi., plus 5.94¢ next 1000 mi., 5.71¢ over 1500 mi. FC = 137–41% of coach. Plus 34¢ security surcharge.	1/29/75 PSA decreased security surcharge to 27¢ and incorporated it into basic fare. Minor increases and decreases in fares to 9.13¢–5.65¢ including security costs.
		7/ 1/75 PSA increased fares to 9.72¢–6.02¢/mi.
	11/15/75 3% increase in coach formula: $14.27 + 8.03¢ + 6.12¢ + 5.89¢ (same mileages as 4/29/75). FC = 137–41% of coach. Plus 34¢ security surcharge.	9/15/75 PSA increased fares to 9.90¢–6.13¢/mi.

2/ 1/76 1% increase in coach formula:
$14.41 + 8.11¢ + 6.18¢ + 5.94¢ (same mileages as 4/29/75).
FC = 137–41% of coach.
Plus 34¢ security surcharge.

3/ 1/76 2% increase in coach formula:
$14.70 + 8.27¢ + 6.31¢ + 6.06¢ (same mileages as 4/29/75).
FC = 137–41% of coach.
Plus 34¢ security surcharge.

4/ 1/76 Security surcharge incorporated in coach terminal charge:
$15.13 + 8.27¢ + 6.31¢ + 6.06¢ (same mileages as 4/29/75).
FC increased to 143–52% of coach.

5/ 1/76 2% increase in coach formula:
$15.43 + 8.43¢ + 6.43¢ + 6.18¢ (same mileages as 4/29/75).
FC = 143–52% of coach.

9/15/76 2% increase in coach formula:
$15.74 + 8.60¢ + 6.56¢ + 6.31¢ (same mileages as 4/29/75).
FC = 143–52% of coach.

1/15/77 2% increase in coach formula:
$16.05 + 8.77¢ + 6.69¢ + 6.43¢ (same mileages as 4/29/75).
FC = 143–52% of coach.

4/ 1/77 FC increased to 150–63% of coach.

4/18/76 16.3% (terminal) and 7% (mileage) increase in coach formula: $24.93¢ + 7.15¢ + 6.61¢ (same mileages as 5/27/75).
FC = 150% of coach.

9/ 1/76 4.5% increase in coach formula: $26.00 + 7.47¢ + 6.91¢ (same mileages as 5/27/75).[i]
FC = 150% of coach.

3/ 1/77 7% increase in coach formula: $27.82 + 8.00¢ + 7.39¢ (same mileages as 5/27/75).[i]
FC increased to 160% of coach.

1/20/76 PSA increased fares to 10.40¢–6.94¢/mi.

5/12/77 PSA increased fares to 10.58¢–7.07¢/mi.

Appendix (Contd.)

*CCA = California Central Airlines; PSA = Pacific Southwest Airlines; SOU = Southwest Airlines.

^aNew class of service resulting in lower fares but not considered a fare *change* for existing services.

^bNew carrier service, not considered a fare *change* for existing services.

^cPrecise date not available.

^dThis fare increase was extended to most city pairs as jet aircraft replaced propeller aircraft between 1958 and the mid-1960s.

^eFare increases in short-haul city pairs held below formula amounts to prevent exceptionally large percentage increases. Also, some "anomaly" fares due to circuitous routings held below fare formula amounts.

^fFares in various short-haul congested city pairs were raised to this level starting October 15, 1970.

^gBased on 241 miles between Dallas Love Field and Houston Hobby Airport. Southwest also provided service during this period between Dallas and Houston Intercontinental Airport (222 miles), Dallas–San Antonio (253 miles), and Houston–San Antonio (192 miles). Since it generally charged the same dollar fares in all airport pairs, the fares-per-mile differed in proportion to the mileage differences. Dallas–Houston Hobby Airport has been the dominant city pair in Southwest's system and is used here to indicate changes in its fares.

^hInitially proposed by Air Canada as a new coach fare formula with a $13.50 terminal charge and line-haul charges of 6.0¢/mi: first 500 miles, 5.5¢ next 500 miles, 5.0¢ next 500 miles, and 4.5¢ for over 1500 miles. This formula would have increased fares under 1100 miles and decreased them over 1100 miles, yielding a net increase in total revenues. CP Air, however, matched the decreases while ignoring the increases and Air Canada felt constrained to do likewise. This resulted in an unintentioned fare decrease.

ⁱMontreal-Toronto fare surcharged $1 over its formula fare. (See also note *e* above.)

Sources: Air Transport Committee, records and files of the Fares, Rates and Service Division; Decisions 4163 (May 26, 1975), 4651 (April 14, 1976), and 5101 (Feb. 24, 1977).

Civil Aeronautics Board (11), pp. 532–545; Orders 69–9–68 (Sept. 12, 1969), 72–8–50 (Aug. 10, 1972), 73–3–46 (March 14, 1973), 73–5–10 (May 3, 1973), 73–11–93 (Nov. 20, 1973), 74–3–96 (March 22, 1974), 74–9–82 (Sept. 23, 1974), 74–11–62 (Nov. 14, 1974), 74–12–109 (Dec. 27, 1974), 75–8–103/4 (Aug. 19, 1975), 75–11–23 (Nov. 7, 1975), 76–1–113 (Jan. 29, 1976), 76–2–120 (Feb. 27, 1976), 76–4–182 (April 30, 1976), 76–8–52 (Aug. 10, 1976), 77–1–93 (Jan. 14, 1977); Press Release 75–81 (April 24, 1974) [Jordan (22), pp. 62–65, 284–287; (26), pp. 25–26]. Public Utilities Commission, Decisions 75899 (July 8, 1969), 76447 (Nov. 18, 1969), 77991 (Dec. 1, 1970), 81390 (May 15, 1973), 81793 (Aug. 21, 1973), 82190 (Dec. 4, 1973), 82280 (Dec. 18, 1973), 82389 (Jan. 22, 1974), 82906 (May 29, 1974), 83415 (Sept. 4, 1974), 83939 (Dec. 30, 1974), 84544 (June 17, 1975), 84767 (Aug. 5, 1975), 85339 (Jan. 13, 1976).

74

FOOTNOTES

The author is professor of Managerial Economics, Faculty of Administrative Studies. This is a revision of a paper presented at the Eleventh Annual Meeting of the Canadian Economic Association on June 13, 1977. The research was supported by grants from the Canada Council and the Faculty of Administrative Studies Research Fund. Of course, neither organization is responsible for the analyses and conclusions of this article.

1. Transport Act, Stat. Can. c. 53 (1938), parts 1–11.

2. Aeronautics Act, Stat. Can. c. 28 (1944–1945). For a description of how the Board of Transport Commissioners' decision regarding the Vancouver-Victoria route resulted in the establishment of the ATB, see Baldwin (7), pp. 34–35.

3. The CTC was established by the National Transportation Act, Stat. Can. c. 69 (1966–1967). The Aeronautics Act remains in force.

4. Civil Aeronautics Act of 1938, 52 Stat. 973. This act was superseded by the Federal Aviation Act of 1958, 72 Stat. 731, with no significant change in the provisions concerning economic regulation. It is necessary to differentiate between economic regulation and the regulation of aircraft operations and safety. All aircraft in both countries are subject to this latter type of regulation.

5. CAB (11), pp. 515, 530. Between 1952 and 1972 the exemption applied to aircraft having a maximum certificated take-off weight of 12,500 pounds or less (equivalent to a maximum capacity of about 20 passengers). The new CAB policy changed this to a 30-seat/7,500 pound-payload limitation. CAB Orders 72–7–61 (July 18, 1972) and 72–9–62 (Sept. 15, 1972).

6. For Canada, this statement applies to the primary east-west routes served by Air Canada and CP Air. The fares for the north-south routes served by CP Air, the small regional carriers, and "bush" operators have not been investigated in this study.

7. Cf. in Douglas and Miller (19), statements on pp. 39 and 145n with those on pp. 41, 131, 139–140, 153, 163, and 168. My own experiences lead to the conclusion that the carriers have been the primary force behind fare changes in the United States with the CAB deciding which of several proposals is to be adopted, or setting the actual fare formula in response to carrier requests for a fare increase.

8. See, for example, ATC Decision 3919 (July 19, 1974).

9. A few fare changes adopted by one or a few carriers for a limited duration are excluded. See Jordan (22), pp. 64–65 for a more detailed listing covering 1946 through 1965.

10. See Appendix, Canadian 1/1/58, 8/5/70 and 10/1/72; U.S. 9/1/48, 4/1/52, 2/1/68, 10/12/74 and 4/29/75; California and Texas 8/25/53, 4/8/54, 2/4/57, 4/20/65, 10/30/72, 2/1/73, 10/1/74 and 1/29/75.

11. Southwest Airlines has largely limited its fare differences to time-of-day or day-of-week criteria rather than on discriminatory type fare differences based on passenger characteristics or excursion travel pattern requirements. See also Jordan (26), pp. 25–26.

12. Another reason for similarities in fare structure could be that the two groups both publish their tariffs through the same agent, Airline Tariff Publishing Company of Washington, D.C. (see, for example, *Local Passenger Fares Tariff No. PF–16*, C.T.C. (A) No. 132, C.A.B. No. 249, 1975). Also, the Canadian carriers are associate members of the Air Transport Association of America, the trade association of the U.S. interstate scheduled passenger airlines; Air Transport Association of America (5), pp. 18–19.

13. Under the provisions of the California Constitution, the California Public Utilities Commission (PUC) has always had jurisdiction over the fares of all scheduled airlines for service within the state. However, the PUC is required to accept the initial tariff of any new carrier (and airline entry was open and unregulated within California

until September 17, 1965), and its approval of fare decreases has been virtually automatic. Thus, in practice, its regulation has been limited to fare increases [see Jordan (22), pp. 2–4]. The Texas Aeronautics Commission (TAC) also has jurisdiction over the fares of intrastate carriers under the Texas Aeronautics Act (V.T.C.S. art. 46c–6–sub. 3), but the frequent fare increases and decreases implemented by Southwest Airlines between mid–1972 and 1974 imply that this regulation has also been limited (see Appendix).

14. As shown in the Appendix, a $1–10 jet surcharge was adopted by U.S. carriers between December 10, 1958, and October 1, 1969. Canadian carriers did not adopt a jet surcharge and Air Canada operated large numbers of turboprop Vanguard and Viscount aircraft substantially longer than the U.S. trunk carriers operated comparable aircraft.

15. It should be pointed out that the relatively low 6.16 cents per mile fare for YUL-YQB was offered by CP Air and that the 6.75 cents per mile fare for YYZ-YQB was obtained by combining Air Canada's 6.94 cents per mile fare for YYZ-YUL with CP Air's 6.16 cents YUL-YQB rate. The other five fares per mile listed for Air Canada in 1946 range from 6.90 cents to 7.18 cents, generally consistent with the conclusion that the average fare per mile in most Canadian city pairs was about 7.0 cents.

16. Statistics Canada (39), pp. 1252–1254 and *Bank of Canada Review* (8).

17. The U.S. federal transportation tax was 15 percent until April 1, 1954, when it fell to 10 percent. Another decrease to 5 percent occurred on November 16, 1962, and the tax was increased to 8 percent effective June 1, 1970 [CAB (11), pp. 534, 538, 543].

18. See Appendix. The rapid expansion of coach service by the U.S. trunk carriers is shown by the following percentages of total available seat-miles produced in coach services: 1949 = 3.2 percent, 1952 = 17.3 percent, 1955 = 33.1 percent, 1958 = 40.0 percent [Jordan (22), p. 46]. Comparable data are not available for Canadian carriers.

19. CAB (11), p. 489. See also *Official Airline Guide* (28), C–308 for March 1960.

20. CP Air received authorization to operate a single daily transcontinental round-trip flight in early 1959. ATB, Decision 1229 (Feb. 19, 1959), p. 3.

21. The 5.7 cent line-haul charge was based on great-circle mileages via the shortest-operated route. This was a change from the previous practice of basing fares on mileages of existing aircraft routings, and it resulted in reduced coach fares in 460 city pairs where traffic density had been light and aircraft routings circuitous, while increasing fares in 150 relatively high-density city pairs where aircraft routings had been more direct. There were no coach fare changes in 26 city pairs. Overall, a majority of passengers experienced a fare increase. Letter to J. P. Lalonde, Secretary, ATC, from C.M. Irwin, Director of Pricing, Air Canada (July 6, 1970).

22. CAB Order 69–9–68 (Sept. 12, 1969). The fares resulting from this formula were later declared unlawful by the U.S. Court of Appeals for the District of Columbia, but following further proceedings these same fares were found by the CAB not to be "unjust or unreasonable, or unjustly discriminatory, or unduly preferential or prejudicial," and they were retained until the across-the-board fare increase of May 7, 1971. See CAB Orders 70–7–128 (July 28, 1970) and 70–9–123 (Sept. 24, 1970).

23. In this case the somewhat higher Canadian fares per mile were not appreciably counteracted by the U.S. transportation tax. On December 1, 1974, Canada introduced a 5 percent transportation tax (with a $5 maximum) and this tax was increased to 8 percent on August 1, 1975 (with an $8 maximum). See *Official Airline Guide* (28) for Dec. 1, 1974, p. 7, and Aug. 15, 1975, p. 7.

24. The Minister requested that the formula fare increases for these short-haul city pairs be held down to a maximum of $5 as opposed to a potential of $10 increase for some city pairs. Letter to J. P. Lalonde, Secretary, ATC, from C. M. Irwin, Director of Pricing, Air Canada (May 12, 1975).

25. During 1966 the rate of return on regulatory investment for system trunks and Pan American was 10.27 percent; in 1975 their rate of return was 2.8 percent. Similarly, Air Canada and CP Air's combined rate of return on noncurrent liabilities, capital stock, and surplus was about 9.1 percent in 1966 and 5 percent in 1975. The lower rates of return in 1975 are especially noteworthy when the effects of inflation are considered. CAB (11), p. 411, and (14). Also, calculated from data contained in Dominion Bureau of Statistics (17) for 1966, pp. 15, 24; and Statistics Canada (36) for 1975, pp. 8, 14.

26. There are two exceptions to this range of percentage increases. The YUL-YQB fare was held to $8 below its formula level resulting in only a 10.4 percent increase over mid-1975. In contrast, a $1 surcharge was added to the formula fare for YUL-YYZ resulting in a 28.6 percent increase in this city pair. Air Canada, *Details of Revised Fare Structure* (Jan. 14, 1977), Table 3.

27. The following is the number of on-line origin and destination passengers flying between these three metropolitan areas for selected years:

Year	LAX-SAN	LAX-SFO	SAN-SFO
1950	81,000	553,000	46,000
1960	363,000	1,461,000	185,000
1970	1,004,000	5,126,000	636,000*
1975	1,050,000	5,944,000	875,000

*12 Months ended June 30, 1971.

Sources: Jordan (22), pp. 307–318.

PUC, Report No. 1511–29 (1970), and 1511–39 (1975);

Exhibit No. 56, Appl. No. 53442 (Oct. 6, 1972).

28. PUC Decision 82280 (Dec. 18, 1973).

29. PUC Decision 85339 (Jan. 13, 1976).

30. PUC Decision 87207 (April 12, 1977). Also see Jordan (22), p. 305.

31. See Eichner *et al.* (20), and *Official Airline Guide* (28) for May 1, 1977.

32. CAB (11), p. 411; (12), p. 105. *Annual Reports*, Air Canada (3) for 1968, pp. 22–23, and 1976, pp. 18–19. Statistics Canada (38), p. 123, and (40), p. 19.

33. See *Annual Reports* for: Air California (1) for 1971, p. 1, and 1976, p. 5; PSA (29); and Southwest Airlines (34) for 1976, p. 4; and Jordan (22), pp. 336–337.

34. The most important domestic capacity agreement was disapproved by the CAB in 1975. CAB Order 75–7–98 (July 21, 1975).

35. Efforts by Air Canada and CP Air to decrease service-quality rivalry are reported in the *Toronto Globe and Mail* (42). Air Canada has capacity or pooling agreements with the airlines of several countries, including Great Britain, West Germany, and Russia [*Toronto Globe and Mail* (43)].

36. In 1977, CP Air converted three of its seven B-737-200s to an all-coach configuration having 107 seats as compared with 12 first-class and 83 coach seats [*Toronto Globe and Mail* (42), p. B13].

37. Data by class of service or area of operation are not published in Canada. Therefore, combined first-class plus coach, system-wide data must be used for Canadian carriers.

38. PSA did not publish its available seat-mile data for those years, therefore the load factors cannot be calculated.

39. Air California inaugurated service in 1967 and Southwest did so in 1971 [Air California (1) and Southwest Airlines (34)].

40. Southwest's load factor for its higher-fare weekday flights was 57 percent in 1976 [Soutwest Airlines (35) for 1976, p. 3].

41. See 1976 *Annual Reports* for Air California (1); PSA (29); and Southwest Airlines (34).

42. See 1973–1976 *Annual Reports* for *ibid.*

43. This is consistent with Davies's (18) finding that in Australia the government-owned Trans-Australia Airlines was less efficient than the privately owned Ansett Australian National Airlines.

44. Air California (1) for 1975, p. 24; Southwest Airlines (35) for 1975, p. 9.

45. See Jordan (22), pp. 23–24; CAB Order 72–4–31/32 (March 28, 1972), pp. 18–33. Merger has also been the major way through which the exit of scheduled airlines has occurred in Canada, even though Air Canada has not participated in mergers nor has CP Air following its formation in 1942 through the merger of nine bush airlines with Canadian Airways. The regional carriers, in contrast, have had active merger histories [Statistics Canada (38), pp. 21, 24].

46. These comparisons are little affected by differences in the values of the Canadian and U.S. dollars. In 1973 these two currencies exchanged roughly at par, in 1974 the U.S. dollar was 2.25 percent below the Canadian dollar, while in 1975 it was about 1.7 percent above [*Bank of Canada Review* (8)].

47. PSA, *First Quarter Report*, March 31, 1971.

REFERENCES

1. Air California. (1971–1976) *Annual Reports*, Newport Beach, Calif., Air California.
2. ———. (October 4, 1976) *Information Statement in Connection with a Special Meeting of Shareholders of Air California to be Held on December 21, 1976.*
3. Air Canada. (1968–1976) *Annual Reports*, Montreal, Quebec, Air Canada.
4. ———. (May 1975) *Enroute*, Vol. 3.
5. Air Transport Association of America. (1974) *Air Transport 1974 Facts and Figures*, Washington, D.C., Air Transport Association of America.
6. AVMARK. (1976) *Commercial Aircraft Fleets, January 1, 1976*, Lolo, Montana, AVMARK, Inc., 3rd ed., pp. 13–15, 80.
7. Baldwin, John R. (1975) *The Regulatory Agency and the Public Corporation.* Cambridge, Mass., Ballinger Publishing Company.
8. *Bank of Canada Review.* (April 1977), p. 65.
9. Civil Aeronautics Board (CAB). (December 1975) *Air Carrier Financial Statistics*, Vol. 23.
10. ———. (December 1972, 1974, 1975, 1976) *Air Carrier Traffic Statistics*, Vols. 18, 20, 21, 22.
11. ———. (1973) *Handbook of Airline Statistics*, Washington, D. C., U.S. Government Printing Office.
12. ———. (1975) *Supplement to the Handbook of Airline Statistics*, Springfield, Va., National Technical Information Service.
13. ———. (September 1974 and September 1976) *Productivity and Cost of Employment, System Trunks, Calendar Years 1972 and 1973* and *1974 and 1975.*
14. ———. (December 1975) *Quarterly Airline Industry Economic Report*, Vol. 8, p. 4.
15. Clifford, R. W., President, Air California. (December 19, 1974) Letter to Senator Edward M. Kennedy, attachment.
16. CP Air. (1975) Information booklet, Vancouver, B.C., CP Air.
17. Dominion Bureau of Statistics. (1954–1968) *Civil Aviation*, Ottawa, Ontario, Queen's Printer.
18. Davies, David G. (April 1971) "The Efficiency of Public versus Private Firms: The Case of Australia's Two Airlines," *Journal of Law and Economics*, Vol. 14: 149–165.
19. Douglas, George W., and Miller, James C. III. (1974) *Economic Regulation of*

Domestic Air Transport: Theory and Practice, Washington, D.C., The Brookings Institution.

20. Eichner, L. J.; Simat, N.S.; Carlson, K.T.; and Sunshine, R. A. (January 1976) *An Analysis of the Intrastate Air Carrier Regulatory Forum*, Technical Report III–22, U.S. Department of Transportation Contract No. DOT–OS–60078.

21. Jordan, William A. (Spring 1973) "Airline Capacity Agreements: Correcting a Regulatory Imperfection," *Journal of Air Law and Commerce*, Vol. 39: 179–213.

22. ――――. (1970) *Airline Regulation in America: Effects and Imperfections*, Baltimore, The Johns Hopkins Press.

23. ――――. (1975) "If We're Going to Regulate the Airlines, Let's Do It Right," in James C. Miller III, ed., *Perspectives in Federal Transportation Policy*, Washington, D.C., American Enterprise Institute for Public Policy Research, pp. 57–70.

24. ――――. (April 1972) "Producer Protection, Prior Market Structure and the Effects of Government Regulation," *Journal of Law and Economics*, Vol. 15: 151–176.

25. ――――. (1975) "Results of Civil Aeronautics Board Regulation," *Hearings before the Subcommittee on Administrative Practice and Procedure of the Committee on the Judiciary*, U.S. Sen., 94th Cong., 1st sess., on Oversight of CAB Practices and Procedures, Vol. 1, pp. 464–487.

26. ――――. (January 1975) "Some Predatory Practices under Government Regulation?" University of Toronto-York University Joint Program in Transportation, Research Report No. 26.

27. Mitchell, George J., Jr. (October 27, 1975) PSA Exhibit No. 17 in PUC Application No. 55160.

28. *Official Airline Guide*, (1948–1977) North American ed., Vols. 4–21 (series 1), 9–18 (series 2), and 1–3 (series 3).

29. Pacific Southwest Airlines (PSA). (1966–1976) *Annual Reports*, San Diego, Calif., PSA.

30. ――――. (March 1976, March 1977) *SEC Form 10–K for the Fiscal Year Ended December 31, 1975 and December 31, 1976*.

31. Peltzman, Sam. (August 1976) "Toward a More General Theory of Regulation," *Journal of Law and Economics*, Vol. 19: 211–240.

32. Posner, Richard A. (Spring 1971) "Taxation by Regulation," *Bell Journal of Economics and Management Science*, Vol. 2: 22–50.

33. ――――. (Autumn 1974) "Theories of Regulation," *Bell Journal of Economics and Management Science*, Vol. 5: 335–358.

34. Southwest Airlines. (1974–1976) *Annual Reports*, Dallas, Texas, Southwest Airlines.

35. ――――. (March 1976, March 1977) *SEC Form 10–K for the Fiscal Year Ended December 31, 1975 and December 31, 1976*.

36. Statistics Canada. (1976) *Air Carrier Financial Statements, 1975*, Ottawa, Ontario, Information Canada.

37. ――――. (October-December, 1973–1975) *Air Carrier Operations in Canada*, Vols. 3–5.

38. ――――. (1972) *Aviation in Canada 1971*, Ottawa, Ont., Information Canada.

39. ――――. (1973) *Canada Year Book, 1972*, Ottawa, Ont., Information Canada.

40. ――――. (December 1971–1976) *Transcontinental and Regional Air Carrier Operations*, Vols. 31–36.

41. Stigler, George J. (Spring 1971) "The Theory of Economic Regulation," *Bell Journal of Economics and Management Science*, Vol. 2: 3–21.

42. *Toronto Globe and Mail*. (Jan. 15, 1977), p. B12; (March 23, 1977), p. B13.

43. ――――. (March 10, 1973), p. 33.

44. *Wall Street Journal*. (Nov. 19, 1973), Midwest ed., p. 16.

AIRLINE MARKET SHARES VS. CAPACITY SHARES AND THE POSSIBILITY OF SHORT-RUN LOSS EQUILIBRIA

James C. Miller III, AMERICAN ENTERPRISE
INSTITUTE FOR PUBLIC POLICY RESEARCH

Some contend that air service is "destructively competitive"—not because of price competition but because of service competition (i.e., the firm with the largest capacity share allegedly garners an even larger share of the traffic). This hypothesis is tested using data from 1967 through 1969. The results suggest that short-run loss equilibria are possible in certain isolated markets. But these are necessary, not sufficient, conditions, and in any event losses would not persist in the long run. Thus, control of capacity directly by the Civil Aeronautics Board or indirectly through carrier agreements is not warranted on efficiency grounds.

Research in Law and Economics, Vol. 1, pp. 81–96.

I INTRODUCTION

In several proceedings before the Civil Aeronautics Board (CAB), most recently in the Capacity Reduction Agreements Case (Docket 22908), some of the larger airlines have contended that air service is inherently "destructively competitive." Their argument is not based on the usual "cutthroat competition" scenario, where because of scale economies, falling or cyclical industry demand, or dissolution of cartel coordination *price* competition drives out all but the strongest firm.[1] Rather, it is based on the notion that *service* competition could lead to the same result, or at least a situation where all carriers lose money.[2] The reason is that in any given market the largest firm allegedly has the easiest time of attracting passengers and thus has the lowest per passenger cost. The policy implication is that the Board must control capacity competition as well as price competition if it is to assure consumers they will receive stable air service and protect carriers from financial losses.

Although the Board has the power to regulate the number of airlines in domestic interstate city-pair markets and the fares they charge, it does not have the authority to regulate *directly* the capacity they provide, once they have received a "certificate of public convenience and necessity."[3] Since schedule frequency is a major determinant of the quality of service, airlines extensively "compete" or "rival" in this service dimension.[4] In fact, the evidence would suggest that this nonprice competition is so extensive that carriers eliminate excess rents by scheduling up to the point where the actual average load factor approaches the break-even load factor.[5]

In early 1971 the Board concluded portions of its Domestic Passenger Fare Investigation (DPFI; Docket 21866) and appeared to concur with this characterization of airline competitive dynamics, stating:

> We find ... that the higher the fare level in relation to cost, the more capacity carriers will offer and the lower load factors will be; and, conversely, the lower the fare level, the less capacity carriers will operate and the higher load factors will be.[6] ... In any given market, the carrier with the greatest number of schedules will normally carry the largest number of passengers. Thus, the desire to maximize market participation creates powerful incentives to add capacity. The countervailing incentive is supplied only by the imperative of economics: Schedules cannot be added indefinitely if the load factors achieved are insufficient, at the prevailing fare levels, to permit the carriers to cover costs and return a profit.[7]

In August of that year, however, the Board approved an intercarrier agreement involving American, TWA, and United in which they agreed to reduce flight capacity between 6 and 38 percent in four of their major markets.[8] Subsequently, the Board approved numerous other capacity limiting agreements and openly considered institutionalizing them as a "regulatory device."[9] One rationale for the Board's action was its concern over "excesses" in service competition; another was the need to conserve fuel.

When, in 1973, the original three-carrier agreements came up for renewal, the Board, now under considerable public pressure, ordered an investigation.[10] In November 1974, Administrative Law Judge Seaver recommended that the Board *disapprove* the proposed extension of the capacity-limiting agreements.[11] In its final order in 1975, the Board accepted Judge Seaver's recommendation, but held open the possibility that such agreements might again be in the public interest at some future date.[12] Importantly, on the basis of evidence presented in the case, both Judge Seaver and the Board rejected the carriers' contention that air service is characterized by destructive competition.[13]

This paper is based on testimony the author presented on behalf of the U.S. Department of Transportation in that case [Miller (12)]. It addresses the destructive competition argument, especially the version which alleges that the result of unrestrained capacity competition is a market equilibrium where, for a time, all carriers lose money.

II NECESSARY CONDITIONS FOR A LOSS EQUILIBRIUM

The sophisticated version of the carriers' argument is based on an ingenious model of the relationship between airline *market shares* (not profits) and airline capacity shares. Drawing on the work of Renard (13) and others at MIT's Flight Transportation Laboratory,[14] they conclude, from cross-section analysis, that in any given market,

$$MS_i = CS_i^a / \sum_{j=1}^{n} CS_j^a, \tag{1}$$

where

MS_i = market share of firm i (i.e., passengers$_i$/total passengers),

CS_j = capacity shares of each of the n firms in the market (i.e., flights$_j$/ total flights or seats$_j$/total seats), and

a = estimated "coefficient of disproportionality," presumably greater than unity.

For a's greater than unity, the implied market share vs. capacity share relationship is as illustrated in the figure. The *a priori* reasoning is that potential travelers in a market learn which carrier offers the greatest capacity, and given the existence of information costs they tend to contact the carrier with the presumed greatest likelihood of having a convenient flight (seat)

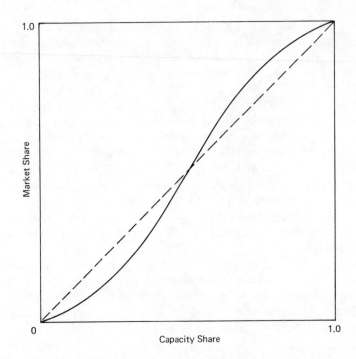

Figure 1. Hypothesized market share vs. capacity share relation, two-carrier market.

available. Consequently, the carrier with a "high" capacity share will have a disproportionately higher market share. This characteristic, in turn, leads carriers to pursue, generally, a policy of maximizing their capacity shares. But since the total market response to greater capacity is inelastic (i.e., market-average load factor falls with increasing capacity, else the market cannot be in equilibrium), load factors fall below break-even and all carriers suffer losses.

As might seem intuitive, the chances of such short-run loss equilibria's obtaining depend upon: (a) what each carrier assumes about the response of other carriers when the initiating carrier changes its capacity; (b) the degree of disproportionality in the market share vs. capacity share relation; (c) the overall market's elasticity with respect to changes in market capacity; and (d) the number of firms in the market. As far as I am aware, the first to express this set of conditions in specific, analytical terms was Joseph V. Yance (17). In that work Yance concluded that *assuming* the extreme case that each carrier proceeds on the basis that no other carrier will respond to its capacity initiatives, then loss equilibria will obtain provided,

$$n > (a - e)/(a - 1), \tag{2}$$

where

e = market capacity elasticity of demand [i.e., $e = (\partial N/\partial C) \cdot (C/N)$,
where N = market passengers and C = market capacity], and
n = number of firms in the market.

In the remainder of this paper I provide estimates of the parameters *a* and *e* as a means of trying to determine the degree to which loss equilibria are *possible* in airline markets.[15] The Appendix, adopted from Douglas and Miller (3), pp. 57–60, formally derives the necessary conditions expressed in Eq. (2). Section III describes ordinary cross-section and cross-section-of-first-difference estimates of *a* and *e*.[16] Section IV summarizes the results and discusses the significance of the loss-equilibria possibility.

III ESTIMATES OF *a* AND *e*

A. Data Source

The data used for generating estimates of *a* and *e* are taken from Bureau of Economics Exhibit BE-6501 in the DPFI. This exhibit summarizes passenger and capacity data for the trunk carriers for the years 1967, 1968, and 1969. (Mid-months of each quarter only were reported.) The exhibit includes information on city-pair market, carrier identification, year, market distance, flights (carrier and total), seats (carrier and total), passengers (carrier and total), as well as other information. These data, representing 256 "competitive" city-pair markets and including the "top 100" markets in terms of revenue passenger miles and also the "top 100" in terms of total revenue passengers, was compiled before any of the capacity agreements went into effect and represents approximately 69 percent of total trunk revenue passenger miles.[17]

B. Cross-Section Analysis

The first task was to duplicate Renard's cross-section estimates of *a*, using this more recent and more complete data. By dividing one carrier's Eq. (1) by that of another, we have:

$$MS_i/MS_k = CS_i^a/CS_k^a, \tag{3}$$

which yields the following estimating equation:

$$\log(N_i/N_k) = a \cdot \log(C_i/C_k), \tag{4}$$

where,

N_i = number of passengers of carrier i in market, and
C_i = capacity of carrier i in market (flights or seats).

Table 1. Cross-Section Regression Analysis of Market Share vs. Capacity Share.

Year	Dependent Variable	Independent Variable	Dispropor- tionality Coefficient (a)	T–Statistic for a = 0	T–Statistic for a = 1	R–Square
1967	$\log (N_i/N_k)$	$\log (F_i/F_k)$	1.133	79.59	9.31	.928
1968	$\log (N_i/N_k)$	$\log (F_i/F_k)$	1.173	68.11	10.06	.904
1969	$\log (N_i/N_k)$	$\log (F_i/F_k)$	1.045	31.94	1.37	.675
1967	$\log (N_i/N_k)$	$\log (S_i/S_k)$	1.120	86.86	9.29	.939
1968	$\log (N_i/N_k)$	$\log (S_i/S_k)$	1.140	72.20	8.86	.914
1969	$\log (N_i/N_k)$	$\log (S_i/S_k)$	1.007	31.53	0.21	.670

The results of a cross-section analysis of all markets is shown in Table 1. In each regression, for all three years, whether carrier capacity is measured in terms of flights (F) or seats (S), a has a positive value and the t-statistics for $a = 0$ are all highly significant. Note also that in each case $a > 1$, meaning that high capacity shares are associated with even higher market shares and conversely (see figure). Moreover, except for the year 1969 the t-statistics for $a = 1$ are all highly significant.

In order to identify the possibility of loss equilibria we must also have estimates of demand capacity elasticity, e. This was accomplished using a very simple model:

$$N = ZC^e, \tag{5}$$

where

N = number of passengers in market;
Z = a constant term, to be estimated;
C = capacity in market (flights, seats); and
e = capacity elasticity of demand, to be estimated.

The estimating equation is thus,

$$\log N = \log Z + e \cdot \log C. \tag{6}$$

A cross-section analysis was made of the DPFI data, and the results are shown in Table 2. Note that the capacity elasticities of market demand, e, are approximately unity, with t-statistics for $e = 1$ that are either insignificant or only barely significant.[18]

C. "Time-Series" Analysis

From the standpoint of the hypothesis being raised about airline competitive dynamics, a more relevant question is the relationship between a *change* in capacity share and the responding *change* in market share. Accepting again that Eq. (1) describes the carriers' underlying market share vs. capacity

Table 2. Cross-Section Regression Analysis of Demand Capacity Elasticity.

Year	Dependent Variable	Independent Variable	Elasticity Coefficient (e)	T–Statistic for e = 0	T–Statistic for e = 1	R–Square
1967	log N	log F	0.944	42.92	− 2.54	0.935
1968	log N	log F	0.952	42.18	− 2.13	0.932
1969	log N	log F	1.007	46.03	0.34	0.943
1967	log N	log S	0.982	48.58	− 0.88	0.948
1968	log N	log S	0.983	48.63	− 0.85	0.948
1969	log N	log S	1.017	50.69	0.86	0.952

share relation, I postulated a consistent cross-section-of-first-difference, or time-series model:

$$MS_{i,t} - MS_{i,t-1} = CS_{i,t}^a / \sum_{j=1}^{n} CS_{j,t}^a - CS_{i,t-1}^a / \sum_{j=1}^{n} CS_{j,t-1}^a. \qquad (7)$$

As before, dividing one carrier's relationship by that of another and simplifying, we have:

$$N_{i,t}/N_{k,t} - N_{i,t-1}/N_{k,t-1} = C_{i,t}^a/C_{k,t}^a - C_{i,t-1}^a/C_{k,t-1}^a. \qquad (8)$$

This specification does not lend itself to estimation by conventional (linear) techniques. Consequently, a nonlinear program was written to iterate over many values of a and then by parabolic techniques to converge on the value of a that minimized the sum of squared deviations. (Iterations were terminated when minimum a was determined to within .001.)

The results of these time-series estimates of a are shown in Table 3. In all cases, a is greater than zero, although the t-statistics for $a = 0$ are grossly insignificant.[19] In four of the six cases, a is greater than unity; in two cases, however, a is less than unity. All of the t-statistics for $a = 1$ are grossly insignificant. The explained variation ranges widely, from approximately 25 percent to over 97 percent.

Time-series (i.e., cross-section-of-first-difference) estimates were also made for demand capacity elasticity, e. Since, *ceteris paribus*, e is closely approximated by

$$e = \{(N_t - N_{t-1})/[(N_t + N_{t-1})/2]\}/\{(C_t - C_{t-1})/[(C_t + C_{t-1})/2]\}, \qquad (9)$$

I used the estimating equation

$$(N_t - N_{t-1})/[(N_t + N_{t-1})/2] = e\{(C_t - C_{t-1})/[(C_t + C_{t-1})/2]\} \qquad (10)$$

to provide first-cut time-series estimates of e.

The results of such a time-series analysis are shown in Table 4. Note that uniformly the t-statistics for both $e = 0$ and $e = 1$ are highly significant. The specific estimates of e range narrowly between .61 and .74 in the case of flight

Table 3. Time-Series Regression Analysis of Market Share vs. Capacity Share.

Time Period	Dependent Variable	Independent Variable	Dispropor-tionality Coefficient (a)	T–Statistic for a = 0	T–Statistic for a = 1	R–Square
1968 vs. 1967	ΔMS	ΔEFS	1.039	0.856	.032	.976
1969 vs. 1968	ΔMS	ΔEFS	0.981	0.555	− .011	.284
1969 vs. 1967	ΔMS	ΔEFS	1.044	0.458	.019	.932
1968 vs. 1967	ΔMS	ΔESS	1.050	1.328	.063	.990
1969 vs. 1968	ΔMS	ΔESS	0.951	0.525	− .027	.246
1969 vs. 1967	ΔMS	ΔESS	1.054	0.484	.025	.938

Note: ΔMS = Change in market share $[\text{i.e., } MS_{i,t} - MS_{i,t-1}]$.

ΔEFS = Change in (exponential) flight share $\left[\text{i.e., } F_{i,t}^a / \sum_{j=1}^{n} F_{j,t}^a - F_{i,t-1}^a / \sum_{j=1}^{n} F_{j,t-1}^a \right]$

ΔESS = Change in (exponential) seat share $\left[\text{i.e., } S_{i,t}^a / \sum_{j=1}^{n} S_{i,t}^a - S_{i,t-1}^a / \sum_{j=1}^{n} S_{j,t-1}^a \right]$.

Table 4. Time-Series Regression Analysis of Demand Capacity Elasticity.

Time Period	Dependent Variable	Independent Variable	Elasticity Coefficient (e)	T–Statistic for e = 0	T–Statistic for e = 1	R–Square
1968 vs. 1967	%ΔN	%ΔF	0.613	14.32	− 9.03	0.612
1969 vs. 1968	%ΔN	%ΔF	0.612	12.99	− 8.22	0.565
1969 vs. 1967	%ΔN	%ΔF	0.741	19.55	− 6.85	0.746
1968 vs. 1967	%ΔN	%ΔS	0.553	15.54	− 12.58	0.650
1969 vs. 1968	%ΔN	%ΔS	0.664	15.95	− 8.07	0.662
1969 vs. 1967	%ΔN	%ΔS	0.645	18.88	− 10.38	0.733

capacity, and between .55 and .66 in the case of seat capacity. The explained variation is from 60 to 70 percent.

IV RESULTS AND INTERPRETATION

Taking the cross-section and time-series estimates of a and e, I used Eq. (2) to compute the *minimum* number of firms in the market necessary for loss

Table 5. Minimum Number of Firms in Market for Loss Equilibria to Obtain
Cross-Section Basis.

Year	Capacity Measure	Estimated Market Share Coefficient (a)	Estimated Demand Capacity Elasticity (e)	Minimum Number of Firms for Loss Equilibria
1967	flights	1.133	0.944	1.4
1968	flights	1.173	0.952	1.3
1969	flights	1.045	1.007	a
1967	seats	1.120	0.982	1.2
1968	seats	1.140	0.983	1.1
1969	seats	1.007	1.017	a/

[a]A demand capacity elasticity, e, greater than unity, together with a disproportionate coefficient, a, greater than unity, automatically leads market capacity to expand without limit. In essence, these results for a and e are irreconcilable.

equilibria to obtain. The cross-section results are shown in Table 5; the time-series results are shown in Table 6. Their differences are striking. Whereas the cross-section results would appear to lend great credence to the loss equilibria hypothesis (that is, two or more firms are sufficient to enable losses), the time-series results would indicate that seven firms are needed before loss equilibria is possible. Notably, not one of the markets in the sample had as many as seven carriers; only Miami-Tampa had six.

Which is to be believed? For several reasons, I suggest that the cross-section results should be given much less weight than the time-series results.

As John Drake (5) has noted, other characteristics of service, such as the timing of flights, the amount of time the carrier has been in the market, the type of equipment used, the amount of advertising, the friendliness of the personnel, and so forth, may be very important in determining the observed S relation.[20] Notably, over the period in question many markets experienced new entry. As a result, the new firms maintained relatively small

Table 6. Minimum Number of Firms in Market for Loss Equilibria to Obtain
Time-Series Basis

Time Period	Capacity Measure	Estimated Market Share Coefficient (a)	Estimated Demand Capacity Elasticity (e)	Minimum Number of Firms for Loss Equilibria
1968 vs. 1967	flights	1.039	.613	10.9
1969 vs. 1968	flights	0.981	.612	–
1969 vs. 1967	flights	1.044	.741	6.9
1968 vs. 1967	seats	1.050	.553	9.9
1969 vs. 1968	seats	0.951	.664	–
1969 vs. 1967	seats	1.054	.645	7.6

levels of capacity, but, understandably, garnered even smaller levels of traffic. In the same manner that a new entrant in any market may encounter information costs and advertise, a new carrier entrant will offer capacity in excess of that which will yield it a market-average load factor.

Second, the cross-section capacity elasticity (e) estimating Eq. (5) contains identification problems. If, as Douglas and Miller (3), ch. 4, have argued, the actual load factor is determined by the break-even load factor and this break-even load factor tends to be reasonably uniform across distances (because of the relationship between costs and the Board's fare-mileage formula), then the ratio of N to C will be very stable and we should not be surprised to find such an e estimate approaching unity, In short, the cross-section analysis of e merely serves to reveal overall average load factor (that is, setting $e = 1$, $N/C = A$).

In conclusion, if the cross-section analysis *overestimates* both a and e, then it *underestimates* the minimum number of firms necessary for loss equilibria to obtain. Thus, the results shown in the last column of Table 5 would appear to be biased on the low side.

Criticisms can also be made of the time-series estimates. While the unexplained variation for a is typically large and the t-statistics for $a = 1$ are very small, one presumes that the "other" factors affecting market share varied less from one time period to the next than they did across markets. Thus, while some bias may exist in these estimates of a, it is probably less than in the cross-section estimates. On the other hand, the time-series estimates of e are undoubtedly biased on the high side. The reason is that there has been a secular rise in air travel due primarily to rising incomes. (This secular increase averaged more than 12 percent per annum during the 1967–1969 period.) Of course, making any downward adjustment in the time-series estimates of e would further increase the minimum number of firms for loss equilibria to obtain.

While the results of the cross-section and time-series analyses do suggest a *possibility* of loss equilibria, it must be stressed that these are *necessary but not sufficient* conditions. The bulk of airline markets certainly are not characterized by loss equilibria. Although in the past few years the airlines have not earned accounting profits consistent with the Board's "reasonable return on investment" (12 percent after taxes but before interest payment on long-term debt, as a percent of equity plus long-term debt), the carriers have been able to expand the industry's investment base quite substantially. In fact, a condition of subnormal industry profits is a signal that airline capacity is overexpanded.[21] It is not an indication of loss equilibria.

Some markets, of course, may exhibit characteristics of loss equilibria. But such behavior may well be a case of predatory service competition.[22] The rationale for the "aggressive" firm(s) is the hope of driving out the competition and then offsetting the short-term losses with long-term excess profits due to the reduced competition. Of course, the reason why this opportunity might afford any hope of success is that the Board can be relied upon to restrain re-entry into the market.

Finally, and most importantly, it must be kept in mind that loss equilibrium is basically a static concept which assumes extremely myopic behavior on the part of airline management. An efficient management presumably would not allow itself to be "caught" in this type of loss situation. When one started to develop, it would cut its losses and attempt to exit the market. (Such an exit would, of course, reduce the possibility of a loss equilibrium's obtaining.) The fact that we do not observe carriers requesting deletion of alleged losing markets is testimony to the absence of loss equilibria. Moreover, carriers do, in fact, take into consideration each other's capacity actions. Indeed, in the absence of a regulatory climate conducive to price competition the carriers have been relegated to competition based on service quality. As the Board has recognized,[23] the use of capacity is one of the most important means carriers have for practicing nonprice competition. Thus, while "loss equilibria" is often raised to justify concerted industry action, the prospect might be better regarded as little more than a theoretical novelty.

APPENDIX: THE NECESSARY CONDITIONS FOR LOSS EQUILIBRIA

This section briefly sketches out the necessary conditions for loss equilibria to obtain.

Equilibrium in a Market with n Firms:

Following Douglas and Miller (3) ch. 4, (*ex post*) market demand is given by

$$N = N(P_0, S), \qquad (A\text{-}1)$$

where P_0 is the given price, and S is total (market) seat capacity. Firm i's demand is given by

$$N_i = \lambda_i N. \qquad (A\text{-}2)$$

Total costs of firm i are

$$TC_i = cN_i + kS_i, \qquad (A\text{-}3)$$

where c is per-passenger traffic cost, k is per-seat capacity cost, and S_i is firm i's seat capacity.* Profits of firm i are thus

$$\Pi_i = P_0 N_i - cN_i - kS_i, \qquad (A\text{-}4)$$

---

*See Douglas and Miller (3), ch. 2.

or

$$\Pi_i = P_0 \lambda_i N - c\lambda_i N - kS_i. \tag{A-5}$$

At equilibrium (that is, first-order profit-maximizing conditions),

$$\partial \Pi_i / \partial S_i = P_0 [N(\partial \lambda_i / \partial S_i) + \lambda_i (\partial N / \partial S)]$$
$$- c[N(\partial \lambda_i / \partial S_i) + \lambda_i (\partial N / \partial S)] - k = 0, \tag{A-6}$$

or,

$$P_0 = c + k\{1/[N(\partial \lambda_i / \partial S_i) + \lambda_i (\partial N / \partial S)]\} = MC. \tag{A-7}$$

Average cost per passenger carried is given by

$$AC = (cN_i + kS_i)/N_i = c + k(S_i/N_i). \tag{A-8}$$

Proportional Market Shares Case:

Let $N_i/Q = S_i/S = \lambda_i$. Then,

$$\partial \lambda_i / \partial S_i = 1/S - S_i/S^2 \tag{A-9}$$

If at equilibrium, $S_i/S = S_j/S = 1/n$, then Eq. (A-7) may be written:

$$MC = c + k/[N/S + (dN/dS - N/S)/n] = P_0. \tag{A-10}$$

The profit margin per passenger is then

$$P_0 - AC = k/[N/S + (dN/dS - N/S)/n] - k/(N/S). \tag{A-11}$$

Since $dN/dS < N/S$, $(P_0 - AC) > 0$, or $P_0 > AC$. However, from Eq. (A-11), $(P_0 - AC)$ approaches zero as n grows large.

Nonproportional Market Shares Case:

Let the firm's relative capacity share be defined as

$$S_i = S_i'/S. \tag{A-12}$$

Let the firm's relative market share be given by

$$N_i/N = S_i'^a / \Sigma S_j'^a, \tag{A-13}$$

where

$$j = 1, \ldots, n$$
$$a \geq 1.$$

Eq. (A-7) now becomes,

$$MC = c + k/\{a[N/S + (dN/dS - N/S)/n]\}. \tag{A-14}$$

Profit margin per passenger thus becomes,

$$P_0 - AC = k/\{a[N/S + (dN/dS - N/S)/n]\} - k/(N/S), \quad (A-15)$$

and is less than the margin given by Eq. (A-11).

Existence of a Loss Equilibrium:

Let market demand be:

$$N = ZS^e, \quad (A-16)$$

where Z is some constant and e is the capacity (seat) elasticity of demand [that is, $e = (dN/dS)/(S/N)$].

$$N_i = (S_i^a/\Sigma S_j^a) \cdot ZS^e. \quad (A-17)$$

The marginal cost of attracting and carrying an additional passenger for firm i is thus,

$$MC_i = c + k(\partial N_i/\partial S_i)^{-1}. \quad (A-18)$$

By symmetry, assume that $S_j/S = 1/n, j = 1, \ldots, n$. Then,

$$N_i = (S_i/S)^a/(n/n^a)(ZS^e) = (S_i/S)^a(n^{a-1})(ZS^e), \quad (A-19)$$

and

$$\begin{aligned} \partial N_i/\partial S_i &= a(S_i/S)^{a-1}(1/S - S_i/S^2)(n^{a-1})(ZS^e) \\ &+ (S_i/S)^a(n^{a-1})(ZeS^{e-1}). \end{aligned} \quad (A-20)$$

Since at equilibrium, $S_i/S = 1/n$,

$$\begin{aligned} \partial N_i/\partial S_i &= a(n - 1/n)(ZS^{e-1}) + (n^{-1})(ZeS^{e-1}) \\ &= ZS^{e-1}[a(1 - 1/n) - e/n]. \end{aligned} \quad (A-21)$$

Average cost per passenger is given by

$$AC = k(S_i/N_i) + c. \quad (A-22)$$

Since $N_i/S_i = N/S$,

$$AC = c + k(S/Z^e) = c + kZ^{-1}S^{1-e}. \quad (A-23)$$

Excess profit exists so long as $(MC - AC) > 0$:

$$MC - AC = Z^{-1}S^{1-e}\{[a(1 - 1/n) + e/n]^{-1} - 1\}, \quad (A-24)$$

which reduces to:

$$MC - AC > 0 \text{ iff } a(n - 1) + e < n. \quad (A-25)$$

In other words, (short-run) loss equilibria is possible if and only if

$$n > (a - e)/(a - 1). \quad (A-26)$$

94 JAMES C. MILLER III

FOOTNOTES

The author is co-director of the Center for the Study of Government Regulation at the American Enterprise Institute for Public Policy Research. This work owes a significant intellectual debt to George W. Douglas and Joseph V. Yance. The author also acknowledges helpful comments from Arthur De Vany, George Eads, Theodore Keeler, and an anonymous referee of this *Review*, and especial appreciation to Eugene Pulley and Nancy Brown for writing the nonlinear regression program mentioned in Section III. The usual caveat applies.

1. Cf. Scherer's discussion (14), pp. 198–206.
2. Cf. CAB Order 73–4–98 (April 24, 1973).
3. Section 401(e) (4) of the Federal Aviation Act states that "No term, condition, or limitation of a certificate shall restrict the right of an air carrier to add to or change schedules, equipment, accommodations, and facilities..."
4. Cf. De Vany (1), Douglas and Miller (2, 3, 4); Eads (6, 7); Jordan (10), ch. 3; White (15); and Yance (16, 17).

Briefly, the passenger's "full cost" of travel consists of the ticket price plus the value of time expended. *Ceteris paribus*, greater schedule frequency lowers (expected) frequency delay (i.e., time waiting for a flight) and expected stochastic delay (i.e., the delay incurred because the preferred flight may be filled). Thus, total schedule delay is an inverse function of schedule frequency, and carriers may lower the "full cost" (or "full price") of service to the passenger by expanding capacity. See Douglas and Miller (3) ch. 6, and (4).

5. Cf. Douglas and Miller (3), ch. 4.
6. CAB Order 71–4–54 (April 9, 1971), p. 23.
7. *Ibid.*, p. 5.
8. Cf. Douglas and Miller (3), pp. 128–134; Eads (6); Jordan (10); and CAB Order 71–8–91 (Aug. 19, 1971). The four markets were New York/Newark–Los Angeles, New York/Newark–San Francisco, Chicago–San Francisco, and Washington/Baltimore–Los Angeles.
9. See CAB Order 73–4–98 (April 24, 1973). Although the Board does not have the authority to regulate carrier capacity directly, it is given very broad power to approve and grant antitrust immunity for intercarrier agreements relating to: "pooling or apportioning earnings, losses, traffic, service, or equipment, or relating to the establishment of transportation rates, fares, charges, or classifications, or for preserving and improving safety, economy, and efficiency of operation, or for controlling, regulating, preventing, or otherwise eliminating destructive, oppressive, or wasteful competition, or for regulating stops, schedules, and character of service, or for other cooperative working arrangements." [Section 412 (a) of the Federal Aviation Act.]
10. CAB Order 73–7–147 (July 27, 1973).
11. Initial Decision of E. Robert Seaver in CAB Docket 22908 (Nov. 18, 1974).
12. CAB Order 75–7–98 (July 21, 1975).
13. Cf. Seaver, *ibid.*, pp. 53–56, and CAB Order 75–7–98, *ibid.*, pp. 9, 10.
14. Also see Fruhan (8), ch. 5.
15. That is, if inequality (2) does not hold and/or if the reactive behavior assumption described above does not obtain, then loss equilibria is said to be impossible.
16. For reasons that will become apparent later, I characterize these later estimates as "time-series" results.
17. BE–T–6501, CAB Docket 21866–6, p. 2. It might be noted that local service carrier participation in these markets was not reported and that trunk carriers having less than 10 percent market share were ignored. However, the sample may be considered representative (and unbiased) for the purpose envisioned here.

18. See comments on these results in Section IV.

19. In the context of this nonlinear estimating equation, it is not at all clear that the conventional t-test is applicable.

20. When Drake added other such variables in a cross-sectional study of local service air carrier markets, the t-statistic for $a = 1$ became no longer "significant" and a approached unity.

21. Cf. Douglas and Miller (3), ch. 6.

22. Cf. Hamilton and Kawahara (9). Another alleged case of predatory service competition arose when American merged with Trans Caribbean in 1971 and then began pouring capacity into the New York–San Juan market. [Cf. CAB Order 72-1-86 (Jan. 25, 1972).]

23. Cf. CAB Order 71-4-54 (April 9, 1971), p. 5.

REFERENCES

1. De Vany, Arthur S. (Spring 1975) "The Effect of Price and Entry Regulation on Airline Output, Capacity, and Efficiency," *Bell Journal of Economics*, Vol. 6, No. 1: 327–345.

2. Douglas, George W., and Miller, James C. III. (Spring 1974) "The CAB's Domestic Passenger Fare Investigation," *Bell Journal of Economics and Management Science*, Vol. 5, No. 1: 205–222.

3. ———. (1974) *Economic Regulation of Domestic Air Transport: Theory and Policy*. Washington, D.C., The Brookings Institution.

4. ———. (September 1974) "Quality Competition, Industry Equilibrium, and Efficiency in the Price-Constrained Airline Market," *American Economic Review*, Vol. 44, No. 4: 657–669.

5. Drake, John W. (1970) "Forecasting Competitors' Market Shares in Local Service Markets, mimeo."

6. Eads, George C. (May 1974) "Airline Capacity Limitation Controls: Public Vice or Public Virtue?" *American Economic Review*, Vol. 44, No. 2: 365–371.

7. ———. (1975) "Competition in the Domestic Trunk Airline Industry: Too Much or Too Little?" in Almarin Phillips, ed., *Promoting Competition in Regulated Markets*. Washington, D.C., The Brookings Institution.

8. Fruhan, William E. (1972) *The Fight for Competitive Advantage: A Study of the United States Domestic Air Carriers*, Boston, Harvard Business School.

9. Hamilton, James L., and Kawahara, Michael K. (1975) "Predatory Nonprice Competition: The Case of Hawaii Inter-island Air Transport," *Antitrust Law and Economics Review*, Vol. 7, No. 1: 82–97.

10. Jordan, William A. (1970) *Airline Regulation in America: Effects and Imperfections*, Baltimore, Johns Hopkins University Press.

11. ———. (September 1973) "Airline Capacity Agreements: Correcting a Regulatory Imperfection," *Journal of Air Law and Commerce*, Vol. 39, No. 2: 179–213.

12. Miller, James C. III. (April 26, 1974) "Testimony," CAB Docket 22908, DOT-T-1 through 4.

13. Renard, Gilles. (September 1970) "Competition in Air Transportation: An Econometric Approach," unpublished MS thesis, Department of Aeronautics and Astronautics, MIT.

14. Scherer, F. M. (1970) *Industrial Market Structure and Economic Performance*, Chicago, Rand McNally.

15. White, Lawrence J. (Autumn 1972) "Quality Variation when Prices are Regulated,"

Bell Journal of Economics and Management Science, Vol. 3, No. 2: 425–436.

16. Yance, Joseph V. (November 1972) "Nonprice Competition in Jet Aircraft Capacity," *Journal of Industrial Economics*, Vol. 21: 55–71.

17. ———. (December 1970) "The Possibility of Loss-Producing Equilibria in Air Carrier Markets."

THE POLITICAL RATIONALITY
OF FEDERAL
TRANSPORTATION POLICY

Ann F. Friedlaender, MASSACHUSETTS
INSTITUTE OF TECHNOLOGY, CAMBRIDGE

Richard de Neufville, MASSACHUSETTS
INSTITUTE OF TECHNOLOGY, CAMBRIDGE

What changes to national transportation policy are possible in the United States? What research is relevant to establishing direction and priorities among these opportunities? This essay proposes a model of American experience in governmental promotion and regulation of transportation that suggests answers to those questions.

We argue first, that, while regulatory and investment policies may often overtly pursue conflicting goals, they have a certain rationality when viewed in the broader context of multiple objectives. The record suggests that these are: Fairness; Support of Rural and Agricultural Interests; Industrial Stability; and Economic Efficiency. We infer from the persistence of these objectives that

Research in Law and Economics, Vol. 1, pp. 97–114.
Copyright © 1979 by JAI Press, Inc.
All rights of reproduction in any form reserved.
ISBN: 0–89232–028–1.

they are thought to be worth the considerable efficiency costs they appear to impose.

Second, we suggest that American pluralist form of government, in which important policy changes can only occur with the acquiescence of diverse groups, promotes political compromise and accommodation. Narrow technical or ideological justifications do not provide sufficient impetus for change.

The issue facing transportation policy is thus not so much whether efficiency savings could be realized, but whether the several regional and economic sectors of our society will find them large enough to overcome the sacrifices these savings would entail. Alternatively, the question is whether new institutional arrangements could be found to reduce efficiency costs while attaining our other objectives.

I INTRODUCTION AND OVERVIEW

The federal government has traditionally played an active and diverse role in domestic transportation. Federal regulatory policies directly affect rates, routes, entry, and mergers in the intercity transportation industries: rail, trucking, and air.[1] The federal government largely determines the quantity, quality, and costs of the infrastructure in the trucking, barge, and air transport industries through its investment and user charge policies. While its role is somewhat less direct, it also affects the quantity and quality of the infrastructure in the railroad industry through its abandonment policies, and, with the establishment of Amtrak and the reorganization of the Northeast railroads into Conrail, is beginning to enter into a new phase of direct subsidy and operations in, at least, rail activities.

Besides these major promotional and regulatory roles, the federal government undertakes a number of other activities that affect the intercity transportation industries. Energy policy directly affects fuel costs and thus the relative costs of the various intercity modes. Environmental controls affect emissions and noise levels of motor vehicles and aircraft and thus their relative costs. Federal policies with respect to safety, union work roles, and loan guarantees can have substantial impacts upon the transportation industries.

With such a diverse spectrum of activities, it would be surprising if all federal policies were aimed at the same goals or affected all transportation industries consistently. Indeed, one need only look at the Preamble in the National Transportation Policy of the Transportation Act of 1940, which called for the Interstate Commerce Commission (ICC) "to preserve the inherent advantage of each mode" and the federal funding of the Interstate Highway System and the extensive network of waterways to realize that these policies may often be in direct conflict.

Nevertheless, it is our belief that while regulatory and investment/user charge policies may often pursue overtly conflicting goals, they have a certain rationality when viewed within a somewhat broader perspective of the multiple objectives of the policy maker. By recognizing that federal transportation policy attempts to satisfy a broad range of goals, which themselves may not be entirely consistent, it is usually possible to explain policy action on the basis of implicit or explicit trade-offs among these several objectives.

The recognition that transportation policy is aimed at multiple objectives is obviously important for policy analysis. If policy makers are concerned about issues of equity and the income distribution, they will tend to discount policy evaluations that concentrate on aggregate efficiency impacts of transportation policy. Conversely, however, to the extent that issues of economic efficiency are important to policy makers, analyses that solely consider the income transfers implied by transportation policies will be inadequate. Insofar as policy makers (whether they be legislators, administrators, or even judges) make implicit or explicit trade-offs among various objectives, their actions may appear to be irrational when viewed from the perspective of any single objective.

A full analysis of the diverse goals and implicit trade-offs associated with the many facets of federal transportation policy is an enormous undertaking that would require the development of a model of regulatory behavior and a quantitative analysis of the policy-maker's objective function and their relevant constraints.[2] While obviously desirable, such an undertaking is beyond the scope of this paper, whose goals are considerably more modest: namely, to suggest the various objectives of transportation policy makers and to indicate the implied trade-offs among them. Thus, rather than develop a behavioral model of transportation policy, we shall attempt to highlight several aspects of transportation policy that have generally been neglected. In particular, it is our belief that questions of income gains and losses to specific groups, of industry stability, and of shipper equity have tended to dominate questions of economic efficiency in regard to regulatory and investment policies.[3] Consequently, although measuring the efficiency impacts of transportation policy is an important activity, it will necessarily fail to consider the full dimension of the problem.

II THE GOALS OF FEDERAL TRANSPORTATION POLICY

Although federal transportation policies encompass a wide range of activities, regulatory and investment/user charge policies dominate the others in terms of their pervasiveness, the magnitude of their impacts, and their political importance. We will consequently focus upon these policies and only discuss other aspects of federal transportation policy when relevant to the objectives contained in regulatory and investment policies.

Identification of the goals of federal transportation policy is made difficult because the American political process tends to make implicit rather than explicit trade-offs and to react to rather ill-defined goals rather than well-defined goals. Thus, it is probably impossible to understand present transportation policy and its evolution without understanding the nature of the political process in the United States.

A. The Politics of Change in the United States

The United States' political system differs sharply from those in other countries, such as Britain or France, in that there is no central authority than can decide upon the desirability of change and then ensure its implementation. Political power in America is deliberately divided among the various branches of government, between the central government and the states, and between the states themselves. Each of these entities has some power to frustrate, delay, and even veto proposals for change. Thus, no regulatory or administrative proposal for major change stands much chance of being implemented unless it commands widespread acceptance by most of the interest groups involved in the issue.

Consequently, widely focused problems must be generally recognized as legitimate and important if they are to receive serious consideration for resolution in the political process.[4] The broad policy problems that will command sufficient attention to attain resolution are, thus, those that arise from broadly based public perceptions of deficiency between what is and what could be. These are the issues on which policy makers may feel are worth spending effort and political capital.

Conversely, policy problems are only rarely, if ever, defined by groups of experts relying solely on their professional standards as to what is right. An economist may see that the regulation of transportation creates inefficiencies. An engineer may find that this same regulation is a barrier to technical innovation. Although both may be correct, little change in policy is likely to result from these observations until public sentiment is sufficiently aroused to motivate the many interest groups to cooperate in doing something about the situation.

While something of an oversimplification, one can argue that changes in transportation policy only come about in time of crisis in response to widely held views that major changes are necessary. Thus, the original passage of the Interstate Commerce Act in 1887 was not so much a response to the specific special interests, but instead a response to a wide range of divergent interests that desired regulation. As Friedlaender (8), p. 2, has stated:

> When regulation of railroads was first introduced in 1887, it was widely supported. Small, isolated shippers wanted it to protect them from the monopoly power of the railroads. Western communities wanted it to limit the railroads' heavy-handed exercise of economic power over rates, routes, and the placement of depots. The general public wanted it to control the frequent rate wars, the watered stock, the irresponsible land speculation, and the many bankruptcies and reorganizations. The federal government wanted it to ensure relatively low freight rates on goods coming from the West to encourage the continued settlement and development of this region. The railroads supported it (or at least acquiesced to it) to formalize the existing rate structure and to end the instability created by frequent rate wars. Thus, the Interstate Commerce Act of 1887 and the regulatory structure it established enjoyed wide support. Regulation controlled the monopolistic excesses of the railroads while permitting them to maintain a rate structure that benefited not only the railroads but society.

For an elaboration of these views see Buck (2), Kolko (17), Benson (1), Tarbell (27), and MacAvoy (18). Similarly, the Transportation Acts of 1935, 1938, and 1940, which respectively introduced the regulation of motor carriers, air carriers, and inland water carriers, resulted from attempts to deal with the crises and disruptions caused by the Great Depression. Faced with bankruptcy of many firms, excess capacity, and cutthroat competition, the carriers favored regulation, which would help control the competitive excesses of the industry and stabilize rates and profits. Shippers favored regulation because it would lead to stability and reduced uncertainty concerning rates. Agricultural interests favored regulation to ensure that the traditional value-of-service rate structure would be maintained.[5] Thus, again, major changes in regulatory practices only came about when a wide consensus developed that existing practices led to intolerable situations as perceived by broad groups of shippers and carriers.

Even in time of crisis that may engender major institutional changes, however, it is only realistic to expect that these changes will be directed toward the issues of the moment. For example, instead of effecting major changes in the regulatory framework, the acts of 1935 and 1940 each brought trucking companies and water carriers under regulation, thus leaving the basic structure of regulation unchanged. Consequently, even if major changes in institutional arrangements occur, it is likely that they will do so in a piecemeal fashion instead of by comprehensive legislation that covers all aspects of transport regulation.

The implementation of change in a piecemeal fashion is also consistent with the tendency of the American political process to compromise and accommodate diverse interests. Since change requires the acquiesence of many different groups, explicit efforts must be made to bridge their differences. This desire for accommodation should affect the nature of the proposals that are acceptable for change. Because policy makers attempt to maximize the political acceptability of innovation, they try to structure the legislation to appeal to as many diverse groups as possible.

This desire for compromise and accommodation was evident in the creation of Amtrak and Conrail. Instead of outright nationalization or abandonment of service, Amtrak and Conrail attempt to preserve service within a private framework. Even though operating companies were formed that belong to the federal government, the autonomy of the private companies was preserved and service was maintained. Although the formation of these companies may well facilitate the eventual nationalization of the rail network and abandonment of service, this change (if it occurs) will necessarily come in a slow and fragmented fashion. Similarly, although the construction of the Interstate Highway System marked a fundamental departure in policy by providing massive amounts of federal funds for the highway infrastructure, which caused a dramatic change in the relative costs of rail and truck transportation, its significance as transportation legislation was minimized by labeling it as a defense measure.

Since the American political process is based upon compromise and accommodation which often attempt to blur the magnitude and significance of the change, it is usually difficult to identify the key motivations for any piece of major transportation legislation or any important regulatory decision. The preambles or rationales for the documents tend to include all the elements that have any political support. Consequently, the major forces leading to regulatory change generally have to be deduced from their ultimate consequences instead of from the documents themselves.

Moreover, since the political process stresses compromise among conflicting forces, the identification of the major themes that have motivated and shaped transportation policy in the United States is essential if we are to develop politically viable alternatives to the existing regulatory structure. Without identifying these themes, it is impossible to understand which problems the public will accept as legitimate and, thus, which problems may present a reasonable possibility for effective political action.

B. Major Issues

The identification of the major motivations that have led to the existing structure of transportation policies is difficult, however, since they are not clearly defined by acts of Congress, the decision of the regulatory agencies, or the rulings of the courts. As suggested earlier, this lack of clarity of purpose is an expected feature of the American political process. Since our system essentially requires that issues be blurred and compromised, it is necessary to interpret the overall patterns that have emerged over time to determine the principal motivations for regulation.

Nevertheless, examination of the record indicates that transportation policy makers have generally been concerned with the following major issues:

- Fairness
- Support of rural and agricultural interests
- Industry stability

Let us consider each of these in turn.

1 *Fairness.* The issue of fairness was a major one in the passing of the Interstate Commerce Act of 1887 and has continued to be a dominant theme in subsequent regulatory changes. Prior to the passage of this act in 1887, the railroad rate structure was characterized by pervasive price discrimination among shippers, localities, and commodities. Small-lot shippers and isolated communities with no alternative means of transport were charged rates far in excess of those charged for comparable service where railroads faced competitive pressures. Large-volume shippers and communities served by several means of transport or alternative sources of supply generally enjoyed low rates, while the railroads exploited their monopoly power with respect to their captive shippers.

Thus, it is not surprising that the bulk of the initial Interstate Commerce Act of 1887 was aimed at the prohibition of discriminatory practices among persons and locations. In particular, this act effectively prohibited the monopoly exploitation of small shippers by requiring that rates be just and reasonable (Section 1), by explicitly prohibiting personal price discrimination (Section 2), undue preference between persons, localities, and type of traffic (Section 3), and the practice of charging more for a short haul than a long haul over a common line (Section 4).

Although the act has been considerably altered during the ensuing 90 years, virtually no efforts have been made to alter its prohibitions against personal price discrimination. Indeed, the market dominance provision of the recent RRRR Act can be interpreted as an effort to ensure that discriminatory pricing will not occur as the railroads undertake more flexibility in rate making.

Nevertheless, it is important to realize that the commission's views of fairness have had a rather limited vision of equity. In particular, it is entirely possible that efforts to maintain the rate structure by permitting blanket rate increases may in fact have created serious inequities with respect to carriers and the consuming public. Indeed, the commission's efforts to maintain a rate structure that favors rural and agricultural interests and to promote industry stability through the implicit cartelization of the surface transport industries have doubtless resulted in instances where certain consumer groups and carriers have been favored at the expense of others.[6] Thus, fairness appears to have been viewed primarily in terms of specific personal price discrimination.

Fairness or nondiscriminatory pricing has also played an important role in the CAB's decisions concerning rate differentials. While it has always been willing to permit rate differentials for service differentials, that is, rate difference for first-class and economy service, it has been somewhat ambivalent about permitting rate differentials for other classes of service. During the past decade the Board has vacillated between permitting rate differentials for less convenient service (e.g., fares requiring advance payment, limiting flexibility for changing plans, or requiring travel by night; student standby discounts), and feeling that these differentials were discriminatory and hence unacceptable. Current policy appears to permit rate differentials that are clearly based on service differentials in terms of convenience, but to prohibit differentials that are based on the characteristics of the traveler. Thus, fares that force the traveler to fly at certain times and to make reservations in advance are acceptable, while student discounts are not.

In addition, the CAB requires a uniform fare taper or relationship between fare and distance. Thus people flying between Grand Forks, North Dakota, and Des Moines, Iowa, face essentially the same fare structure as those flying between Boston and Washington, D. C., even though the airlines are able to achieve substantial economies of density on the heavily traveled routes. Since rate differentials based on route density would appear discriminatory, even though they would in fact reflect cost differentials, the CAB has resisted them.

Nevertheless, price discrimination is pervasive in the transportation industries; price-marginal cost ratios differ among different types of commodities and different types of users. The value-of-service rate structure is frankly discriminatory and the cross subsidization between passengers and freight, and between various types of traffic in the air and surface freight industries is widely recognized and accepted. Thus, while considerations of fairness prohibit certain forms of price discrimination, they do not prohibit all of them. It is consequently instructive to analyze the nature of the permissible price discrimination, which will indicate the role that regulatory practices have played in supporting agricultural and rural interests.

2 *Support of Rural and Agricultural Interests.* Value-of-service pricing is a key characteristic of the freight rate structure in the United States. Under this structure low-value agricultural and bulk commodities are charged low

rates relative to costs while high-value manufactured commodities are charged high rates relative to costs. Thus, although the Interstate Commerce Act of 1887 prohibited all forms of personal price discrimination, it permitted the retention of a major form of discriminatory pricing in the value-of-service rate structure.

Since the value-of-service rate structure clearly favors rural and agricultural interests and the interests of other bulk shippers, it is entirely consistent with a more general public policy that has tended to favor these interests. Indeed, the support of agricultural and rural interests has been a dominant theme of American political life. Thus, just as direct price supports or subsidies can be viewed as vehicles of income maintenance for agricultural and rural groups, so can the maintenance of value-of-service rate structure, the agricultural exemption in trucking regulation, the construction of the Interstate Highway System, and the construction of the extensive waterway network with its lack of user charges.

When regulation was initially instituted, the value-of-service rate structure met a number of important goals. It not only made sense as a vehicle for social policy by ensuring relatively low rates on agricultural commodities but also made sense from the point of view of the railroads which could obtain higher profits with a discriminatory rate structure than a nondiscriminatory one. As Friedlaender (8), p. 16, has argued: "The rate structure that maximized the railroads' profits was also the one that encouraged the development of the West. At that time regulation unquestionably served important social goals and created few, if any, losses in terms of economic efficiency."

Nevertheless, with the growth of truck competition, the value-of-service rate structure was no longer the profit-maximizing rate structure. Nelson and Greiner (22) have argued convincingly that the railroads consistently attempted to raise rates on noncompetitive agricultural commodities between the passage of the Transportation Act of 1920, which in principle permitted rate-of-return rate making,[7] and the passage of the Transportation Act of 1935, which brought motor carriage under regulatory control. Nevertheless, the ICC consistently prevented these rate increases, citing the depressed state of agriculture and the Hoch-Smith resolution of 1925 which gave a clear legislative sanction to the value-of-service rate structure. Indeed, the extension of regulation to motor carriers and water carriers can be interpreted as an effort to maintain the traditional rate structure in the face of competitive pressures that would otherwise have eroded it.

In this connection, the agricultural and bulk exemptions provided by the Transportation Acts of 1935 and 1940 are interesting. In particular, the exemption of agricultural commodities by motor carriers is entirely consistent with efforts to maintain relatively low agricultural rates as is the exemption of rate regulation for barge tows which contain less than three commodities. Both instances reflect legislative concern with agricultural rates and a belief that competitive pressures can act as a supplement to regulation. Thus, the structure of regulation that seems to have evolved is one in which rail rates on agricultural commodities are kept at relatively low levels through regulatory and competitive pressures.

Federal investment and user charge policies are also consistent with efforts to provide the railroads with competition on their bulk and agricultural traffic and thus to ensure that market forces will help maintain relatively low freight rates on these commodities. In several cases, high freight rates are explicitly cited as the rationale for construction of inland waterways; see The Doyle Report (28), p. 95, for example. Moreover, the procedures used by the Corps of Engineers to measure benefits are frankly related to the railroad rate structure. Because benefits are measured by the differentials between rail rates and barge costs, there is a clear presumption that waterway construction will lead to lower rates to producers of bulk agricultural commodities. Since one of the goals of waterway construction is reduced freight rates, it would thus be counterproductive to impose user charges that would tend to offset these rate reductions. Consequently, the federal investment and user charge policy in waterways has a clear political rationale, if not an economic one.

Although the Interstate Highway System was sold in terms of its general national impacts upon all regions of the country, it seems clear that it has dramatically improved the accessibility of rural areas and reduced, if not eliminated, the latent monopoly power of the railroads with respect to rural and agricultural areas that do not enjoy water competition. While the completion of the urban segments of the Interstate System has often been delayed by excessive costs and local opposition, the rural segments of the system have largely been completed on schedule. Thus, virtually all areas of the country now have a viable (if more expensive) alternative to rail transportation.

Whether considerations of the traditional rate structure entered explicitly into the decision-making calculus of the legislative process when the Interstate Highway Act was passed in 1958 is impossible to say. It is clear, however, that by virtually any cost/benefit calculus, much of the rural Interstate System was not economically justified; see for example, Friedlander (7). From this we can only infer that accessibility and low-cost transport to rural areas were viewed as being sufficiently important to merit the construction of a large number of links of questionable merit in terms of economic efficiency.

Finally, the abandonment provisions of the Railroad Revitalization and Regulatory Reform Act of 1976 also indicate that a concern with rural and agricultural interests still persists. As high-value traffic has increasingly been diverted to trucks at the expense of the railroads (partially due to the lowered trucking costs occasioned by the Interstate Highway System), increasing amounts of rail lines have been subjected to falling traffic densities. Since considerable evidence shows that there are substantial economies of density—see Keeler (15), Caves and Christensen (3)—this means that costs have risen substantially on these lines. Because the railroads are prevented from raising rates on this traffic, either by regulatory controls or by truck or water competition, it is likely that much of this traffic has become uneconomic for the railroad to carry. The rational behavior of the railroads in this situation would be to abandon this traffic. Thus, if the railroads were free of all capacity controls, it is likely that they would abandon a substantial amount of their light-density lines.

However, the Revitalization and Regulatory Reform Act of 1976 has made abandonment considerably more difficult than it previously has been. Specifically, the act prevents abandonment in the face of sufficient shipper opposition and instead provides modest subsidies for the continuation of service. Since rural and agricultural interests would presumably be the hardest hit by massive abandonment of light-density lines, this provision is clearly consistent with the traditional stance in favor of these interests at the expense of urban and suburban interests.

Finally, the structure of air rates has also discriminated in favor of rural areas. While there is a certain amount of controversy concerning the existence of cross subsidies between rural and urban interests in the sense that the airlines actually suffer losses on their light-density traffic—see Douglas and Miller (5), Eads (6)—it is generally agreed that a cross subsidy exists in the sense that compared to rates between major cities, rates to rural areas are lower and service is higher than each would be in the absence of regulatory controls. In addition, the Board grants explicit subsidies to local carriers.

The problem facing the airlines is quite similar to that facing the railroads. In both cases, economies of density would dictate a rate structure that was characterized by lower rates on high-density traffic characterized by large traffic volumes over a given link. In fact, however, rates for "similar" routes are comparable regardless of the traffic density. Thus, the rate structure discriminates in favor of the low-density areas since the price-marginal cost ratios they experience for the same load factor are much lower than those associated with high-density areas.[8]

In the absence of regulation, it is highly likely that the airlines would either reduce service or raise rates (or both) to low-density regions to make their returns on this traffic commensurate with the returns to other traffic. This, of course, would not be in the best interests of these rural communities which have enjoyed service on a general parity with other regions. Thus, again we see that regulation has tended to favor these regions relative to urban areas.

In sum, it seems clear that one of the major themes of transportation policy has been the support of rural and agricultural interests. The freight rate structure and the air rate structure discriminate in favor of small communities and rural regions. The federal investment and user charge policies in highways and waterways can largely be explained in terms of a desire to provide alternative sources of transportation to regions that are subject to potential monopoly power on the part of the railroads. The abandonment provisions of the Railroad Revitalization and Regulatory Reform Act of 1976 serve to ensure continued rail service to rural regions that generate light-traffic density.

Income redistribution from urban and suburban areas to rural and agricultural regions has also been a major theme of American public policy. The farm subsidy and the stockpiling procedure for raw materials have also been designed to aid rural and agricultural groups. Thus the income redistribution implicit in the transportation policies concerning rates and infrastructure is entirely consistent with broader policy goals and actions.

This indicates, however, that in the absence of a major shift in public policy, any changes in transportation policy that adversely affect rural and agricultural interests will probably not be politically or socially acceptable.

3 *Industry Stability.* Although probably somewhat less important than fairness or support of agricultural and rural interests, the issue of industry stability has consistently been a concern of regulatory authorities. The following from the *Railway Review* of 1886, quoted in Kolko (17), p. 40, expresses the general attitude toward stability quite well:

> The rate wars which have of late years so devastated the finances of the railroad companies, are all inaugurated and carried out upon interstate traffic ... they introduce elements of chance into the transactions of business. ... In the interests of the producer, transporter and consumer, governmental regulation of interstate traffic is necessary and desirable.

Congress has repeatedly endorsed the notion of price stabilization (or fixing) in transportation. The Transportation Act of 1920 established regulation of minimum rates for railroads and reinforced the railroads' capacity to prevent rate wars and set prices. Later, when these practices came under attack under the antitrust laws, Congress exempted them from these statutes through the Reed-Bulwinkle Act of 1948.

More recently, Congress has endorsed the notion of price stability in the surface freight industries in the Transportation Act of 1958 and the RRRR Act of 1976. In the first case, Congress flirted with passing legislation that specifically prohibited umbrella rate making, under which rates of the low-cost carrier are maintained to protect the high-cost carrier; for a full discussion see Friendly (10). However, when it become clear that the passage of such legislation would free the railroads to reduce rates to attempt to capture the high-value traffic, Congress retreated from this position.[9] The recently passed RRRR Act is rather ambiguous on this point. Although it does permit railroads to charge rates within a 7 percent band, it can prevent these changes in the face of market dominance, which presumably means situations in which such rate reductions would hurt competitors. Thus, concern with industry and market stability still appears to be very strong.

Generally, the regulatory agencies have acted to preserve the status quo and to maintain threatened firms or industries. The Civil Aeronautics Board has repeatedly attempted to save specific airline firms from collapse by giving troubled airlines advantageous routes.[10] When all else fails, the Board is the matchmaker for rescuing mergers, as it was between Capital and United and between Northeast and Delta. Similarly, the Interstate Commerce Commission carefully examines proposed railroad rates to see if they might lead to "destructive competition" and impose a risk of driving a competitor or competing mode out of business.

The ICC has also been extremely reluctant to grant certification of entry to motor carriers in new markets. Even if existing shippers argue that existing service is inadequate, the commission will generally refuse to grant a new certificate in the face of opposition from existing carriers; for discussions, see Fulda (11) and Williams (29).

The way in which regulatory agencies respond to innovations further illustrates their desire to prevent rapid dislocations. It takes years for them to incorporate threatening new technology into the pattern of service. The Interstate Commerce Commission long resisted the introduction of the "Big John" railroad cars. This was only accomplished after protracted legal maneuvers which eventually permitted the railroads to operate these cars; but only under conditions that prevented the railroads from fully exploiting their economic advantage. Difficult as it is for existing modes of transportation to introduce new technology, it appears even more difficult for new modes or forms of transport to gain recognition. The nonscheduled airlines in the United States have, for example, been trying for decades to inaugurate the kind of charter services so common in Europe. The Civil Aeronautics Board has resisted these proposals and today similarly resists the proposals of Federal Express to provide all-cargo service with large aircraft.

It is clear, however, that the carriers are as eager to maintain stability as the regulatory agencies and Congress. Proposals for deregulation have consistently met opposition from the various modes. The trucking industry is unanimous in its condemnation of regulatory reform that would ease present restrictions concerning rates and entry in the trucking industry.

The airlines have consistently voiced strong opposition to the deregulation of airline fares and entry. They assert that deregulation would encourage airlines to desert routes during off seasons when traffic is light, thus failing to provide adequate service to the public.[11] Although the airlines are ostensibly complaining on behalf of their passengers, the lack of concern about deregulation from consumer groups—indeed, their general endorsement of this proposal—leads one to suspect that the airlines are really concerned about instabilities they themselves might encounter.

This concern with stability on the part of the Congress, the regulatory agencies, and the carriers has prompted numerous critics to argue that regulation has resulted in the cartelization of the transportation industries; see Huntington (12). Thus, it is argued, regulation does not really serve the public interest, but the interests of the regulated industry.

While being outwardly appealing, this argument is probably too simplistic. Although regulation does indeed increase the stability of the regulated carriers, it also ensures the other goals of fairness and support of rural and agricultural interests, which are also benefited by industry stability. Since, for example, instability with respect to rates of entry could threaten the traditional rate structure or encourage the industry to attempt new and novel ways of price discrimination, it appears that the other two goals are entirely consistent with industry stability. Indeed, present regulatory practices are such as to ensure that the goals of fairness, support for agricultural and rural interests, and industry stability generally act in harmony.[12]

III THE EFFICIENCY COSTS OF REGULATORY AND INVESTMENT POLICIES

Although these three goals are generally consistent with each other, in recent years an extensive literature has developed which indicates that these goals are not consistent with economic efficiency. Since the efficiency costs of regulatory and investment policies have been extensively documented elsewhere,[13] we need only summarize what should be now be a well-known argument.

With respect to intercity freight transportation, it is generally agreed that present regulatory practices encourage excess capacity and an inefficient rate structure. Specifically, because the railroads are constrained from abandoning their unprofitable track, they are forced to operate along an inefficient short-run cost curve instead of an efficient long-run cost curve. Since the railroad trackage was built for volumes far in excess of those that now exist, a rationalization of the roadbed could lead to annual savings of $2 to $3 billion; for discussion, see Keeler (15) and Friedlaender (9). Moreover, because of the rate differentials between high-valued manufactured commodities and low-valued bulk commodities, it has been estimated that society incurs a dead weight loss of approximately $500 million. Thus, it is argued, a rationalization of the rate structure in conjunction with appropriate abandonment could lead to annual resource savings in excess of $3 billion; see Keeler (16).

Regulation also encourages excess capacity in the air and trucking industries. Although regulatory authorities control the rate structure, they fail to control the level of service or number of vehicles utilized by any given firm. Since firms believe that their market share is associated with frequency of service, they have an incentive to offer more trips. Thus, firms will tend to provide excess capacity and eliminate the potential profits associated with the regulated rate. Consequently, service and capacity will be directly linked to the regulated rates. Since the regulated rates are greater than those expected under competition, excess capacity is also greater than that expected under competition. Consequently, regulation not only imposes a dead weight loss from the rate structure but also imposes a capacity cost. In a deregulated environment, it is likely that air and trucking rates would be lower and that there would be less excess capacity; for a full discussion see Douglas and Miller (5).

Finally, it is well documented that investment and user charge policies are inefficient; see Friedlaender (7), Meyer *et al.* (19), The Doyle Report (28). With respect to investments, a large number of inland waterways and links on the Interstate Highway System have been shown to be uneconomic in terms of the usual cost-benefit criteria. With regard to user charges, it is generally agreed that the lack of user charges on inland waterways distorts relative costs in favor of barges. Moreover, there is some evidence that heavy diesel trucks do not pay their full share of highway costs. Consequently, the private costs of barge and trucking activities fail to reflect their true social costs.

Since the present regulatory and investment policies appear to impose considerable efficiency costs upon society, we can only infer that the attainment of the goals of fairness, support of agricultural and rural interests, and industry stability are thought to be worth these efficiency costs. Thus, the issue facing regulatory and investment policy is not so much whether it leads to efficiency costs, but whether the attainment of these goals is deemed sufficiently important to warrant the present magnitude of these efficiency costs. Alternatively, we can also ask whether new institutional arrangements could be found that would reduce these efficiency costs while permitting the achievement of the other goals.

The recent experience in the railroad and airline industries indicates that such change may be possible. The pricing provisions of the RRRR Act permit railroads to set rates freely within a relatively broad rate band so long as rates are above long-run marginal cost and below the monopoly levels implied by "market dominance." These bands are not sufficiently broad, however, to alter the traditional rate structure. Furthermore, the market dominance provision prevents monopoly exploitation, while the rate floor ensures industry stability. Thus, the three basic goals of regulatory policy are not threatened in this act. Nevertheless, the rate freedom permitted in this act should lead to increases in efficiency and a more rational rate structure.

The pending Cannon-Kennedy legislation regarding airline regulation similarly represents a piecemeal approach to change. By relaxing constraints upon rate differentials for different kinds of service, it should increase efficiency and give consumers a much broader choice than they presently have. By relaxing restrictions on routes and entry, it should similarly permit more varied service. But it is unlikely that the act would alter the elements of cross subsidy in the rate structure with respect to the fare taper and traffic density. Thus, while the passage of the act will doubtless lead to much more choice in the areas of service and fares, it will probably not fundamentally affect the regional fare structure that permits rural, light-density areas to enjoy lower fares relative to costs than urban, high-density areas.

In conclusion, then, it appears that change is quite possible if it is consistent with the goals of fairness, rural income maintenance, and industry stability. Within these constraints, there are probably a number of changes that could be made that would reduce the efficiency costs of present policies. Nevertheless, it is also clear that major changes that would have an adverse effect upon these goals are not possible. Thus, we should probably concentrate on piecemeal changes that can increase efficiency while not threatening the other goals.

FOOTNOTES

Work on this paper was supported by the Department of Transportation, Office of University Research, Grant # DOT–OS–52039. We are grateful to Alan Altshuler, Ernst Frankel, James Sloss, Robert W. Simpson, Joseph Vitteck, and a referee for the insights they provided.

1. In addition, the ICC exercises limited regulation over traffic on inland waterways.

2. For a general statement of such an approach see Peltzman (23), Stigler (26), and Posner (25).

3. Although we focus upon these three major areas, this list is not meant to be exhaustive. For example, Moore (21) has recently argued that regulatory policy has also contributed to high teamster wages. In addition, transportation investments are often defended in terms of national defense.

4. Of course, there are also numerous administrative and political decisions that are narrowly focused and benefit selected members of society. Typical of these are the numerous tax provisions that benefit very specific groups. Similarly, narrow regulatory decisions typically do not concern themselves with the general interest.

5. To further protect the agricultural interests and to ensure that agricultural rates were kept at competitive levels, the Motor Carrier Act of 1935 permitted an ag.icultural exemption, under which all agricultural products carried by truck are exempt from regulation.

6. As discussed below, the rate structure appears to discriminate in favor of areas characterized by light-density service and against carriers specializing in this service.

7. The Transportation Act of 1920 established "fair return on fair value" as the rule of rate making to be followed by the ICC.

8. The actual price-marginal cost ratio depends, naturally, on the average load factors on the route. Note, however, that if the load factor is raised—thus lowering the marginal cost—the passengers are typically inconvenienced with greater difficulty in booking flights, less frequent service, etc., resulting in a greater perceived cost to them.

9. This retreat could also be interpreted as an effort to maintain the traditional rate structure.

10. For example, the CAB gave Northeast lucrative routes to Florida and arranged temporary route exchanges between TWA and Pan American to bolster their international operations.

11. Of course, airlines still attempt to forsake low-density, especially rural, routes with regulation. Allegheny, for example, spun off many such routes to a variety of air taxi operators offering less reliable and less secure service.

12. However, it should be recognized that increased competition leading to a rate structure based on marginal costs could lead to reduced price discrimination and reduced agricultural rates. Hence, in the short run, at least, industry stability and the resulting cartelization may not be consistent with the other two goals.

13. See, for example, Meyer *et al.* (19), Friedlaender (8), Moore (20), Keeler (15, 16), Jordan (13), Eads (6), Douglas and Miller (5).

REFERENCES

1. Benson, Lee. (1965) *Merchants, Farms, and Railroads: Railroad Regulation and New York Politics, 1850–1887,* Cambridge, Mass., Harvard University Press.
2. Buck, Solon Justus. (1965) *The Granger Movement, 1870–1880,* Cambridge, Mass., Harvard University Press.
3. Caves, Douglas W., and Christensen, L. R. (September 1976) "Modeling the Structure of Production in the U.S. Railroad Industry," Mimeo.
4. Cherry, Russel C. (Spring 1975) "On the Economic Efficiency of Inefficient Regulation," *New England Journal of Business and Economics,* Vol. 1, No. 2.
5. Douglas, George W., and Miller, James C. (1974) *Economic Regulation of Domestic Air Transport,* Washington, D.C., The Brookings Institution.
6. Eads, George. (1972) *The Local Service Airline Experiment,* Washington, D.C., The Brookings Institution.
7. Friedlaender, Ann F. (1965) *The Interstate Highway System.* Amsterdam, North-Holland Publishing Co.
8. ———. (1969) *The Dilemma of Freight Transport Regulation,* Washington, D.C., The Brookings Institution.
9. ———. (May 1971) "The Social Costs of Regulating the Railroads," *American Economic Review,* 226–234.
10. Friendly, Henry J. (1962) *The Federal Administrative Agencies,* Cambridge, Mass., Harvard University Press.
11. Fulda, Carl. (1961) *Competition in the Regulated Industries: Transportation,* Boston, Little, Brown.
12. Huntington, Samuel P. (April 1952) "The Marasmus of the ICC: The Commission, the Railroads, and the Public Interest," *Yale Law Journal,* Vol. 61: 467.
13. Jordan, William A. (1970) *Airline Regulation in America: Effects and Imperfections,* Baltimore, John Hopkins University Press.

14. Keeler, Theodore E. (Autumn 1972) "Airline Regulation and Market Performance," *Bell Journal of Economics and Management Science*, Vol. 3:399–424.
15. ———. (May 1974) "Railroad Costs, Returns to Scale, and Excess Capacity," *Review of Economics and Statistics*, Vol. 56: 201–208.
16. ———. (September 1976) "On the Economic Impact of Railroad Freight Regulation," Working Paper No. 52–7601, University of California, Berkeley.
17. Kolko, Gabriel. (1965) *Railroads and Regulation*, Princeton, N.J., Princeton University Press.
18. MacAvoy, Paul W. (1965) *The Economic Effects of Regulation: The Trunk-Line Railroad Cartels and the Interstate Commerce Commission before 1900*, Cambridge, Mass., MIT Press.
19. Meyer, John R. *et al.*, (1959) *The Economics of Competition in the Transportation Industries*, Cambridge, Mass., Harvard University Press.
20. Moore, Thomas Gale. (1972) *Freight Transportation Regulation: Surface Freight and the I.C.C.*, Washington, D.C., American Enterprise Institute.
21. ———. (1977) "The Beneficiaries of Trucking Regulation," Hoover Institution on War, Revolution and Peace, Stanford, California, No.'77–17, Mimeo.
22. Nelson, Robert A. and Greiner, William R. (1965) "The Relevance of the Common Carrier under Modern Economic Conditions," in *Transportation Economics*, New York, Columbia University Press for the National Bureau of Economic Research, pp. 351–374.
23. Peltzman, Sam. (August 1976) "Toward a More General Theory of Regulation," *Journal of Law and Economics*, Vol. 19: 221–240.
24. Phillips, Almarin, ed. (1975) *Promoting Competition in Regulated Markets*, Washington, D.C., The Brookings Institution.
25. Posner, R. A. (Spring 1971) "Taxation by Regulation," *Bell Journal of Economics and Management Science*, Vol. 2: 22–50.
26. Stigler, George J. (Spring 1971) "The Theory of Economic Regulation," *Bell Journal of Economics and Management Science*, Vol. 2: 2.
27. Tarbell, Ida. (1904) *The History of the Standard Oil Company*, New York, Macmillan.
28. U.S. Senate, Committee on Interstate and Foreign Commerce (1961) *National Transportation Policy*. (The Doyle Report).
29. Williams, Ernst W., Jr. (1958) *The Regulation of Rail-Motor Rate Competition*, New York, Harper & Bros.

A NEW REMEDY FOR THE FREE RIDER PROBLEM?— FLIES IN THE OINTMENT

Roger C. Kormendi, UNIVERSITY OF CHICAGO

This paper analyzes some properties of a newly developed taxation method for solving the classical free rider problem—the Demand Revealing Process. The main problem is shown to be that the taxes required for maintaining the incentive mechanism for truthful revelation of demand necessarily constitute a deadweight loss to society. The result follows that the possibility of a net social loss to using the Demand Revealing Process instead of the free rider alternative cannot be precluded. The implications for the likelihood of such a net social loss for a given project are then examined. Finally, it is shown that there is an underlying free rider problem associated with setting the agenda of public projects for consideration that increases the likelihood that

Research in Law and Economics, Vol. 1, pp. 115–130.
ISBN: 0–89232–028–1.

using the Demand Revealing Process will yield aggregate net social losses. Thus, for many individual public projects and for the aggregate set of public projects, the Demand Revealing Process cannot be expected to do better than the free rider alternative.

In a recent set of articles, Clarke (1, 2), Groves and Loeb (7), Groves and Ledyard (5), and Tideman and Tullock (11) exhibit and analyze a new process for making social choices.[1] The most important claim made is that the process, which following the literature we call the Demand Revealing Process, solves the free rider problem. It does this by providing incentives in the form of special taxes that induce individuals to reveal truthfully their valuations of the objects of social choice, such as a public good or an externality. The focus of these articles has been on the allocative efficiency that can be achieved using this incentive mechanism, and the strong conclusion that emerges is that the Demand Revealing Process can be used successfully to deal with the problem of making efficient social choices.

We will argue in this paper that, in the eagerness to exhibit the allocative virtues of the Demand Revealing Process, some disturbing flaws have been overlooked and that these flaws undermine its usefulness to deal with the problem of making social choices. In Section I we will reconstruct the elements of the Process in the context of a setting in which the choice is whether or not to undertake a public project. In Section II we will illustrate in this same context a basic problem with the Demand Revealing Process. In Sections III through V we will introduce some related issues and discuss the implications of problems that we uncover. Finally, we summarize our results and discuss their relationship to the general models discussed in the literature.

I THE PROCESS

Let us first quickly construct the Demand Revealing Process for the simple case of deciding as to whether or not some social project is to be undertaken; such as whether or not a public good is to be produced.[2] Let the true valuation of the project in question for individual i be denoted by V_i. Let there also be a cost associated with the project, C. In the Demand Revealing Process, this cost must be apportioned across all individuals in a manner independent of their revealed valuations; otherwise, each individual would have an incentive to understate his valuation, yielding the classical free rider problem. We will denote the arbitrary assignment of individual cost shares by C_i, such that $\sum_i C_i = C$. Table 1 illustrates for three individuals their valuations and their cost assignment in columns (1) and (2), respectively.

Given the individual data on V_i and C_i, two things should be noted.

Table 1. Valuations and Their Cost Assignment for Three Individuals.

Individual	(1) V_i	(2) C_i	(3) $V_i - C_i$	(4) T_i	(5) $V_i - C_i - T_i$
1	55	20	35	25	10
2	15	20	-5	0	-5
3	0	20	-20	0	-20
Σ	70	60	10	25	-15

First, as long as $\sum_i V_i > C$, the project "should" be undertaken in the sense
that there is some way of allocating total cost, C, among the individuals such
that everyone is better off; that is, Hicks compensation is possible. Second,
an arbitrary assignment of cost shares, C_i, will *not* necessarily satisfy this
condition. That is, since an arbitrary assignment of cost shares is required
in the Demand Revealing Process, Pareto optimality cannot be guaranteed.[3]
This possibility is illustrated in the third column of Table 1, where $V_i - C_i$
is negative for individuals 2 and 3.

After the arbitrary assignment of cost shares, each individual is told that
he will be taxed or assessed an amount that would just compensate the
others in society for the effect of his *revealed* valuation on the ultimate
decision. Letting R_i be individual i's revealed valuation and $R \equiv \sum_i R_i$, the
ultimate decision rule is: "accept the project if $R > C$ and reject if $R \leq C$."
Defining $D \equiv R - C$ and $D_{(i)} \equiv \sum_{j \neq i} R_j - \sum_{j \neq i} C_j$, the tax for individual i is:

$$
T_i = \begin{cases}
0 & \text{if (a) } D_{(i)} > 0 \text{ and } D > 0 \\
|D_{(i)}| & \text{if (b) } D_{(i)} > 0 \text{ and } D < 0 \\
|D_{(i)}| & \text{if (c) } D_{(i)} < 0 \text{ and } D > 0 \\
0 & \text{if (d) } D_{(i)} < 0 \text{ and } D < 0
\end{cases}. \tag{1}
$$

Thus, $T_i = |D_{(i)}|$ when adding individual i would change the decision from
that made in the absence of i, that is, if $D_{(i)}$, the revealed net value of all
agents other than i, and D, the revealed net value of all agents, are of different
sign. In column 4 of Table 1, we show the relevant taxes under the assumption
that $R_i = V_i$, that is, that all agents reveal their true valuation.

It remains to argue that *regardless* of the revealed valuation of others,
individual i always has the incentive to reveal his valuation truthfully.
That is, regardless of $D_{(i)}$, $R_i = V_i$ is at least as good as any other R_i for all

individuals. Let individual i choose R_i so as to maximize:

$$U_i(R_i) = \begin{cases} V_i - C_i - T_i & \text{if } D > 0 \\ -T_i & \text{if } D < 0 \end{cases}. \tag{2}$$

Noting that $D = D_{(i)} + R_i - C_i$, we can utilize (1) and (2) to derive $U(V_i)$, that is, utility when $R_i = V_i$:

$$U_i(V_i) = \begin{cases} V_i - C_i & \text{if (a) } D_{(i)} > 0 \text{ and } D_{(i)} > C_i - V_i \\ -|D_{(i)}| & \text{if (b) } D_{(i)} > 0 \text{ and } D_{(i)} < C_i - V_i \\ V_i - C_i - |D_{(i)}| & \text{if (c) } D_{(i)} < 0 \text{ and } D_{(i)} > C_i - V_i \\ 0 & \text{if (d) } D_{(i)} < 0 \text{ and } D_{(i)} < C_i - V_i \end{cases}.$$

For simplicity, denote by $U_i^a(V_i)$ the utility associated with case (a); similarly for $U_i^b(V_i)$, and so on.

For case (a), $U_i^a(R_i) = U_i^a(V_i) > -|D_{(i)}|$ for all $R_i > C_i - D_{(i)}$, and $U_i^a(R_i) = -|D_{(i)}|$ for all $R_i < C_i - D_{(i)}$. Thus, $U_i^a(R_i) \le U_i^a(V_i)$ all R_i. For case (b), $U_i^b(R_i) = U_i^b(V_i) = -|D_{(i)}|$ for all $R_i < C_i - D_{(i)}$, and $U_i^b(R_i) = V_i - C_i < -|D_{(i)}|$ for all $R_i > C_i - D_{(i)}$. Thus, $U_i^b(R_i) \le U_i^b(V_i)$ all R_i. The same reasoning holds for cases (c) and (d), so that $U_i(V_i) \ge U_i(R_i)$ all R_i and any $D_{(i)}$. Thus every individual can do no better, *and may do worse*, if he fails to reveal his true valuation.

So far so good. The use of the Demand Revealing Process definitely provides the incentive to each individual to reveal truthfully his valuation of the public project. At the same time, the imbedded ultimate decision rule, adopted if $R > C$, yields what *seems* to be the correct decision as regards adoption of the project. In the next section, however, we will argue that this seemingly correct decision rule has a crucial flaw.

II THE DECISION RULE

Before proceeding, let us put aside some issues regarding the use of the Demand Revealing Process that are important but that we do not wish to address directly. It is obvious that the Process requires what seem like rather large administrative costs, where these include the calculation costs of both the individuals involved and the agency that "tallies the vote," the enforcement costs of the taxes, and whatever transition costs are inherent in moving from one policy system to another. The authors involved in this literature are correct in ignoring these costs. A necessary condition for considering any proposed policy change to effect public decisions, including one such as using the Demand Revealing Process, is that *in the absence of the administration and transition costs* the proposed policy has certain desirable properties. Once these properties are established, the issue becomes whether the gains from implementation justify the previously ignored costs.[4]

The arguments above do *not*, however, hold for costs directly associated with the structure of the policy proposal. Tideman and Tullock, for example, argue that the taxes associated with the Demand Revealing Process should be ignored as simply part of the administrative costs of reaching a decision. But whereas the effect of the Demand Revealing Process can be analyzed independently of, say, the enforcement costs associated with collecting the taxes, it cannot be analyzed ignoring the taxes themselves. Our procedure then in analyzing the Demand Revealing Process will be to ignore the secondary administrative costs as part of the "rules of the game," while taking into account explicitly the direct costs of the Process.

So far, our analysis has shown that it is a property of the Demand Revealing Process that (1) no individual is worse off after the assessment of the taxes *and* the decision to adopt the project or not (based on the value $R - C$) than he would be *if he had no say in the decision.* This is simply saying, however, that the Process fulfills a necessary condition for having the proper incentives to reveal truthfully one's valuation of the project (for abstaining is identical to registering $R_i = 0$). It is *not* a property of the Demand Revealing Process, however, that (2) *everyone* is better off with the Process than without. Assume for convenience that without the Process the public project would not be undertaken (perhaps due to the "free rider problem"). Even ignoring the payment of the taxes, $V_i - C_i$ will in general be negative for some individuals, depending upon the allocation of C across the population.

These two properties have been generally recognized in the literature. They give rise, however, to the following interesting but disturbing property of the Demand Revealing Process that has been overlooked. (3) *It is not in general the case that the sum of the gains associated with the Demand Revealing Process outweighs the losses.*[5] To illustrate this, consider column 5 in Table 1, in which the net value of the decision of the Demand Revealing Process is recorded for each individual inclusive of the taxes he has to pay, that is, $V_i - C_i - T_i$. Assuming that the Process is used, no individual is worse off participating than not participating; this is property (1) and reflects the fact that $T_i < |V_i - C_i|$. But the absence of property (2) implies that $\Sigma(V_i - C_i - T_i)$, the net social gains from the Demand Revealing Process, may be negative! (This is property (3), reflected in the -15 at the bottom of column 4.)

III GIVING BACK THE TAXES

Obviously, the implication of property (3) depends crucially upon the fact that the sum of the taxes, $T = \sum_i T_i$, is positive, and that they do not find their way back to the individuals in any way. Clearly, if T is returned in some pattern dependent upon revealed valuation, the whole incentive mechanism will be thwarted.[6] Consider, however, any way to divide up T

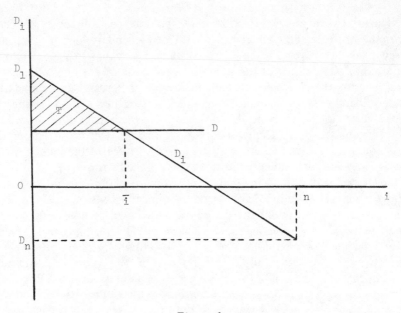

Figure 1.

among individuals that is *not* dependent upon revealed valuation. Let α_i, $i = 1,\ldots,n$, be the proportion of T going to individual i where $\sum_i \alpha_i = 1$.

Clearly $\alpha_i T \neq T_i$ in general, and we require simply that α_i not vary with R_i or with anything that is correlated with R_i (such as T_i).

It will be important for our immediate analysis, and for what follows later, to examine what determines the level of T, and thus $\alpha_i T$, under the Demand Revealing Process. Since under the Process $R_i = V_i$, we will modify our notion slightly. Let $D_i \equiv V_i - C_i$, $V \equiv \sum_i V_i$ and $D \equiv \sum_i D_i = V - C$.

We can order D_i for all individuals in any way without loss in content; therefore, let $D_1 \geq D_2 \geq \ldots \geq D_n$. This allows us conveniently to graph D_i as a decreasing function of i. (Note that D_i is really a step function that we draw as continuous for convenience only.) We can also represent $D = \Sigma D_i$ on this diagram as a function independent of i. In Figure 1, we exhibit the case $0 < D < D_i$.

In terms of our earlier analysis, if $D > 0$ and $D_{(i)} < 0$, then $T_i = |D_{(i)}|$. Notice, however, that $D_{(i)}$ is simply $D - D_i$. Thus, $T_i = D_i - D$ for those agents with $D_i > D$, and $T_i = 0$ for those with $D_i < D$. In terms of our diagram, $T = \Sigma T_i$ is simply the shaded area, the sum of $D_i - D$ in the region of $D_i > D$.

We can now use the model above to show why the Demand Revealing Process breaks down if T is given back, even in a manner unrelated to R_i.

Consider individual 1 first, who has $D_1 = V_1 - C_1 > D$ and is paying $T_1 = D_1 - D$. Suppose he reveals an $R_1 \neq V_1$. Let $D_1(R_1) \equiv R_1 - C_1$ and $D(R_1) \equiv \sum_{i=2}^{n} D_i + D_1(R_1)$. Clearly, regardless of the value of $D_{(1)} = \sum_{i=2}^{n} D_i$, $T_1(R_1) \equiv D_1(R_1) - D(R_1) = D_{(1)}$ is independent of the revealed valuation R_1. However, $\partial D(R_1)/\partial R_1 = 1$, implying that the revealed valuation R_i has an effect on T through $D(R_1)$.

Let $\bar{\imath}$ be the solution to $D_i - D = 0$ as illustrated in the figure. We would like to know the effect on T of R_1, holding D_i, $i = 2, \ldots, n$ constant. From our earlier results, we can derive the expression:

$$T(R_1, \ldots, R_N) = T_1(R_1) + \sum_{i=2}^{\bar{\imath}} [D_i(R_i) - D(R_1, \ldots, R_N)],$$

where $D(R_1, \ldots, R_n) = \sum_i D_i(R_i)$.

Differentiating T with respect to R_1 yields:

$$\partial T/\partial R_1 = \partial T_1/\partial R_1 - (\bar{\imath} - 1)\partial D/\partial R_1$$
$$= -(\bar{\imath} - 1).[7]$$

In words, the effect on T of individual 1 *understating* his true valuation by one dollar is to *increase* T by $(\bar{\imath} - 1)$ dollars, that is, by one dollar times the number of other individuals being taxed. Since individual 1 gets $\alpha_i T$ redistributed back to him, he clearly has an individual incentive to understate his true valuation even if T is distributed back independent of R_i.

The analysis carried out above for individual 1 holds true for every individual, in the context of the competitive (Nash) experiment of holding the actions of all others constant. The incentive of individual i to underreveal is $I_i = \alpha_i \partial T/\partial R_i = -\alpha_i \bar{\imath}$ for all $i = \bar{\imath}, \ldots, n$ and $I_i = \alpha_i(\bar{\imath} - 1) \approx -\alpha_i \bar{\imath}$ for all $i = 1, \ldots, \bar{\imath}.[8]$ But if everyone understates his true valuation, we are simply back to the free rider problem again. Thus, in seeking to increase the rebate coming to him, each individual will understate his true valuation, regardless of the method of redistributing T across agents.[9] By how much will a given individual understate his true valuation? Let the expectation of individual i about the level of $D_{(i)}$ be $D_{(i)}^*$. If he is risk neutral, he will simply set his R_i equal to $-D_{(i)}^* + \varepsilon$, where ε is a small positive number.[10]

The above analysis implies that T must be "wasted" in order to preserve property (1), and, hence, the negative implication of property (3) remains a significant problem with the use of the Demand Revealing Process to make social decisions. The key to the extent of the problem, however, is in the allocation of cost shares across individuals. By the very nature of the problem, when $V - C > 0$, there always exists *some* assignment of cost shares that makes everyone better off than if the project were not adopted. In this case, unanimity would rule, $T = 0$ *a fortiori*, and the Demand Revealing Process would, for that assignment, yield the "desirable" choice—$V - C - T > 0$. Thus, we must look deeper into the effects of the initial assignment of cost shares on the Demand Revealing Process.

IV THE ASSIGNMENT OF COST SHARES

To see the effect of the assignment of cost shares on the Demand Revealing Process, in particular on property (3), we continue to exploit the model of the last section. Since the main problem in utilizing the Process is in the size of T relative to D, we will focus our attention on the effect of the assignment of cost shares on T, for any given value D.

Consider now breaking down the D_i function developed earlier into its components. In particular, let us focus first on V_i, ordering it so that $V_1 \geq V_2 \geq ... \geq V_n$. In general, V_i may be less than zero (the project harms some individuals absolutely), but we will assume for convenience that $V_i \geq 0$ all i. The assignment of costs can be viewed as choosing an allocation $\{C_i\}$ whose sum over i is equal to C. The case in which $C_i = kC$, $k = 1/n$, is shown in Figure 2 along with the resultant D_i.

As long as $V - C > 0$, there must be some $\{C_i\}$ such that $D_i > 0$ for *all* individuals. In particular, $\hat{C}_i = (V_i/V)C$ will achieve such a solution. The cost allocation $\{\hat{C}_i\}$ is particularly interesting, because $D > D_i$ all i by construction. In fact, it is clear that there are many $\{C_i\}$'s such that $D > D_i$

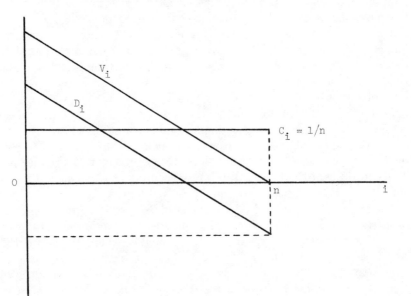

Figure 2.

all i. The class of these $\{C_i\}$, call it ξ, has the property $T_i = 0$ all i, and hence $T = 0$. That is, for *any* initial pattern of preferences, $\{V_i\}$, there is a nonempty class of cost allocation functions such that $T = 0$ under the Demand Revealing Process.[11]

The above result is a very weak one, however. It simply says that if $D > 0$ and one knows $\{V_i\}$ then a $\{C_i\}$ *can* be found such that everyone is better off. This is simply echoing the very first element behind the decision rule: that as long as $D > 0$ the project *should* be adopted. In fact, there is an expanded class ξ' that has the property that $V - C - T > 0$ for all assignments $\{C_i\} \in \xi'$. The critical weakness of the result, however, is that the complement of the class ξ', $\bar{\xi}'$, contains many cost allocations, each of which has the implication that $D - T < 0$, that is, net social losses to using the Demand Revealing Process. How can one be assured that an initial cost allocation is chosen from ξ', and not from $\bar{\xi}'$, in order to avoid the negative implications of property (3)?

This question has been dealt with casually by both Groves and Loeb (7) and Tideman and Tullock (11). The former attempt to argue that a *collective* decision on $\{C_i\}$ arrived at among the n individuals could establish a $\{C_i\} \in \xi'$, since there are many $\{C_i\}$ in ξ' each of which makes everyone better off. This does not deal with the issue, however, because the same free rider incentives to have "someone else" pay C exist as in the initial public project adoption problem. The latter devise an ingenious method that (with some modification) will minimize T, subject to the information individuals already have. Start with an arbitrary cost share assignment, $\{C_i\}$. Then allow each individual to bid an amount, F_i, for the right to alter the cost shares of everyone other than himself, where he will receive $F_i - \beta T$, $\beta > 0$ fixed in advance as payment for his decision if his bid is chosen. The individual with the lowest F_i is chosen. The individual with the most *ex ante* "information" about $\{V_i\}$ will be able to submit the lowest bid. However, there is no a *priori* reason to believe that $V - C - T > 0$ would result, since even the most informed individual may be poorly informed.

In any case, the essence of the decision on the adoption of a public project is that $\{V_i\}$ is not known. Furthermore, the information required to assure $\{C_i\} \in \xi'$ cannot be obtained with any reference to R_i, or the incentive for revealing true valuations will be lost. Thus, the effect of property (3), that the Demand Revealing Process will not in general yield $V - C - T > 0$, remains an important problem with the Process, one that to this point has clearly not been appreciated.

In the analysis so far we have purposefully excluded the possibility of a large number of agents who receive no benefit from the public project, if undertaken. To focus on the problem that arises when we combine lack of knowledge about $\{V_i\}$ with large numbers of agents who have $V_i = 0$, we will adapt the model we have been working with as follows. Start with a set of

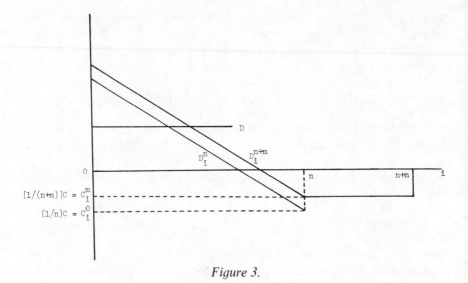

Figure 3.

n agents, all of whom have $V_i > 0$, and order them $V_i \geq V_2 \geq ... \geq V_n \geq 0$ as before. Now consider adding m individuals for whom $V_i = 0$ to this group of n, so that there are n + m individuals. Since by the structure of the problem we do not know what specific individual's true valuations are, we will let $C_i^m = k_m C, i = 1, 2, ..., n + m$ where $k_m = 1/(n + m)$; that is, we are allocating costs across all n + m individuals equally.[12] We can show the effect of moving from n to n + m individuals according to this scenario in Figure 3.

Adding m individuals reduces the costs per person and thereby raises D_i by the difference $C_i^0 - C_i^m$. *The effect of this reduction in cost per person is to increase the sum of taxes, T*, since D is unchanged by adding people for whom $V_i = 0$. The implication of this result is that the more people there are who receive little or no benefit from the project, the larger will be T, and the more likely it is that $V - C - T < 0$, even given that $V - C > 0$. In connection with the previous result, we now see that more people with $V_i = 0$ (or close to zero) decreases the likelihood that $\{C_i\} \in \xi'$ in the absence of prior information on V_i.[13]

V THE ANALYSIS FOR A SET OF PROJECTS

Up to this point we have focused our analysis on one project. However, in the absence of *a priori* information as to the value $V - C$, any single project must properly be considered to be a draw from some population of all possible projects that generally includes negative as well as positive values for $V - C$. Furthermore, if the Demand Revealing Process were to be used generally, the full set of projects involved (a sample drawn in some manner from the population of all possible projects) would be the relevant unit of analysis.

Therefore, consider a set of projects, $p = 1, 2, \ldots, P$, that might be under consideration in some relevant time period. Suppose for the moment that each project has $V^p - C^p > 0$. Suppose further that $\{V_i^p\}$ and $\{C_i^p\}$ are different across projects. Our analysis so far shows that even though for *some* projects $V^p - C^p - T^p > 0$, for others one can expect $V^p - C^p - T^p < 0$. Summing over all p, $\sum_{p=1}^{P} (V^p - C^p - T^p)$ may be positive or negative, depending upon the set of $\{V_i^p, C_i^p\}$ involved. There is, however, another important consideration that must be brought in. If the set of projects under consideration indeed had $V^p - C^p > 0$ all $p = 1, \ldots, P$, there would be no necessity for the Demand Revealing Process; adopt all P projects would be the simple, costless decision rule. In fact, in general one can expect that some subset of projects have $V^p - C^p < 0$.

Consider, therefore, a set of P projects ordered as follows: $D^1 \geq \ldots \geq D^{P'} > 0 > D^{P'+1} > \ldots > D^P$. From our earlier analysis, the net loss of using the Demand Revealing Process is $- T^p < 0$ for each $p = P' + 1, \ldots, P$. That is, for the $P - P'$ projects with $V^p - C^p < 0$, there are *only* net social losses to using the Demand Revealing Process instead of the free rider alternative. Clearly, as $P - P'$ gets larger relative to P', it becomes *more likely* that

$$\sum_{p=1}^{P'} (V^p - C^p - T^p) + \sum_{p=P'+1}^{P} (-T^p) < 0.$$

How large is the set of projects for which $V^p - C^p < 0$? This question is related to the general problem of choosing an "agenda," that is, the set of projects that will be considered under the Process. Suppose for the moment there are no costs of submitting a project for consideration and no administrative costs associated with using the Demand Revealing Process. Under the Process each individual will have the incentive to submit for consideration all projects for which $D_i > 0$ *for him*. This is because he bears no cost if the project is rejected, whereas he gains $D_i > 0$ if it is accepted. When the analysis of the previous sections is brought in—that the nature of the Demand Revealing Process will have agents with low valuation generally bearing disproportionately more costs—we clearly have the free rider problem operating in the incentive to submit projects for the agenda. Thus, the Demand Revealing Process provides no incentive to prevent projects with $V - C < 0$ from being placed on the agenda.[14]

The general problem of setting an agenda is, of course, not specific to the Demand Revealing Process. Since any individual generally bears only a small portion of the administrative costs of a social choice process, his incentive is to submit for consideration any project with net benefits to him, regardless of the net social benefits. The problem specific to the Demand

Revealing Process is that additional deadweight costs are imposed, both in accepting desirable projects and rejecting undesirable projects. Abstracting from administrative costs, under other social choice processes, an agenda with many undesirable projects presents no special problems. Under the Demand Revealing Process, the existence of undesirable projects on the agenda involves additional net social loss in the form of the deadweight taxes, T^q. Since with limited information an agenda will generally have many undesirable projects in it, $\sum_{p=1}^{p'} (V^p - C^p - T^p) + \sum_{p=p'}^{p} T^p < 0$ is an important possibility, especially when the free rider incentive involved in setting the agenda is taken into account.

VI SUMMARY AND COMMENTS ON THE CONTINUOUS PUBLIC GOOD CASE

We have analyzed in considerable detail a newly proposed method of making social decisions that purportedly solves the classical free rider problem by inducing agents to reveal their true valuation. The literature has so far concentrated on exhibiting the incentive structure and showing that the new mechanism does indeed create the incentive for true revelation of valuation. In this paper, we have focused on some issues that have been to date overlooked.

Three main results came to light under our analysis. First, one cannot in general preclude the possibility that $V - C - T$, the net social gain of using the Demand Revealing Process, is negative, even if $V - C$, the *potential* gain, is positive. Giving back the taxes independent of revealed valuation does not solve the problem, because an incentive then arises to reveal incorrect valuations.

Second, as long as $V - C > 0$, there are, in principle, many cost allocations $\{C_i\}$, such that $V - C - T > 0$. The problem is that finding one depends crucially upon *knowing* V_i, and knowing V_i or even that $V - C > 0$ would remove the problem of having to induce individuals to reveal their true valuations in the first place. More importantly, the more people there are who receive little or no benefits from the project, the more likely is it that $V - C - T < 0$ will be the case. The implication here is that for a large class of public projects the Demand Revealing Process cannot be expected to do better than the free rider alternative!

Third, there are incentives for agents to try to get *their* projects included in the set of projects to be considered, regardless of $V - C$. This is due to the inherent cost-sharing feature of the Demand Revealing Process when $\{V_i\}$ is unknown. Whenever $V - C < 0$, the net social gains from using the Demand

Revealing Process are always negative, since the taxes are a deadweight loss to the system. Thus, in the absence of *a priori* information that allows projects to be (correctly) excluded, the free rider incentive to get projects included regardless of V − C increases the likelihood that the net social gains over any set of projects under consideration is negative.

These results are rather strongly negative as regards the efficacy of using the Demand Revealing Process to make even the simple type of choice we considered—whether or not to adopt a public project. In the more general setting, that of a continuous public good, analogous arguments to those in this paper can be shown to hold. There is one argument, however, that has appeared in the literature so far that should be dealt with in the context of this more general model.

Tideman and Tullock (11), and Clarke (1,2) before them, argue that in the continuous case, the size of the aggregate tax can be shown to be small relative to the total cost of producing the optimum level of the public good, under reasonable assumptions. In fact, what is crucial given our analysis is the size of the taxes relative to the net surplus achievable at the optimum level of production. Net surplus (equal to $\int_0^{\hat{Q}}[V(Q) - C(Q)]dQ$, where $V(Q) = \sum_i(V_i(Q))$ is the sum of individual valuation functions, $C(Q)$ is the marginal cost function and $\hat{Q}$ is the optimum) bears no particular relation to total production costs. Demand Revealing Taxes that are "small" relative to total costs may be large relative to net surplus.

More to the point, however, is that the relevant comparison should not in fact be Net Surplus since that presumes that the alternative social choice mechanism always arrives at Q = 0 as the decision. Suppose instead that there are alternative mechanisms that do not involve the deadweight losses of the taxes but that do not guarantee $Q = \hat{Q}$. Let $\bar{Q}$ be the choice of the "best" alternative decision process where $\bar{Q} < \hat{Q}$ for convenience (though $\bar{Q} > \hat{Q}$ may clearly be the result of some choice processes).[15] The size of the taxes, T, is clearly not affected by the alternative choice process, but the relevant point of comparison is. Whether the Demand Revealing Process is viable depends upon T relative to $\int_{\bar{Q}}^{\hat{Q}}[V(Q) - C(Q)]dQ$, that is, the difference between Net Surplus under the Process and Net Surplus under the alternative.[16] Thus, the analog to V − C − T in our simple model is $\int_{\bar{Q}}^{\hat{Q}}[V(Q) - C(Q)]dQ - T$. That this value may be negative for many public goods, even if $T/C(\hat{Q})$ is small, is clearly possible. From this starting point the analysis undertaken in the simple model of above follows naturally.

FOOTNOTES

I wish to thank Daniel Benjamin, Robert Dolan, Nicholas Gonedes, Michael Mussa, George Neumann, Charles Stuart, Nicolaus Tideman, and Gordon Tullock for helpful comments. Any errors that remain are my own.

1. The work by Clarke, on the one hand, and Groves and Loeb on the other, was done independently. The Tideman and Tullock paper was basically an exposition of Clarke's results. The mechanism exhibited by Groves and Loeb is slightly different from Clarke's, but in essence it is the same. Groves and Ledyard (5) extend the Groves-Loeb mechanism to a general equilibrium setting. Finally, Dolan (3,4) independently developed a similar mechanism in the context of queuing theory.

2. This simple discrete setting was first utilized by Clarke (2) and then analyzed by Tideman and Tullock (11). In Section VI we will consider the continuous case. The simple example we illustrate in Table 1 was adapted from the Tideman and Tullock paper.

3. The deep proposition that there is no "individually incentive compatible" mechanism that yields a Pareto-optimum allocation of a public good was proved by Hurwicz (8).

4. It may also be the case, of course, that there are interactions between the costs we have labeled administrative and the properties of the pure policy. Such interactions, however, are usually treated as second order effects.

5. We have set up as a bench mark the free rider decision that the project will be rejected, but any decision process would serve with similar results *as long as no direct* (*i.e.*, "*nonadministrative*") *costs are involved.* Without prior knowledge as to individuals' true valuations, the Demand Revealing Process will not in general yield net gains over the alternative. In a recently published paper, Groves and Ledyard (6) make a similar point using majority rule as the bench mark. Kormendi (9) analyzes the general relationship between majority rule versus the Demand Revealing Process as a mechanism for making social choices.

6. See footnote 8 *infra.* Clarke (1) suggests that T be given back to individuals through lump sum transfers. Tideman and Tullock (11) suggest either that the taxes be "wasted" or that governments "exchange" their tax proceeds. The implications of wasting T have already been discussed with respect to property (3). If "exchange" between governments takes place, either a dollar for dollar *quid pro quo* is guaranteed, in which case the exchange is exactly like a simple distribution of T, or the combined policy of the Demand Revealing Process and exchange of taxes does not get around the implication of property (3). In fact, such a scheme provides a government with the incentive to "undertax" their people in order to give up less in the exchange.

7. In general, $\bar{\imath}$ may increase with a small decrease in R_1, thus further increasing T. This effect will generally be of second order, and since it would only reinforce our analysis we ignore it for simplicity.

8. If $\alpha(R_i)$, $\partial\alpha_i/\partial R_i \neq 0$, then $I_i = (\partial\alpha_i/\partial R_i) T - \alpha_i\bar{\imath}$ would be the case. To preserve the incentive to reveal truthfully, $I_i \equiv 0$ must hold, which can happen if and only if $\partial\alpha_i/\partial R_i = \alpha_i\bar{\imath}/T$. Since $\bar{\imath}$ depends upon $(D_i, ..., D_n)$, setting $I_i \equiv 0$ requires knowing $(D_1, ..., D_n)$, and hence D, in which case, of course, the Demand Revealing Process would not be required.

9. The question may arise at this point as to whether this incentive to understate one's true valuation depends on the number of individuals involved. In particular, does this incentive diminish with increased numbers of individuals, so that it may be feasible to give back the taxes when large populations are involved? The sense of this question comes from looking at the rebate share α_i, which must decrease as the population

increases. Looking only at α_i, however, ignores the effect of increasing the population on $\bar{\imath}$.

Let $\alpha_i = 1/n$ and consider increasing the population, holding the distribution of individuals constant in that the same *proportion* of the population are paying taxes. Thus, $\bar{\imath} = \rho n$, when ρ is the proportion of individuals who are being taxed by the Demand Revealing Process. Clearly, then, the incentive of any individual i is $I_i = \alpha_i \bar{\imath} = 1/n \cdot \rho n = \rho$, which is independent of the size of the population. The incentive to underreveal thus depends upon the proportion of the population being taxed, which in turn depends, as we shall see later, upon the assignment of cost shares.

10. This incentive does not depend upon $D_i > D$, only upon each agent being able to effect D by his revealed valuation. It does, however, assume that individuals believed that $D > 0$. Suppose instead that $D < 0$ was expected to prevail (and in fact would under true revelation). Then the diagram would look as below, and the incentive would clearly

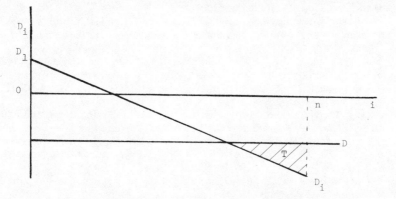

be for individuals to *overstate* the true valuations (following a similar argument as we used above for $D > 0$). Clearly, a full analysis cannot be carried out independent of the structure of expectations that individuals have about the ultimate outcome of the decision and hence complex strategic interaction. In any case, however, if T is returned, property (1) of the Demand Revealing Process, that individuals have incentives to reveal their true valuation, is overturned.

11. This is in essence the same result that Groves and Loeb (7) present as their final proposition. It is also implicit in the Tideman-Tullock (11) discussion of the Lindall solution.

12. It can be shown (see Kormendi (9)) that, under no *a priori* information, the cost allocation that minimizes expected taxes, T, is in fact an equal division of the cost across the population.

13. One might be tempted to say that those with $V_i = 0$ should simply be excluded from the social choice process since they have no stake in the outcome. The problem is not inclusion or exclusion but in the cost assignment. If exclusion means $C_i = 0$ for those agents with $V_i = 0$, once again the free rider problem comes into play, since many agents with $V_i > 0$ but $V_i < C_i$ would like to be excluded, and hence would reveal $R_i = 0$, or do whatever would exclude them. This, of course, would again break down the Demand Revealing Process.

14. It should also be clear that nothing is gained by using the Demand Revealing Process to determine spots on the agenda.

15. Majority voting, dictatorship, committee decisions (representation) all will in

general have some $\bar{Q} \neq \hat{Q}$, but not necessarily $\bar{Q} = 0$. Furthermore, a "Cheap Rider" solution may have $\bar{Q}$ close to $\tilde{Q}$; see Stigler (10).

16. See Kormendi (9) for an analysis of the general relationship between Majority Rule and the Demand Revealing Process as a mechanism for making social choices.

REFERENCES

1. Clarke, Edward. (Fall 1971) "Multipart Pricing of Public Goods," *Public Choice* Vol. 11: 17–33.
2. ———. (1972) "Multipart Pricing of Public Goods: An Example," in *Public Prices for Public Products*, S. Mushkin. ed., Washington, D.C., Urban Institute.
3. Dolan, Robert. (1976) "Priority Pricing Models for Congested Systems," Ph.D. dissertation, University of Rochester.
4. ———. (1977) "Public Goods Incentive Mechanisms Applied to Priority Queueing Problems," unpublished paper, University of Chicago (forthcoming, *The Bell Journal of Economics*).
5. Groves, Theodore, and Ledyard, John. (May 1977) "Optimal Allocation of Public Goods: A Solution to the 'Free Rider Problem,'" *Econometrica*, Vol. 45: 783–809.
6. ———. (June 1977) "Some Limitations of Demand Revealing Processes," *Public Choice*, Vol. 29–2: 107–124.
7. Groves, Theodore, and Loeb, Michael. (August 1975) "Incentives and Public Inputs," *Journal of Public Economics*, Vol. 4: 211–226.
8. Hurwicz, Leonid. (1972) "On Informationally Decentralized Systems," in *Decision and Organization*, R. Radner and B. McGuire, eds., Amsterdam, North Holland Pub.
9. Kormendi, Roger. (1977) "Majority Rule *Versus* the Demand Revealing Process as Social Choice Mechanisms," unpublished paper, University of Chicago.
10. Stigler, George. (Autumn 1974) "Free Riders and Collective Action: An Appendix to Theories of Economic Regulation," *The Bell Journal of Economics*, Vol. 5: 359–365.
11. Tideman, T. Nicolaus, and Tullock, Gordon. (December 1976) "A New and Superior Process for Making Social Choices," *Journal of Political Economy*, Vol. 84: 1145–1159.

TOWARD A THEORY OF
GOVERNMENT ADVERTISING

Kenneth W. Clarkson, UNIVERSITY OF
MIAMI SCHOOL OF LAW

Robert Tollison, VIRGINIA POLYTECHNIC
INSTITUTE AND STATE UNIVERSITY

Elements of a theory concerning the nature and extent of advertising by government as well as some preliminary data on implications of the theory are presented in this paper. Among the variables considered are government concentration of advertising efforts, budget maximization by bureaus, location of public spending, degree of classified information involved, antitrust exemption, and others. Existing pricing regulations and other constraints that directly or indirectly affect advertising expenditures are examined. The analysis has implications for variations in advertising expenditures as well as the extent to which the public good characteristic influences government advertising activities. In view of the analysis here, Galbraith's "dependence effect" by

Research in Law and Economics, Vol. 1, pp. 131–143.
Copyright © 1979 by JAI Press, Inc.
All rights of reproduction in any form reserved.
ISBN: 0–89232–028–1.

which there is an oversupply of private relative to public goods may be irrelevant or in fact work in reverse.

The size of the public sector in democracies has become the object of a great diversity of opinion. A fairly extensive literature analyzes the size of the public sector from various perspectives; see Amacher, Tollison, and Willett (1, 2).

Galbraith (8) argues that a systematic imbalance between the private and public sectors persists because of heavy advertising in the private sector. In Galbraith's view, heavy advertising for private goods presumably leads to an overabundance of private goods and to too few goods provided by government. Implicit in this argument is the view that government does not advertise or has some inherent disadvantage relative to the private sector in its advertising efforts.

A potentially strong counterargument to Galbraith's notion is suggested by Demsetz (7), who notes that lobbying and public relations by public agencies and their suppliers and free press coverage of proposed government policies are all functional equivalents of private advertising activity. We shall pursue this counterargument in some detail here. Our objective is to suggest a theory of elements concerning the nature and extent of advertising by government and to offer some preliminary data on several implications of the theory. We assume that government advertising is directed toward lobbying for future budgets or other benefits that can be captured by government decision-makers. Contrary to the arguments of Galbraith, we conclude that government advertising has several inherent advantages over private advertising, a situation which can bias resource allocation between the private and public sector and within the public sector.

The elements of our theory are presented in the first section. Data on several empirical implications of the theory are presented in Sections II, III, IV, with some concluding remarks offered in Section V.

I ELEMENTS OF A THEORY OF GOVERNMENT ADVERTISING

We start from a simple premise. Advertising by private firms can be verified through consumer experience with goods; advertising by government offers no such yardstick. Mises (12), p. 318, makes the point clearly:

> In political matters experience is always the experience of complex phenomena which is open to different interpretations; the only yardstick which can be applied to political doctrines is aprioristic reasoning. Thus political propaganda and business propaganda are essentially different things, although they often resort to the same technical methods.

With this premise firmly in mind, what are some of the elements of a theory of government advertising?

As stated above, we assume that advertising is directed toward increased budgets. Profit maximization implies that private firms will advertise to increase profits. Budget maximization implies that government bureaus will advertise when such activity adds more to the budget than it adds to bureau costs. Meeting any other condition would lower the bureau's budget, which is inconsistent with the assumption of budget maximization. The bureaucrat thus has a different objective than the businessman, but each will treat advertising expenditures as part of their relevant constraint sets. In this view it does not matter that the bureaucrat does not personally fund the advertising expenses of the bureau. We can proceed to ask, then, what is the nature of the advertising constraints faced by a bureau, especially as compared to those faced by a private firm?

Bureaus have one source of special efficiency compared with private firms—they do not have to advertise their output directly to all potential consumers. Representative democracy allows them to concentrate their propaganda on a relatively small number of effective decision-makers, primarily key members of legislative committees. Bureaus can thereby achieve substantial economies in advertising for budgets, in contrast to private sector advertising, which is directed at more diffuse and less easily identifiable groups of potential consumers. Compare, for example, the problem facing the Department of Defense in lobbying for a new budget with that of the cereal maker introducing a new breakfast item.

With representation based upon geography and influence in the legislature based upon seniority, the *location* of public expenditures becomes an important element of bureau advertising activity. We know from related work that the location of public expenditures is explained not by fiscal efficiency criteria but primarily by the seniority of state House and Senate delegations; see Stigler (15), Crain and Tollison (6). In our theory, the important decision-makers are the senior members of the legislature. Consequently we must ask if they will permit budget maximization by the bureaus they oversee. Our theory predicts that they will, because bureaus control the location of public spending and because public expenditures in a representative's home district are associated with his ability to combine legislative service with outside earnings; McCormick and Tollison (11). For example, expenditures may be directed to local firms in which the legislator has a financial affiliation. The point is that expenditures by bureaus may be directed to the districts of important representatives, where the valuable by-products of such activity are outside earnings and enhanced re-election prospects for the incumbent legislator. Support for budget extension may thereby be secured. Such an approach seems imminently plausible as an invisible hand mechanism in bureau lobbying for future budgets. Violation of fiscal efficiency criteria is likely to be severe in this process, whereas with private firms an efficient relation between location of output and the distribution of demand is typical.

This is a simple but plausible theory of the budgetary process, which obviates most of the problems raised by Thompson (16) in his review of Niskanen's (13) fundamental work on bureaus as budget-maximizing entities. Niskanen stresses that the output of the budget-maximizing bureau will be "too large" socially because of the inherent all-or-none monopoly power embodied in the exchange of bureau output for a total budget. Thompson argues that Niskanen's implication of a too-large budget is the result of his assumption that the bureau is in a superior bargaining position relative to its trustee, such as a congressional committee. Thompson argues that the situation is more analogous to bilateral monopoly and that the size of the budget will depend, in this setting, on how good the bureaucrat is at misrepresenting expected costs and outputs. Our approach is different from Thompson's. We stress the possibility of collusion between the congressional committee and the bureaucrat and provide a mechanism in the location of public spending by which bureaus may behave as Niskanen predicts. In effect, then, our theory is observationally no different from Niskanen's. It simply extends his budget-maximization approach by suggesting its implications for the location of bureau output. We note again that the empirical evidence on this matter seems to be on Niskanen's and our side; see Plott (14), Crain and Tollison (6).

Several other aspects of bureau advertising might be added as extensions of our theory. However, we will confine ourselves to just two additional points before we turn to several empirical implications of our analysis.

First, note that bureaus often advertise with classified information. For example, secrecy in the military area allows the Department of Defense to release sensitive information on Russian threats prior to important votes on the defense budget. Furthermore, since in many cases bureaus are the only possessors of certain types of information, it is difficult to challenge the credibility of their estimates when made public. Of course, consumers and decision-makers can generate their own estimates and make their own judgments, but there is no direct way to check the credibility of such statements. Similar situations can arise in private markets, especially with new products where the technology is complex and information costs are high, but consumers have recourse to direct consumption to judge the new product, an option which they do not have with the defense budget.

Second, a type of special efficiency which government bureaus can achieve in advertising arises from their exemption from antitrust law. Consider the analogy of the private industry problem of the interfirm *versus* intra-industry effects of advertising. For example, there are strong empirical reasons for viewing the cigarette industry as an example of uncoordinated advertising tending to reduce industry profits, because a large portion of each firm's advertising increases its cost without expanding the demand for cigarettes; Grabowski and Mueller (9). Under these circumstances, industry collusion will lead to lower levels of advertising, lower prices, and higher profits, yet antitrust law makes this impossible for firms in the private sector. However, it is entirely feasible within a bureau to coordinate the advertising efforts of its component parts. Since we know that the component parts of bureaus are competitive, it is an important empirical question whether or not advertising by the component parts of bureaus is competitive or complementary. For example, does the expansion of one defense bureau tend to result in the expansion or contraction of other defense bureaus? This is analogous to estimating cross elasticities of demand for public outputs.

We do not intend this discussion to be an exhaustive treatment of government advertising. It is meant only to suggest one approach to this topic, and does not take up some important aspects of these activities.[1] Our main point here is that a consistent theory indicates that government advertising has certain inherent advantages that private advertising does not have. One conclusion is that one should not be deluded by the fact that government agencies may spend less on advertising activities than private firms. Comparisons of this sort can be extremely misleading since government advertising will achieve more impact per dollar of expenditures than private advertising.[2] Yet this is not all that our theory suggests. We now examine several empirical implications of this discussion.

II PRICING IN GOVERNMENT

Before we turn our attention to some of the more important elements of advertising or nonprice competition in government, it is necessary to identify the constraints governing price competition in bureaus. The basic nature of the nonprofit status of government suggests that pricing constraints in bureaus will differ from those constraints in private concerns.

As expected, pricing in government differs from pricing in private organizations. Government agencies produce and sell thousands of different products and services. Some of the major products and services provided by these bureaus and their associated receipts for fiscal year 1970 are shown in Table 1. Most of these goods and services are offered at prices below market clearing levels to increase the number of users. The primary regulations governing price or user charges are contained in the Office of Management and Budget Circular A-25. This document provides guidelines for developing "an equitable and uniform system of charges for certain governmental services and property."[3] In general, the regulations permit and even encourage the establishment of prices below market clearing levels. For example, when

Table 1. User Charge Receipts, Fiscal Year 1970.

Government Activity	Amount ($ Millions)
Regulated resources	
Civil Aeronautics Board[a]	$ 1.2
Federal Aviation Administration	13.7
Federal Communications Commission	4.6
Federal Maritime Commission	0.0
Federal Power Commission	4.7
Interstate Commerce Commission	1.5
Securities and Exchange Commission	23.5
Permits and licenses	
Admission and recreation fees	9.4
Commission on business concessions	13.0
Immigration, passport, and consular fees	45.0
Patent and copyright fees	28.2
Other permits, registrations, and licenses	56.2
Rents and royalties	
Royalties	141.2
Rent of real property	221.4
Rent of equipment	38.6
Sale of products	
Timber, wildlife, agricultural and other land products	362.9
Minerals and mineral products	5.1
Power and other utilities	285.9
Publications and reproductions	13.5
Miscellaneous products and by-products	32.0
Miscellaneous fees and charges	
Testing, inspections, and grading services	1.1
Administrative, judicial, and professional services	40.4
Communication and transportation services	6.3
Subsistence, laundry, and health services	7.7
Miscellaneous services	28.1

Source: Receipts credited to agency accounts from U.S. Department of the Treasury, *Combined Statement of Receipts, Expenditures, and Balances of the U.S. Government, Fiscal Year 1970.*
[a]Exclusive of payments to air carriers.

the good or service provides special benefits to identifiable recipients, Circular A-25 provides that a charge should be imposed to recover the average cost of governmental services. Cost estimates, however, are based on historical, not replacement costs, and exclude the value of resources such as land or other assets acquired from previous periods.[4] The net result of such regulation is that most user charges result in prices far below market clearing levels. When benefits are distributed over a large population, the regulations permit the agency to establish a zero price.

> No charge should be made for services when the identification of the ultimate beneficiary is obscure and the service can be primarily considered as benefiting broadly the general public (e.g., licensing of new biological products).[5]

Such policies are consistent with budget maximization by the bureau. Lower than market clearing prices will induce more consumption and larger budgets and also imply that consumers will not properly validate the effectiveness of bureau advertising expenses since they do not bear these costs in the prices they face. The latter point, in particular, is illustrated by the laws concerning the volume of self-promotion by government agencies.

III CONSTRAINTS ON GOVERNMENT ADVERTISING

Advertising by bureaus may take the form of agency reports, pamphlets, periodicals, educational advertisement, press releases, and other forms, and has grown much faster than have the regulations controlling it. There are various statutory requirements for annual reports from executive agencies, for statistical publications, and for bulletins from various services.[6] The content of these publications is limited by law, however, to that which is "necessary to the public business."[7] All printing must be authorized in writing by department chiefs.[8] Cost, the use of illustrations, and form and style are also regulated by statute to be in keeping with the "public business."[9]

Thus, the laws concerning the volume of self-promotion by government agencies appear to have little impact beyond the minimum reporting requirements, which would probably be exceeded in any case. The upper limit on this pursuit is some nebulous concept of the public business and the size of the agency budget.

These constraints, however, only represent a lower bound on the amount of advertising among agencies. According to *Advertising Age*, governmental advertising in written publications amounted to approximately $113 million in 1975. The actual amount of advertising varies substantially among the different publications. For example, Table 2 shows the most recent expenditures by U.S. government agencies for a wide variety of magazines. This table reveals that governmental advertising expenditures ranged from 1.1 percent of total advertising expenditures for *Boys' Life* to 10.15 percent for *Sport* magazine in 1973.

These expenditures, however, merely hint at the magnitude of advertising

Table 2. U.S. Government Spending in Selected Magazines in Recent Years.

Year (Date)	Government Advertising Expenditures ($ Thousands)	Government Advertising as a Percentage of Total Expenditures
Argosy (1973)	$ 70.8	2.25%
Black Enterprise (1973)	105.7	4.02
Boys' Life (1973)	36.3	1.08
Car & Driver (1973)	234.8	4.68
Car Craft (1973)	115.9	5.50
Cosmopolitan (1972)	170.2	1.23
Ebony (1973)	805.9	6.39
Field & Stream (1973)	464.8	4.26
Esquire (1973)	249.3	1.42
Glamour (1973)	303.1	1.94
Grit (1972)	67.0	3.13
Guns & Ammo. (1973)	71.1	5.21
Hot Rod (1973)	380.0	6.21
Mademoiselle (1973)	118.4	1.23
Mechanix Illustrated (1973)	252.4	4.02
Motor Trend (1973)	277.8	5.36
National Geographic (1973)	241.1	1.48
Outdoor Life (1973)	459.8	4.19
Playboy (1973)	840.3	1.98
Popular Mechanics (1973)	181.6	2.24
Popular Science Monthly (1973)	534.6	5.98
Presbyterian Life (1967)	7.2	1.30
Reader's Digest (1973)	1,152.8	1.56
Road & Track (1973)	86.8	3.38
Scholastic Magazines (1964)	149.8	5.27
Scientific American (1973)	35.7	1.50
Seventeen (1972)	230.7	1.39
Skin Diver (1973)	31.5	3.39
Sport (1973)	575.7	10.15
Sports Illustrated (1973)	1,262.1	1.71
Sports Afield (1973)	361.7	5.38
Together (1967)	3.2	1.08
True (1973)	78.3	1.99
TV Guide (1973)	1,654.9	1.45

Source: Advertising Age, Vol. 48 (Feb. 14, 1977): 53–54.

by governmental programs, since they only include newspapers, magazines, radio and television expenditures. A more extensive investigation would surely reveal forms of advertising that have a functional equivalence to private advertising. For example, the Food and Nutrition Service (U.S. Department of Agriculture) spent more than $26 million for the food-stamp outreach activity in 1972. The outreach activity is explicitly designed to find potential recipients and to encourage them to participate in the food-stamp program. Expenditures on the outreach program alone accounted for approximately 18 percent of the total administrative costs for the food-stamp program in 1972.[10]

As noted earlier, governmental agencies distribute information about public programs and other governmental activities to newspapers and other media in the hope of receiving zero-priced publications. Consequently, an investigation of advertising expenditures relative to total expenditures yields highly biased results. The extent of these biases can be obtained by examining a random sample of news items devoted to various governmental, private, and other news stories. During late May and early June 1977, an investigation of seven newspaper days representing approximately 25,500 column inches revealed that 19 percent of the news stories was devoted to governmental programs.[11] This compares with 11 percent of the column inches devoted to information about private companies or products for those dates. The remaining 70 percent of space was devoted to sports (though we note that sports is a business) or information about other events involving individuals, the weather, or other noninstitutional information.

In sum, government agencies have clear incentives to expand their budgets by selling their outputs at less than market clearing prices and in the process advertising their virtues. In combination, these two policies virtually ensure that consumers will have little incentive to contradict the advertising claims of government.

IV VARIATIONS IN ADVERTISING EXPENDITURES

Without a more formalized theory of advertising pricing, output and input selection, it is difficult to identify differences in advertising activities between bureaus and private concerns. Yet, despite these problems, some constraints governing bureau behavior are so powerful that they can be used to predict outcomes of advertising in these organizations.

In the private sector there is considerable variation in the amount of resources devoted to advertising. Table 3 gives the proportion of total expenditures spent on advertising (as a percentage of net sales) for a number of representative U.S. industries. This table reveals considerable variation in advertising expenditures among private industries. For example, the pharmaceutical industry, which heads the list, spends more than ten times as much on advertising per dollar of sales as firms in the aerospace industry. An examination of Table 3 also reveals that in those industries where there is a high degree of substitutability or high elasticity of demand, the percentage of net sales devoted to advertising expenditures is relatively higher than in industries that have been characterized as being relatively less competitive. It is also true that in those industries where products have a shorter economic

Table 3. Advertising as Percentage of Net Sales. 1949–1971,
by Industry

Industry	Advertising as Percentage of Net Sales
Pharmaceuticals	3.7
Chemicals	3.7
Foods	2.3
Electrical machinery	1.6
Rubber products	1.5
Office machinery	1.0
Motor vehicles	0.8
Paper	0.7
Petroleum	0.5
Ferrous metals	0.3
Aerospace	0.3

Source: Clarkson, K. W., Intangible Capital and Rates of Return (Washington, D.C., American Enterprise Institute, 1977), p. 60.

life span, such as individual pharmaceutical products or chemicals, advertising is greater.

These general characteristics also hold in an examination of advertising expenditures in governmental bureaus. In Table 4, a representative number of governmental bureaus and their total advertising expenditures and total expenditures (including the percentage of advertising expenditures relative to total expenditures) are shown. An inspection of this table generally reveals greater advertising by those agencies that face a relatively more elastic, grossly defined demand curve. In addition, those firms whose products or programs are relatively older devote a smaller total percentage of their total budget to advertising activities. An examination of Table 4 also reveals that in situations where the bureau provides products that generally have more of the public good characteristic, the amount of expenditures devoted to advertising is relatively less than those where the private good characteristic is more prominent. These observations, of course, are only initial, and our evidence collected to date does not permit us to engage in systematic tests of the differences between these organizations.

We do note that advertising expenditures exhibit considerably more variation among bureaus than among private firms. This is a direct implication of our theory, which suggests that it will be more costly for consumers to validate the claims of most government advertising through direct consumption experience.[12]

Table 4. Advertising Expenditures as Percentage of Expenditures
Selected Federal Agencies, Fiscal Year 1974.

Agency, Branch, or Department	Advertising Expenditures ($ millions)	Total Expenditures ($ millions)	Advertising as Percentage of Total Expenditures
Army	$ 49.5	$ 22,162.4	0.22%
Navy	28.0	21,745.8	0.13
Air Force	19.2	23,163.6	0.08
Marine Corps	14.3	2,165.9	0.66
Coast Guard	1.5	850.5	0.18
Postal Service	6.8	11,295.3	0.04
Amtrak	3.0	529.6	0.57
Energy Research and Development Administration	3.6	2,308.3	0.16
Law Enforcement Assistance Administration	1.1	770.4	0.14
Department of Transportation (News & Information Division)	2.0	7,253.7	0.03
Manpower Administration	1.5	8,681.6	0.02
U.S. Travel Service	3.3	10.9	29.94
Housing and Urban Development	4.6	4,785.8	0.10
Consumer Product Safety Commission	1.4	18.7	7.40
Environmental Protection Agency	3.0	2,030.1	0.01
Veterans Administration	1.0	13,336.9	0.00
American Revolution Bicentennial Administration	1.2	5.1	23.92
NASA (Office of Public Affairs)	8.6	3,252.3	0.26
Internal Revenue Service	3.3	1,595.4	0.21
Bureau of the Mint	1.0	22.2	4.63

Sources: U.S. General Accounting Office, *Survey of Public Information Expenditures*, Office of Management and Budget 1975; *The Budget of the United States Government, Fiscal Year 1976* (Washington, D.C.: Government Printing Office, 1975); U.S. Postal Service, *Annual Report of the Postmaster General 1974–1975;* and U.S. National Railroad Passenger Corporation, *1975 Amtrak Annual Report*, p. 25.

V CONCLUDING REMARKS

We have only scratched the surface of government advertising in this paper. For example, we omit completely the myriad of rules controlling government procurement of goods and services,[13] disposal of goods and property,[14] and provision of services and information.[15] We have limited our purpose to suggesting an economic approach to government advertising and to illustrating a couple of its implications.

The economics profession has devoted a relatively large amount of attention to advertising by private firms. We find that many of the concepts that economists have sought to apply to the private sector, but for which only scanty empirical evidence has been found, appear to apply forcefully to the public sector as well, for example, economies of scale in advertising and monopoly power in the private sector. We think there is a clear link between advertising and monopoly in government. In the final analysis, it may be that, when read carefully, Galbraith's dictum about social balance applies exactly in reverse.

FOOTNOTES

Kenneth W. Clarkson is professor of economics, Law and Economics Center, University of Miami School of Law. Robert Tollison is professor of economics, Center for Study of Public Choice, Virginia Polytechnic Institute and State University.

1. For example, Amacher, Tollison, and Willett (1, 2) and Greene (10) emphasize the effects of uncertainty in increasing the size of the government budget in a democracy.
2. See Clotfelter (5) for an example of the pitfalls one can fall into along these lines.
3. OMB Circular A–25, § 1 (1959).
4. OMB Circular A–25, § 5 (1959).
5. OMB Circular A–25, § 3b (1959).
6. 44 U.S.C. 13. Translations of these statutes cannot be found in the Code of Federal Regulations for the various departments. The bulk of the regulations in the Code concerns procedures of compliance with the Freedom of Information Act, not the provision of promotional information. See 5 U.S.C. § 552 (1976).
7. 44 U.S.C. § 1102 (1968).
8. *Ibid.*
9. 44 U.S.C. § 1105.
10. Expenditures on outreach for fiscal year 1972 represent 1.3 percent of the total administrative costs plus the value of bonus food stamps; Clarkson (3), p. 29.
11. *Miami Herald*, May 13, 21, 23, and 31, and June 1 and 2, 1977.
12. See Clarkson (4) for additional discussion of why bureaus would predictably exhibit greater variation in input categories.
13. See, for example, 41, U.S.C.A. § 5, 6, 240, 252; 44 U.S.C.A. § 3701–3703 and 41 CFR § 1–1.3, 1–2.2, *et seq.*
14. See, for example, 40 U.S.C.A. §484; 43 CFR §5410, 5430.
15. See, for example, 5 U.S.C.A. §552 (FOIA); 44 U.S.C.A. §11, 13; 7 CFR §295; 21 CFR §4.1; 45 CFR §17.

REFERENCES

1. Amacher, R., Tollison, R., and Willett, T. (April 1975) "Budget Size in a Democracy: A Review of the Arguments," *Public Finance Quarterly*, Vol. 3: 99–122.
2. ———. (1976) "Risk Avoidance and Political Advertising: Neglected Issues in the Literature on Budget Size in a Democracy," in R. Amacher, R. Tollison, and T. Willett, eds., *The Economic Approach to Public Policy*, Ithaca, N.Y., Cornell University Press.

3. Clarkson, K. (1975) *Food Stamps and Nutrition,* Washington, D.C., American Enterprise Institute.
4. ————. (October 1972) "Some Implications of Property Rights in Hospital Management," *Journal of Law and Economics,* Vol. 15: 363–384.
5. Clotfelter, C. T. (July 1976) "The Scope of Public Advertising," paper presented at the Conference on the Political Economy of Advertising, Washington, D.C., at the American Enterprise Institute.
6. Crain, W. M., and Tollison, R. D. "The Influence of Representation on Public Policy," *Journal of Legal Studies,* forthcoming.
7. Demsetz, H. (May 1970) "Discussion," *American Economic Review,* Vol. 60: 481–484.
8. Galbraith, J. K. (1958) *The Affluent Society,* Boston, Houghton Mifflin.
9. Grabowski, H.G., and Mueller, D.C. (Summer 1971) "Imitative Advertising in the Cigarette Industry," *Antitrust Bulletin,* Vol. 2: 257–292.
10. Greene, K. (April 1973) "Attitudes Toward Risk and the Relative Size of the Public Sector," *Public Finance Quarterly,* Vol. 2: 205 – 218.
11. McCormick, R., and Tollison, R. D. "Legislatures as Unions," *Journal of Political Economics,* forthcoming.
12. Mises, L. V. (1949) *Human Action,* New Haven, Yale University Press.
13. Niskanen, W. A. (1971) *Bureaucracy and Representative Government,* Chicago, Aldine.
14. Plott, C. R. (May 1968) "Some Organizational Influences on Urban Renewal Decisions," *American Economics Review,* Proceedings, Vol. 58: 306–321.
15. Stigler, G. (January 1976) "The Sizes of Legislatures," *Journal of Legal Studies,* Vol. 5: 17–34.
16. Thompson, E. (September 1973) "Review of Bureaucracy and Representative Government by W. A. Niskanen," *Journal of Economic Literature,* Vol. 11: 950–953.

PROTECTING THE RIGHT TO BE SERVED BY PUBLIC UTILITIES

Victor P. Goldberg, UNIVERSITY OF CALIFORNIA, DAVIS

The administered contracts approach to regulation focuses attention on adjusting relationships over time. One recurring problem concerns the possible termination of service to a customer class. Customers would desire mechanisms which balance the benefits of encouraging reliance on continued provision of the service against the costs of decreased flexibility and increased short-term misallocations. In the terminology of Calabresi-Melamed, standard economic analysis and current policy call for "property rules" for protecting the right to be served. This paper explores the merits of using "liability rules" and suggests that a combination of liability rules is likely to yield satisfactory results.

Research in Law and Economics, Vol. 1, pp. 145–156.
ISBN: 0–89232–028–1.

In an earlier paper I developed the concept of administered contracts and suggested that it would provide a useful framework for understanding and analyzing economic institutions, particularly regulation; see Goldberg (9). Regulation can be viewed, in effect, as a long-term, collective contract for provision of a changing set of services. This formulation raises a rather different set of policy issues than the static efficiency matters (for example, marginal cost pricing) generally raised by economists. Instead, it directs attention to the "constitutional" problems inherent in designing and adjusting the regulatory arrangement over time.

A particularly sticky set of questions concerns the conditions under which a service can be terminated. This can be subdivided into three different types of problems. First, if some (or all) of the utility's customers have a more attractive option (such as microwave transmission), should they be allowed to take advantage of that option; that is, how ought the *producer's* right to serve the market be protected? Second, if a utility alleges that a customer has failed to pay bills or has misused the service, what procedures must it follow before terminating service; that is, how ought the *individual's* right to be served be protected? Third, if service to a particular customer class proves unduly expensive, can the producer discontinue service to that class; that is, how ought the *collective* right to be served be protected? Here I want to consider only the third question. While the subject matter is termination or abandonment by public utilities, the same issues arise in other administered contract contexts—for example, the treatment of "runaway shops" in collective bargaining agreements.

In the next section I will explore the customers' interest in protecting the right to be served. The problem can be partitioned by initially suppressing the collective aspects of the relationship and assuming that there is only a single customer; this enables us to focus on the "relational" aspects of the implicit regulatory contract. The complications arising from multiple customers are then introduced. In Section II mechanisms for giving some protection to that right will be considered.

I THE RIGHT TO BE SERVED

Relational Contracts

In discrete transactions, on which economists focus most of their attention, the parties are more or less indifferent to each other's identity. Y produces for the market and X buys from the market. If one party ceased to exist there would be little or no effect on the affairs of the other. In such transactions the benefits to one party of imposing penalties for breach on the other party are minimal. In relational contracts, on the other hand, one party (or both) will rely to some degree on the continuation of the exchange relationship between the two parties.[1] X, for example, might have to invest in the formation of physical or human capital the value of which is contingent, in part, on the continuation of the relationship. In such cases X would find it important to try to protect itself from a severing of the relationship by Y (or from the threat of such severance).

Consider a single customer faced with the problem of designing a relationship with a potential supplier of electricity. While there is some *ex ante* competition among potential suppliers, *ex post* the provider will be rather isolated from competition.[2] Assume for convenience that the customer has the ability to bargain intelligently on the shape of the contract and that the costs of so doing are a minor factor. The parties will establish a set of prices — or a flexible pricing rule[3] — for the duration of the contract. However, if after performance has begun, honoring the contract conflicts with the provider's perceived self-interest, he might choose to breach the agreement. It is necessary, therefore, for the customer to include protection from this contingency in the initial agreement, while recognizing that increased protection does not, generally, come free.

The customer's first concern is the "hold up" problem — its vulnerability to arbitrary, capricious, or opportunistic behavior by the other party.[4] The provider could threaten to curtail the supply unless the customer agreed to a substantially higher price — a price which it never would have agreed to at the formation stage. That is, once the customer agrees to the contract, the customer has an *ex post* demand substantially greater than the *ex ante* demand. It is in the provider's short-run interest to exploit its position; it is also (probably) in the long-run interest of *both* parties to restrict the provider's ability to exploit that position. Designing restrictions which will protect the vulnerable party from being held up but which will not have further unfortunate consequences is a nontrivial problem, as is evidenced by the difficulties courts have had in dealing with such problems — witness such doctrinal morasses as duress of goods, pre-existing duty, unconscionability, and good faith modification.[5]

The second concern — on which I will concentrate my attention — is the problem of reliance.[6] The customer must make long-term investment decisions relying on the continued availability of the service at reasonable prices. It will want to impose contractually on the provider an obligation to take that reliance into account when the provider weighs the benefits of performing or breaching.[7] The level of protection afforded the consumer will influence pretermination behavior. Thus, if compensation were minimal we would expect lower levels of relation-specific investment by customers than we would if it were generous. Likewise, increases in protection should result in higher costs for providers which would be passed on to customers in the form of higher prices at the formation stage.

The customer's loss if there is a breach is the future earnings that would have accrued to him had the provider been compelled to perform—the expectation interest. At the formation stage it is reasonable to suppose that the customer expected a normal rate of return on his capital—that he would be indifferent between the earnings foregone and the capital invested. That is, the expectation interest and the reliance interest would be the same. At the time at which termination is to be considered, however, the sunk costs (reliance) and future earnings foregone (expectation) need not be the same. The divergence between these two interests will be of importance in the subsequent discussion.

Multiple Customers

The preceding discussion presupposed that there was but one customer and that the customer was in a position to bargain on the precise terms of the relationship. However, since regulation typically gives substantial protection to the utility's right to serve, the customer's ability to bargain over price is in fact severely constrained.[8] Furthermore, there exist substantial advantages to mass production of contract terms, especially for nonbusiness customers; see Goldberg (7), pp. 483–491. Instead of customizing terms to each customer's idiosyncratic needs, it will be necessary to lump customers together into classes of "equals" (with a class of "all customers" being the extreme case).

The utility does not confront customers with a set of future prices but with a price-setting process; they need a flexible pricing rule to adjust price over time in the face of changing conditions. Private parties use many techniques for attaining such flexibility—indexation, arbitration, percentage of the gross pricing, prices keyed to an outside price, and so forth; see Goldberg (9). Under regulation the price for the *collective* contract (that is, the rate level) is determined largely on a cost-plus basis with rate of return regulation. Rarely is it feasible to use comparability to outside prices.[9] That is not true, however, for prices faced by individuals or customer classes. The prices charged other customers can serve as an indicator[10] of changing conditions common to all customers, and therefore a commitment to a reasonably stable price structure might establish a satisfactory bench mark for price adjustment.[11]

Furthermore, the customers will often be at least as interested in the prices charged competitors as those they face. It is not unusual for private contracting parties to attempt to protect themselves in this dimension by utilizing "most favored nation" clauses or by keying the price to an outside market-related price.[12] By committing themselves in advance to a rate structure providing for equal rates (or constant rate differentials) over time, customers can mitigate the risks arising from this source.

J. M. Clark (3), p. 358, makes this point graphically:

Another of the general principles governing the social interest in rate making is that existing channels of trade and locations of production are to be given the benefit of all reasonable doubt, since the livelihood of communities has come to depend on them, not to speak of the value of large capital investments. Where cities are in close competition with each other, especially in types of business in which a small difference in rail rates might be decisive, business adjusts itself to the existing rate differentials, whatever they may be, and any change is a misfortune. Hence these relationships should be preserved, as far as possible, through all changes in rates, unless it becomes perfectly clear that they are unjust or uneconomical in such a substantial degree as to warrant the injustice and economic loss which would result from a change.[13]

There are, therefore, a number of forces encouraging the grouping of a public utility's customers into classes of individuals to be treated equally[14] and the maintenance of a reasonably stable rate structure. Since termination of a customer class is the equivalent of setting an infinite price for that class, the argument applies as well to attempts by utilities to terminate or abandon service.

If the rate *level* is allowed to change enabling the regulated firm to recover a reasonable rate of return, then an important distinction between the single customer and the collective case emerges. In the earlier discussion, price stability came largely at the expense of the provider's flexibility in adapting to changed circumstances. Here the utility's earnings are more or less unaffected,[15] and the costs of providing unprofitable services are shifted to other customers; in addition, if the price structure is prevented from adjusting to short-run changes in supply and demand conditions, there will be persistent (and probably growing) short-term resource misallocation. The relevant trade-off now concerns the customers' reliance on the rate structure and the misallocations rate structure stickiness entails.

The foregoing understates the complex nature of the trade-off in that it implies that, in the absence of rate structure stickiness, prices would be closely related to costs. Such need not be the case. Rather, the rate structure might have internal subsidization—Posner's (18) "taxation by regulation"—built into it by design.[16] Certain groups of customers will, as a matter of policy, be favored with service at a subsidized price. Changes in rate structure will reflect not only changes in underlying costs, but also changes in the underlying political structure. This complication would be very serious if the analysis centered on standard efficiency issues. However, my prime concern is in searching for mechanisms facilitating adjustment to changed circumstances; the source of that change is not of great consequence. People do, after all, come to rely on the continuation of certain subsidies even though such subsidies might seem ill-conceived to the observer.[17]

II PROTECTING THE RIGHT TO BE SERVED

How, if at all, should the right to be served be protected? Economic analysis, by ignoring relational issues, implies that there should be no protection—the firm should have the right to terminate service if it sees fit.[18] This "cold turkey" solution might be desirable for two quite different reasons. First, the relevant decision-makers might feel that protection is not merited—people should not have relied on continued service. Second, even if the interest deserved protection, the agency might not be trusted to provide that protection intelligently—the cure is apt to be worse than the disease.

At the other extreme, the customers might be given the right to enjoin any "taking" of their right to be served. That is, the provider would not be permitted to raise the class's relative rates or terminate service. This is essentially the I.C.C.'s position in abandonment cases.[19] A railroad serving a light-density, money-losing route must petition the I.C.C. for permission to abandon that route; if the petition is opposed by shippers who would be hurt by that abandonment, the Commission must determine whether to grant or deny that petition. If an abandonment is contested, the I.C.C. has been very reluctant to grant the petition and thereby harm the protesting customers.[20]

These alternatives correspond to what Calabresi and Melamed (2) refer to as "property rules" for protecting an entitlement. The entitlement in the former case is the producer's right to terminate, and in the latter case it is the customers' right to be served. Protection need not, however, be an either/or affair. Less drastic alternatives are available in the form of what these authors call "liability rules." That is, the entitlement would be assigned initially to either the producer or the customers but the other party would be permitted to "take" that right provided that it paid compensation.

The variety of feasible compensation schemes is great and it is perhaps artificial to confine the discussion to the Calabresi-Melamed framework. Nevertheless, I believe this to be a useful vehicle both for raising the essential issues and for introducing a rather novel proposal.[21] Consider first the case in which the customers have a right to be served protected by a liability rule. The producer can terminate service provided that it pays damages to the customers. The damages are, in effect, the price the producer must pay for the taking. If that price exceeds the savings arising from termination, the producer would find it less expensive to continue service (and vice versa).

That is, the damage rule should ideally measure the losses stemming from good faith reliance, tempered by administrative expediency. The loss is the unamortized cost of capital expenditures that could not be offset by mitigation (resale, partial use, or relocation).[22] It is important to realize that the actual protection of the right to be served depends on the computation of damages. By using conservative measures, the regulators can, in effect, deny the protection that was seemingly granted by vesting the right with the customers. While in some instances a fairly straightforward estimate of the cost of reliance could be made with tolerable accuracy, it will in many cases be wiser to establish rather crude schedules of stipulated damages as—it should be noted—is frequently done by private parties at the formation stage of a long-term, complex contractual relationship.[23] The simplest approach would be to set a price for termination at the time the service is extended to a class. But this might not always be practical; it certainly is not feasible for termination proceedings concerning service that is *currently* being provided. More complex rules might base compensation (for commercial customers) on a percentage of the gross sales or on some multiple of the previous year's expenditures on the service. Such "flexible termination benefit" rules are singularly inelegant but might well represent a reasonable balancing of accuracy and administration costs.[24]

Consider now the case in which the producer has the right to terminate protected only by a liability rule. That is, if termination is proposed the customers can enjoin it provided that they are willing to pay for the producer's damages.[25] If the customers find continuation of the service sufficiently valuable, they will pay the costs of forestalling termination. Compensation would take the form of a higher unit price reflecting changes in the relative cost of service to the class or a changed perception of that class's "deservingness." For most reasonable measures of damages, this second rule gives less protection of customer reliance and more protection of producer flexibility than does the first rule. This might, paradoxically, mean that it would result in too little change. Regulators perceiving the unpopularity of such a change are apt to be reluctant to initiate termination proceedings in such circumstances (much like in the case of "property" protection discussed above).

Consider finally a third alternative, a variant on the Calabresi-Melamed scheme which combines the two rules [see Ellickson (5), pp. 738–761]. Give the customers a *choice* between (1) termination with compensation for reasonable reliance and (2) enjoining termination, but paying damages (a higher price) to the producer. Customers are not worse off than they would have been with only the first liability rule, since they still have the opportunity to choose that; if the continued service is of great value to the customers (or their actual reliance interest exceeds the measured damages), they can choose the latter option. Since the total compensation paid to terminated customers should in the long run be less with this option, the "insurance premium" included in the price structure would be lower. However, if the rule encourages more terminations and if termination proceedings are expensive for the firm, some of the savings will disappear.

The merits of the rule depend on a number of practical problems. Who is to represent the customers in making the choice? What will trigger the termination process? How are damages to be determined? Implementation of any of the compensation mechanisms will require workable solutions to problems of this sort. Because of the exploratory nature of this essay, I leave such important questions aside. If such problems proved insurmountable, then, surely, further theorizing on the merits of the various compensation rules would be of little use. By encouraging further exploration of the merits, I implicitly assume that these questions can be answered tolerably well.

III CONCLUDING REMARKS

It might well be that the efficiency case for administered contracts is flawed. That is, while the results might exceed those arising from the private market alternative[26] if the agents (regulators, union leaders) were both extremely clever and faithful representatives of their constituency, the opposite might be true in a world in which mere mortals play the agent's role. But that is largely beside the point. Administered contracts will play a significant role in the resource allocation process in the future whether we like it or not, and it is therefore incumbent on economists to develop tools for analyzing problems inherent in that mode. This essay should be viewed as one step in that direction.

The central concern in the preceding discussion was the balancing of good faith reliance against the need for flexibility. This is a recurrent problem in social relations and at its deepest level concerns the balancing of the need for order and continuity against the necessity of change; see Goldberg (10), pp. 884–886.

Thus, if instead of the "right to be served" we substituted the "right to pollute an air basin," the problem of terminating or otherwise altering that right would raise essentially the same set of problems—a set radically different from those economists are accustomed to treating. The economist's normal reaction to the problem would be either to ask the comparative statics question: on whom should the right be conferred (regardless of the initial placement), or to insist upon the importance of defining the right unambiguously so that private parties could subsequently rearrange the ownership of rights by voluntary exchange. Both approaches presume that the decision can be made *ex ante*, before anyone has come to rely on any particular definition of rights; the latter approach presumes additionally that once the decision has been made, reliance on that definition should be protected. I am presenting a bit of a caricature, but I believe this captures the spirit of the economist's usual approach. The fundamental problem of redefining rights in an ongoing society is ignored, yet policy prescriptions imply that it has been taken into account. The approach taken here explores, albeit in a narrow context, the merits of facing the redefinition problem directly. The results, while tentative, suggest that this is a fertile area for further search.

FOOTNOTES

The author is currently professor of economics, University of California, Davis. Part of the work on this paper was done while the author was a visiting fellow at the Center for Study of Public Choice, Virginia Polytechnic Institute and State University and while he was visiting associate professor at the Law School, University of California, Berkeley. An earlier draft of this paper was presented at seminars at Yale University, University of California (Berkeley), University of Virginia, and Virginia Polytechnic Institute and State University. The author would also like to thank Thomas Borcherding, Richard Danzig, Melvin Eisenberg, Robert Ellickson, Lee Friedman, William Hallagan, Friedrich Kessler, Arthur Leff, Ian Macneil, Alan Olmstead, David Warner, Oliver Williamson, Richard Zerbe, and two anonymous referees.

1. For a detailed cataloging of the differences between discrete transactions and relational contracts, see Macneil (17), pp. 735–805.

2. The isolation from competition could be the result of purely technical considerations (the other local suppliers of electricity might cease to exist if they fail to receive enough contracts initially); it might, however, be due in part to the customer's granting substantial protection to the producer's right to serve; see Goldberg (9). It must be remembered that conceptually designing protection for the rights to serve and be served are distinct problems; it is feasible that parties might quite rationally choose to give great protection to the one and little to the other. It is, however, also true that in some instances an increase in protection of the right to serve will make it desirable for the customer to insist upon greater protection for the right to be served.

3. In long-term relationships, the parties often will choose to agree not on a set of prices but on a procedure for altering prices through time; for a discussion of the whys and wherefores of flexible pricing rules, see Goldberg (9), pp. 436–438.

4. This is a manifestation of what has been referred to as the "small numbers" and "opportunism" problems; see Williamson (26) pp. 26–30.

5. See Dawson and Harvey (4), pp. 467–644. The "hold up" problem can be dealt with by noncontractual methods. Vertical integration is one (possibly costly) alternative; see Williamson (26), pp. 82–131, and Richardson (20). It is also possible to rely on long-term, noncontractual relationships which can be roughly summed up in the amorphous phrase "maintenance of good will." In many instances this can indeed be a powerful sanction, but it is doubtful that most economic actors (or economists) would put *exclusive* reliance on it. For a valuable discussion of the subordinate role of formal contracts in governing ongoing relationships, see Macaulay (15).

6. While I will not consider the "hold up" problem in detail, the *possibility* of hold up is a fundamental condition of the subsequent discussion; see note 7.

7. If there were costless bargaining and no opportunism, then the value of the customer's reliance would be an opportunity cost for the firm. (Likewise, the costs of the provider's foregone flexibility would be an opportunity cost to the customer.) The costs of reliance would, *ex hypothesis*, be communicated to the provider. This mechanism only works, however, if the costs are accurately perceived at the formation stage of the relationship and if there is no opportunism within the relationship after it has begun. Relational exchange transforms *ex ante* large number bargaining to *ex post* small number bargaining. Hence, the theoretical and practical difficulties arising from small numbers exchange [on which see Williamson (26), pp. 26–30; Arrow (1); and Regan (19)] are seen to be endemic to a world of relational exchange.

8. For discussion of protection of the right to serve, see Goldberg (9), pp. 432–436. In legal jargon, contracts between utilities and individual customers would be referred to as contracts of adhesion; see Slawson (23).

9. The relationship between TVA and private electric utilities would provide a partial exception.

10. These prices are a good indicator only for the common costs; if noncommon costs or demand conditions differ substantially between customers, then problems arise.

11. A stable price structure also makes it more difficult (economically and politically) for producers to single out individual customers with prices aimed at capturing their *ex post* consumer surplus.

12. Cost equalization would seem to be a reasonable explanation of the gasoline industry's dependence on the spot market price in long-term contracts. See *U.S. v. Socony Vacuum*, 310 U.S. 150 (1940).

13. I would suggest that historically much of the outcry against price discrimination has been concerned with such dynamic *reliance* issues, not with the problems illuminated by the traditional comparative static analysis.

14. These forces exist outside the public utility sector as well. Consider, for example, the ASCAP consent decree which provided: "When a reasonable fee has been finally determined by this Court, defendant ASCAP shall be required to offer a license at a comparable fee to all other applicants similarly situated who shall thereafter request a license of ASCAP." The decree is quoted at length in Timberg (25), p. 308. Wage structures provide another instance. See, for example, Yandle's (27), pp. 506–507, discussion of "property rights" in wage structures.

15. Rate of return regulation does not provide an absolutely binding earnings ceiling; for a discussion of the mechanics of rate of return regulation, see Joskow (13).

16. Note that in my conception some observed internal subsidization is functional, being a by-product of the protection of customer reliance.

17. I am using the concept of "subsidy" loosely here. It implies that there is a normal alternative that could be identified as not entailing a subsidy independent of the social context. For criticism of this notion, see Goldberg (6, 11); Samuels (21); and Samuels and Mercuro (22).

18. The Task Force on Railroad Productivity (24), p. 169, notes: "[M]ost firms in a market economy, such as that of the United States, are free to withdraw their product or service from any market in which they cannot sell at a profit and to relocate their factories as markets and technology change without regard for the economic welfare of the town from which they are departing. Clearly, a different morality has been imposed on the railroad industry since passage of the Transportation Act of 1920 which requires a 'certificate of public convenience and necessity' in order to abandon." However, the Task Force does give some attention to the problems of customer reliance, compensation, and the smoothing of the adjustment to abandonment.

19. For discussion of the mechanics of current abandonment proceedings see Jones (12), pp. 333–339, 420–437, and Task Force (24), pp. 157–186.

20. Although there are about 100 abandonment cases decided each year by the I.C.C., most of them involve situations in which there is little or no opposition by shippers; see Task Force (24), pp. 165–169. Failure to grant the petition will generally result in further losses for the railroads. Five of the railroads with a substantial share of the country's light density, unprofitable operations are in bankruptcy; see Task Force (24), pp. 160–162.

21. The mechanism has been proposed in other contexts; see Ellickson (5), pp. 738–761, and Goldberg (10), p. 886.

22. To facilitate damage mitigation, the producer's right to serve should be taken simultaneously. That is, the customers should be free to receive service from other providers who had previously been barred from the market.

23. For a discussion of termination benefits in the sale of nuclear power plants, see Kwitny (14), p. 38; Macaulay (15), pp. 90–91, summarizes the termination benefits in automobile franchise contracts.

24. Also, they might not. These rules are only meant to be suggestive of the types that might enable the regulators to take the reliance interest into account, while not being so unwieldy as to be impractical.

25. The first liability rule had a straightforward counterpart in tort law: If X's car hits Y, X pays damages. The second rule is less common; see, however, *Spur Industries, Inc. v. Del. E. Webb Development Co.*, 494 P. 2d 700 (1972).

26. It is somewhat misleading to contrast administered contracts with private market alternatives. Private transactions take place within a legal framework which can be viewed as an administered contract; see Goldberg (8), pp. 52–54 and (9), pp. 429–430. See also the following paragraph in the text.

REFERENCES

1. Arrow, K. J. (1969) "The Organization of Economic Activity," in *The Analysis and Evaluation of Public Expenditures: The PPB System*, Vol. 1. JEC, 91st Congress, 1st Session, pp. 47–64.
2. Calabresi G. and Melamed, A. D. (April 1972) "Property Rules, Liability Rules and Inalienability: One View of the Cathedral," *Harvard Law Review*, Vol. 85: 1089–1128.
3. Clark, J. M. (1939) *Social Control of Business*, 2nd ed., New York, McGraw-Hill.
4. Dawson, J. P. and Harvey, W. B. (1969) *Cases on Contracts and Contract Remedies*, 2nd ed., Mineola, N.Y., Foundation Press.
5. Ellickson, R. C. (Summer 1973) "Alternatives to Zoning: Covenants, Nuisance Rules, and Fines as Land Use Controls," *University of Chicago Law Review*, Vol. 40: 681–781.
6. Goldberg, V. P. (September 1974) "Public Choice-Property Rights," *Journal of Economic Issues*, Vol. 8: 555–579.
7. ———. (October 1974) "Institutional Change and the Quasi-Invisible Hand," *Journal of Law and Economics*, Vol. 17: 461–492.
8. ———. (March 1976) "Toward an Expanded Economic Theory of Contract," *Journal of Economic Issues*, Vol. 10: 45–61.
9. ———. (Autumn 1976) "Regulation and Administered Contracts," *Bell Journal of Economics*, Vol. 7: 426–448.
10. ———. (December 1976) "Commons, Clark, and the Emerging Post-Coasian Law and Economics," *Journal of Economic Issues*, Vol. 10: 877–893.
11. ———. (March 1977) "On Positive Theories of Redistribution," *Journal of Economic Issues*, Vol 11: 119–132.
12. Jones, W. K. (1976) *Regulated Industries, Cases and Materials*, Mineola, N.Y., Foundation Press.
13. Joskow, P. L. (October 1974) "Inflation and Environmental Concern: Structural Change in the Process of Public Utility Price Regulation," *Journal of Law and Economics*, Vol. 17: 291–327.
14. Kwitny, J. (May 1974) "Combustion Engineering's Order Surge May Have Been Based on Risky Deals," *Wall Street Journal*, Vol. 91: 38.
15. Macaulay, S. (February 1963) "Non-Contractual Relations in Business: A Preliminary Study," *American Sociological Review*, Vol. 28: 55–67.
16. ———. (1966) *Law and the Balance of Power: The Automobile Manufacturers and Their Dealers*, New York, Russell Sage Foundation.

17. Macneil, I. R. (May 1974) "The Many Futures of Contract," *Southern California Law Review*, Vol. 47: 691–816.
18. Posner, R. A. (Spring 1971) "Taxation by Regulation," *Bell Journal of Economics and Management Science*, Vol. 2: 22–50.
19. Regan, D. H. (October 1972) "The Problem of Social Cost Revisited," *Journal of Law and Economics*, Vol. 15: 427–437.
20. Richardson, G. B. (September 1972) "The Organization of Industry," *Economic Journal*, Vol. 82: 883–896.
21. Samuels, W. J. (November 1974) "An Economic Perspective on the Compensation Problem," *Wayne Law Review*, Vol. 21: 113–134.
22. ———. and Mercuro, N. (1978) "The Role and Resolution of the Compensation Principle in Society," in *Research in Law and Economics*, Vol. I.
23. Slawson, W. D. (January 1971) "Standard Form Contracts and Democratic Control of Lawmaking Power," *Harvard Law Review*, Vol. 84: 529–566.
24. Task Force on Railroad Productivity. (November 1973) *Improving Railroad Productivity*, Final Report to the National Commission on Productivity and the Council of Economic Advisers, Washington, D.C.
25. Timberg, S. (Spring 1954) "The Antitrust Aspects of Merchandising Modern Music: The ASCAP Consent Judgment of 1950," *Law and Contemporary Problems*, Vol. 19: 292–322.
26. Williamson, O.E. (1975) *Markets and Hierarchies*, New York, Free Press.
27. Yandle, B. (September 1975) "Property in Price," *Journal of Economic Issues*, Vol. 9: 501–514.

THE ROLE AND RESOLUTION OF THE COMPENSATION PRINCIPLE IN SOCIETY: PART ONE—THE ROLE

Warren J. Samuels, MICHIGAN STATE UNIVERSITY

Nicholas Mercuro, UNIVERSITY OF NEW ORLEANS

The compensation problem is explored in light of radical indeterminacy, selective perception, and the nature and operation of the legal system. The compensation principle is shown to be functional as psychic balm and legitimation of the institution of property and the basic organization of society, and not the protection of particular property rights, except selectively. Conventional legal and economic treatment of compensation issues—for example, the conflicting, conclusionary and tautological taking issue—thus is shown not to reach the fundamentals of the system of property, the legal system, and the roles thereof in society.

Research in Law and Economics, Vol. 1, pp. 157–194.
Copyright © 1979 by JAI Press, Inc.
All rights of reproduction in any form reserved.
ISBN: 0–89232–028–1.

Private Property: ... which consists in the free use, enjoyment, and disposal of all his acquisitions, without any control or diminution, save only by the laws of the land. ... that sole and despotic dominion which one man claims and exercises over the external things of the world, in total exclusion of the right of any other individual in the universe. [W. Blackstone, in Ehrlich (29), pp. 51, 113.]

The real question that has to be decided is: should A be allowed to harm B or should B be allowed to harm A? [Coase (18), p. 2.]

When reason argues about particular cases, it needs not only universal but also particular principles. [St. Thomas Aquinas, in Viner (107), p. 47.]

General propositions do not decide concrete cases. [Oliver Wendell Holmes, *Lochner v. New York*, 198 U.S. 45, 74 (1905).]

One generation's misfortune is a later generation's cause of action. ... [R. Smith (95), p. 122.]

Any radical change in the structure or content of law expropriates former holders of power. [Friedman (41), p. 47.]

In the past it was the railroad's responsibility for protection of the public at grade crossings. This responsibility has now shifted. Now it is the highway, and not the railroad, and the motor vehicle, not the train which creates the hazard and must be primarily responsible for its removal. [Interstate Commerce Commission, quoted in Van Alstyne (106), p. 50n. 232.]

All we can seek is consistency, coherence, order. The question for the scientist is what thought-scheme will best provide him with a sense of that order and coherence, a sense of some permanence, repetitiveness and universality in the structure or texture of the scheme of things, a sense even of that one-ness and simplicity which, if he can assure himself of its presence, will carry consistency and order to their highest expression. Religion, science and art have all of them this aim in common. The difference between them lies in the different emphases in their modes of search. [Shackle (92), p. 286.]

The purpose of this article is to explore the role of the compensation principle in the legal and property systems of society. The discussion is analytical and nonnormative; there is no effort to establish or assess any particular test of "taking" or compensability. The analysis is developed primarily with regard to the taking clause of the Fifth Amendment[1] but has wider applicability. The materials covered include both case and statute law but also "nondecisions"—areas and issues wherein the compensation problem either does not explicitly arise or does not receive formal, written, legal disposition. The problem of prediction—that no singular or simple explanation suffices for the imposition or nonimposition of the compensation requirement—arises in a manner which reaches to the fundamentals of the system of property, the legal system, and the roles thereof in society.

Section I summarizes various aspects of the problem of compensation. Sections II and III explore radical indeterminacy and selective perception, respectively, as fundamental explanatory principles. Section IV presents a general theory of the relevant nature and operation of the legal system, in part with regard to property rights and regulation, in respect to the role of the compensation requirement. Section V explores the several specific roles of the compensation principle in society.

I THE PROBLEM

It is possible to secure a number of different handles on the compensation problem.[2] In each respect, the problem is seen as intractable.

From an analytical perspective, the compensation problem is ubiquitous; uncompensated takings are inevitable; there is no analytically significant distinction between legally and nonlegally imposed changes; and analytically equivalent situations inevitably receive different normative treatment. These conclusions are predicated upon the dual nature of rights and the reciprocal character of externalities.[3]

From a practical perspective, widely stated findings show that no clear rule exists to rationalize the taking-compensation, or eminent domain-police power, cases[4] and that the decisions are conflicting, essentially tautological, and frequently transparently conclusionary.[5] Indeed, the reality is that almost every decision has an opposite number.[6] There are different holdings in almost every taking area, including inverse condemnation, even in the same state, with regard to similar fact situations.[7] Several different possible perceptions of loss or "takings" are possible [Kramon (57), pp. 149, 158, 160, 161]: The polluter's actions[8] [Michelman (65), p. 1236], the inaction or lack of government control [Large (61), pp. 1062, 1069–1070, 1077, 1083; Kramon (57)]; and the legal control of the polluter.[9] Each may be perceived as constituting a taking. It *is* impossible to formulate a rule which will compensate for all losses in a world of reciprocal externalities and dual rights. The legal system can appear to do so only by not recognizing certain losses as losses. Yet even without this understanding, and offering no other rationale, both the courts and commentators stress the helter-skelter situation in the cases.

The predicament extends further than the absence of any clear, dispositive or explanatory rule and reliance upon conclusionary and tautological language. Compensation is a universally recognized principle; its universal recognition is stressed in the literature: Cormack (21), p. 221; Costonis (22), pp. 1026, 1032; and ample literature emphasizes the propriety of compensation: Furubotn and Pejovich (44), p. 1142; Stoebuck (100), pp. 606–608; Buchanan and Tullock (16); Michelman (65). Yet the literature also contains admonitions that it is impractical and undesirable to compensate for all losses;[10] that there is in fact not only a ubiquitous compensation problem— (Olson (72), p. 447—but a wide array of inevitable uncompensated losses: Sax (88), p. 53; Michelman (65), p. 1258; Downs (27), pp. 71–90; Costonis (22), p. 1075; and Note (115); that "it is universally agreed that not every harm caused by governmental activity should be compensated for" [L. Berger (8), p. 169]; and, *inter alia*, that the always-compensate rule is one "which, manifestly, society has rejected" [Williamson (110), p. 124]. Moreover, there is an asymmetry between payment for losses (itself capricious) and recovery of windfall benefits and gains. Persons equally injured in some sense are not equally compensated. "In many situations, the injury or loss to the individual is exactly the same, and whether he recovers or not depends wholly on how the court characterizes the exercise of governmental power involved" [Elias (31), p. 31]. Locally concentrated losers are not compensated, for example, out of funds raised by special taxes upon locally concentrated gainers. "The absence of both of these devices can be considered indirect evidence that the public affected prefers to risk suffering uncompensated losses in order to have a chance to benefit from unrecaptured gains" [Downs (27), p. 92]. Given the widely perceived capriciousness in the area of compensation, the lottery interpretation is not inapposite.

The compensation principle thus seems both visionary and capricious. The Lockean desideratum of protecting property through the compensation requirement seems vacuous and impossible. In what context does the compensation principle have meaning and to what is that meaning restricted?

II RADICAL INDETERMINACY IN SOCIETY

The compensation predicament is one manifestation of a deeper and enveloping existential problem. Society is neither given nor fixed but open, with its future created through human action, choice, and interaction, specifically with regard to the details of individual and organized life. For reasons of personal psychology and social control, pretense often is maintained concerning the absoluteness, finality, pre-existence, and pre-eminence to man of social arrangements; see Levi (63), p. 1. Human society and organization, including law, does exist. *Ex post*, social arrangements are determinate. *Ex ante*, however, society is radically indeterminate and open. Making and remaking social arrangements, including law, is the existential burden of man. In so doing, man neccessarily confronts certain fundamental problems. One of them, the "problem of order," is discussed below. In general it can be said that there are "eternal issues or problems . . . in the sense [of] . . . formulations of human dilemmas on so high a level of abstraction that they cannot ever really be resolved"; see Friedman (40), p. 828. In attempting partial, halting, and limited resolutions of these issues, problems, and dilemmas man makes and remakes society.

In every society, throughout time, a sense of order and coherence is imposed upon both the physical and social worlds by man, a major function of ideologies, religious, economic, social, and political. Individuals are thus provided comfort in an otherwise ambiguous and changing world. "Institutions are now experienced as possessing a reality of their own, a reality that confronts the individual as an external and coercive fact"; see P. L. Berger and Luckmann (10), p. 58. Such social definitions are opaque in places, but they nonetheless are transmitted through socialization processes. Each system is defined on its own (current) terms. It is accordingly difficult to differentiate between the objectivity of natural phenomena and the objectivity of social formations, including the concepts through which they are reified (p. 59).

However, social arrangements are in fact artifactual, made and remade by man. "Social order is a human product, or, more precisely, an ongoing human production. . . . Social order exists *only* as a product of human activity" (p. 52). "Neither God nor a mystical 'Natural Force' created society; it was created by mankind"; see Mises (67), p. 515. "Culture exists or operates in human beings, who, by their patterned conduct and way of life, create whatever order there is. . . . Social order arises, therefore, not from some mysterious cosmic mechanism but from the patterning of human behavior into the conduct approved by the group traditions"; see L. K. Frank (37), pp. 550, 551. The order which man perceives as given and even externally generated is thus a creation of man himself. That creation is a product of both deliberative and nondeliberative decision-making. The institutional order is the result of slow accretion. Normally changes occur gradually and incrementally, in part through direct confrontation with issues resulting in change but also in part through halting and tortuous adjustments which combine to effectuate changes of substance and/or direction. (This is particularly true of the common law system.) Moreover, as studied in the social sciences and in jurisprudence, all such decision-making, that is, change, occurs within the constraints and regularities of behavior and interaction. It is from these changes that determinate solutions and thereby social reality exists, that is, the changing status quo point through time. All this is true of both the economy and the legal system. Over time, both are made, not found, so far as humanity as a whole is concerned. The social reality which is thereby constructed is heterogeneous, ambiguous, and marked by unresolvable dilemmas and conflicting subordinate principles and tendencies.

The existential burden of man is the process of choice, including the choice of constraints upon choice. Indeed, there is an infinite regression of choice encountered in analyzing human arrangements and institutions. "Facts" on one level tend to be grounded on choices at some deeper level.

Given the radical indeterminacy-choice nature of society, the most relevant social process is the identification, confrontation, clarification, and selection of values. Choices must be made, and the valuation process operates, among other things, to treat what may be analytically equivalent as normatively unequal. Externalities may be reciprocal but the valuation process adjudges one visitation of harm to be superior, or of greater propriety, than the other. Compensation rules function as part of the valuation process to differentiate normatively between applications both among the compensation rules themselves and among other rules which compete with them. Out of these processes and applications, society is made and remade. *Ex post* determinateness is achieved through coming to grips with *ex ante* radical indeterminacy, openness, and the necessity of choice.

Part of the processes outlined above is the rationalization, legitimation, and sanctioning of the choices made, including, and for present purposes especially, the choices of rights and exposures to rights. Legitimation will be further discussed below.

The legal system, then, participates in the overall valuation process with regard to norms, rules, and choices. There is, in fact, necessary incremental legal choice making and remaking the structure of socioeconomic-legal relations so typically articulated in terms of rights. Both social control and our own psyches induce us to believe in final, definitive rights but such is impossible. Among other things, change produces new Alpha-Beta conflicts and the problematical legal and economic significance of rights. Legal terminology, the necessity of decisions, and deterministic economic theory together operate to create the appearance of precision and certainty; moreover, the legal and economic systems do provide determinate results *ex post*. Conflicts between rule and discretion approaches are complicated by the plurality of rules. There is a high demand for a sense of operational certitude, which would psychologically compensate for, yet conflicts with, the imprecise nature and nonmechanical application of rules and the inevitable roles of discretion and uncertainty as between rules; see Friedman (40), pp. 789–794, 829–837. On the level of jurisprudential philosophy, analytical jurisprudence conflicts with legal realism.[11]

As a consequence of the operation of the legal system, there is a normative structure—a chosen structure—of society organized in part through legal rights. This normative structure governs the distribution of power, the disaggregation of scarcity and, *inter alia*, the distribution of the burdens of uncertainty and sacrifice. There is differential capacity among people to insulate themselves from adverse changes and to capture the benefits of change. This differential capacity is a partial function of the randomness or capriciousness of results, radical indeterminacy, and the chosen normative structure.

In short, radical indeterminacy signifies both a necessity of choice marked by inconsistency, as the unresolvable must somehow be given more or less temporary and partial solutions, and an arbitrariness, as those solutions, as functional as they may be, have no ultimate rationale or foundations but instead depend upon and reflect human choice.

III SELECTIVE PERCEPTION

The fundamental force at work in the resolution of the compensation problem is *selective perception*. Beyond the complex process of choice itself, the general phenomenon pervading the entire compensation problem is the differential perception of analytically equivalent situations capable of different and contradictory identifications depending upon perspective. The valuational element contained in underlying selective perceptions enables decision-makers to go from ostensible *is* propositions to *ought* conclusions. One cannot derive an *ought* from an *is* alone; the way in which it is often done is through selective, and therefore valuational, perceptions and identifications contained in the *is* part of the analysis. This process is present in all takings cases and reasonably clearly evident in at least some. Selective perception is functional for normative differentiation, and the normative conclusion drawn is likely to be tautological with an antecedent premise involving selective perception.

Each society has a socially constructed, subjective definition of reality which each member of society internalizes as part of his/her mental equipment. Sociologically, we share a subjective consciousness acquired through societization and inculcated and reinforced through ideology, material interests, and social sanctions. Psychologically, this subjective consciousness involves personal identity definitions, motivational orientations, and specific attachments of individual psychic meaning which help define the self and one's place and role in the social system, in which societization is both internalized and individualized. Actual objective social reality develops and changes as individuals and groups act on their particular subjective view of social reality, both giving effect to and altering its subjective construction; see P. L. Berger (9), P. L. Berger and Luckmann (10). Each individual has a complex and changing personal attitudinal structure from which arises selective perception of relevant events. Social and legal development is at least in part a process of restructuring perceptions as well as giving effect to them. This process is multifaceted and involves the evolution of norms and conceptions of entitlement and propriety; see Tapp and Kohlberg (103), pp. 85–86 and *passim*.

In partial analytical amplification, the following may be noted. First, a large number of losses are not perceived as such by decision-makers (or by the losers themselves). Typically, one person in an Alpha-Beta conflict is perceived not to have a loss vis-à-vis the other's deemed entitlement; similarly, this is true with respect to parties in reciprocal externality conflicts. Second, it is difficult to differentiate between active perceptions and the arguments manipulated by skilled advocates. Third, it is difficult to differentiate selective perception as such from the form which it takes—private versus public, harm-benefit tests, or benefit-cost calculations. Fourth, selective perception may inform the analyst as much about the person undertaking the perception as the object or event identified. Finally, in part because individuals have differential "sensitivity" and values [Laitos (59), pp. 448, 449 and *passim*], the goal of "greater sensitivity"[12] may not yield the same lessons or perceptions to all parties.

There are a multiplicity of instances[13] in which courts, legislatures, and commentators make conclusionary and tautological assertions. In each case, the words give effect to an underlying selective perception. Some interests are recognized as rights and others not, although both may have had previous putative legal status and protection. Some losses are perceived as such and others not. Decisions are rendered in each conflict, often by divided courts or narrow legislative majorities. Selective and conflicting perceptions are inevitable, ubiquitous, and reflected in the incoherence and inconsistency of decisions, statutes, and tests of "taking."

Perhaps the most important respect in which selective perception and identification is exercised is in regard to "injury," "damage," and "loss." The definition of injury, evidence of injury, and the criteria of compensability for injury—that is, the fact, nature, and degree of harm [C. J. Berger (7), p. 823; Levi (64), pp. 404–405; Funston (43), p. 277]—are all subject to selective perception.[14] The widely cited common-law maxim *sic utere tuo ut alienum non laedas*—use your property as not to injure the property of others—requires an additional, or independent, determination of injury, and, indeed, there has been changing perceptions of injury in relation thereto; see J. Smith (94), pp. 389–390; Carmichael (17), p. 759. Similarly, the *de minimis* rule is subject to selective interpretation and application, as is the *damnum absque injuria* (damage without legal injury) rule.[15] What Holmes called the "petty larceny" of the police power is not petty to all participants and observers in particular cases; see Van Alstyne (106), p. 4.

Perception of injury may correlate with selective perception of rights. Judgment as to the reasonable use of property may be seen as justification for damages to a neighbor, but "harmful" or "noxious" use may permit control without compensation; Kratovil and Harrison (58), p. 627. Injury may be perceived of as a *de facto* vis-à-vis the *de jure* taking date; Sackman (79) pp. 163, 169, 170; Arnebergh (3), p. 324. Different attitudes may be held with regard to injury consequent to breach of contract; Birmingham (11), pp. 283ff. Injury may be seen as incidental or material enough to destroy the essential elements of ownership, or as necessarily incident to the ownership of property [Sackman (79), pp. 163–173, 179–181], or as already capitalized in the market. Injury may be seen as capricious, disproportionate, and unprincipled exploitation; Michelman (65), pp. 1217, 1230. Unemployment or inflation may be seen as injury and either or both may be seen as a function of policy decisions, as systemic, or as aberrational; Ackerman (1a), pp. 146ff; Cohan (19); Spengler (98), p. 538. The sense of entitlement, vis-à-vis which injury tends to have meaning, likely will differ between wetlands and marshes [Ackerman (1a)], nonreturnable bottle production and use, billboards, breweries, and massage parlors or pornographic book businesses. Amortization for the recapture of investment may be seen as inadequate vis-à-vis loss of use and business opportunity; Holme (51), p. 284; Van Alstyne (106), pp. 44ff. Damage may be perceived as substantial or incidental, permanent or temporary; Ruegsegger (77), pp. 336, 340, 341. Rendering of property totally useless for economic purposes may or may not be perceived as a legal injury requiring compensation.[16] Access loss may be perceived as substantial or incidental; Sackman (80). "Deprivation" may be seen as lawful and thus not legally injurious; Sackman (79), p. 182. Transfer of development rights (TDR's) may or may not be seen as constituting uncompensated loss to development zone landowners; Barrows and Prenguber (6), pp. 549ff. Damages may be seen as consequential (meaning incidental to government action and compensable) or as inconsequential (remote and noncompensable).[17] In all these and many other respects, selective perception is exercised in Fifth Amendment taking cases (and other areas of the law of damages) and in the relevant interpretive literature. [In general, see Lesser (62), p. 144; Ditwiler (26), pp. 669, 671; Large (61).] In each instance, more than one party can complain of injury, and choice has to be made and usually is made with selective perception.

The role of selective perception and identification also applies to the frequent dictum that cases are, and should be, decided on the basis of the "facts." In numerous cases, the validity of regulation is said to depend "upon the facts in each particular case," that is, "each case must be decided on its own facts" [see cases quoted in Lesser (62), pp. 136, 137, and Van Alstyne (106), p. 45]. On the other hand, commentators have remarked that factual assessments are "subjective" [Harris (50), p. 667], and that "facts" are real and certain only to the extent that they go unchallenged; Friedman (40), p. 805. There are numerous cases wherein two fact situations (that of the instant case and that of a possible precedent) are interpreted differently by majority and minority, with no appreciable difference in their respective treatment of the governing law but with opposite holdings as to takings and therefore compensation.[18] *Res ipsa loquitur*,[19] but differently to different persons.

IV THE NATURE AND OPERATION OF THE LEGAL SYSTEM

Within the context of radical indeterminacy and the principle of selective perception, we present here an analysis of the nature and operation of the legal system as the necessary context of meaning of the compensation principle and the roles which it performs. Some of the statements made herein are dependent on chains of reasoning, some are statements of observable fact, and others are essentially interpretive. In every regard the intent is positive description and interpretation; in no respect are specific normative implications intended.

The role of the legal system, including both common and constitutional law, is to provide a framework or process for conflict resolution and the development of legal rights; see Tribe (104), p. 556. This is the primary mode through which Alpha-Beta rights conflicts are formed and resolved. There is a fundamental and ineluctable necessity of choice with regard to inconsistent or competing interests, in part, with allocative and distributive consequences [Keeton (55), p. 1333; Sax (89), p. 174; Samuels (82, 83, 84)]. It is not surprising, then, that different and conflicting views of law develop. Law is in fact both a mechanism for sanctifying what is perceived or advocated as tradition and a resource for facilitating what is perceived or advocated as desirable change; see Tapp and Kohlberg (103), p. 89. Given the dual nature of rights and ubiquitous reciprocal externalities, there will be legal change, and change of the interests to which government gives its protection regardless of which perspective one adheres to. That there are different attitudes toward government (state, law) is understandable: Law is a source and/or enforcer and protector of rights and it is also an infringer on rights. It is a universal father-figure with both negative and affirmative images [Freud (38); Laitos (59), p. 430]. There is desire both to use and to limit use of the state. There has been a greater policy consciousness [Friedman (41), pp. 37–38] during recent centuries, although this must be juxtaposed to the continued pretense of, and apparent desire for, finality which is at least in part a function of a desire to promote continuity and to legitimize decisions. But policy consciousness cuts two ways: Along with clearer appreciation of the artifactual and therefore normative and contingent character of arrangements has come a sharper sense of loss (which no longer is attributed to nature and perceived as inevitable) and thereby resort to government for redress of felt loss and iniquity.

Change and Conflict

Two characteristics of legal history have been *change* and *conflict*. Apropos of the former, there has been continuous change, typically of an incremental or gradual character. There have been ubiquitous changes of rights (among other things) by common, statute, and constitutional law. The legal system has initiated, reacted to, and ratified change originating within other sub-processes of society. Rights and principles of law have undergone historical evolution. New technology has elicited new bodies of law, new rights, and changes in the consequences of old rights and principles; see Friedman (41), p. 26. Law has been made through judicial decisions (although the Fifth Amendment just compensation provision has not been applied to common-law legal change); Sax (88), p. 51; (89), p. 180 and n. 64; Kratovil and Harrison (58), pp. 614, 632, 645; Michelman (65), p. 1181. However, most legal change has not been perceived as change.[20]

Although the process of legal change has been gradual, it has been continuous and accordingly has led to major transformations of the legal system and of the patterns of rights and, thereby, of the systems of economic organization and control. Large-scale systemic evolution has resulted in every field of law and of the economic system; Laitos (59), p. 426, n. 9; Horwitz (53); Commons (20). The real world of law and economics has been transformed from an agrarian to an industrial capitalist, nonlanded property system with an emphasis on capital accumulation. Present concepts and doctrines have been adapted from a simpler, agrarian society [Costonis (22), p. 1038]; but changing society always has meant changing rights; Dales (23), p. 503. Consequently, the process of change has involved a continuous interaction between legal and economic systems (Laitos (59), pp. 424, 429; Samuels (82), with the economic role of government having changed significantly in the process; Laitos (59), pp. 423ff; Auerbach (5); Solo (96).

Change has meant, perhaps inevitably, conflict over costs and benefits. American legal history is also characterized by conflict between gainers and losers, or over escaping costs and capturing gains; Friedman (42); Horwitz (53); Commons (20); Schumpeter (91). There has been conflict both about and through the legal system, conflict over legal change and the broken eggs of economic development;[21] Fusfeld (45), p. 905. Some, but by no means all, conflict has arisen over the fact and consequences of inequality of income and wealth. Attention to conflict should not obscure the fact that relative harmony or social peace has prevailed and endured in American society. But it should be noted that these conditions are sustained only through the successful resolution of conflict. The realities and pretenses of harmony should not obviate the realities of conflict, which is what controversy over the compensation principle is largely about. Scarcity has meant conflict which has contributed to the inability of rights to be absolute or fully protected, especially in a changing world. The legal system has been unable to avoid controversy, in part because of its deep involvement in the distribution of sacrifice—Michelman (65), p. 1258—and advantage[22] in society, whether through legal or market change (the latter involving differential legal protection).

The Problem of Order

In every society there is a fundamental "problem of order"—Spengler (97), the necessity for a continuing reconciliation of freedom with control, change with continuity, and hierarchy with equality. "Order" can be defined under any of these six terms; which definition is adopted and followed influences one's conception of law; Friedman (41), p. 15 and *passim*. There is great tension between the principles representing each of the terms comprising the three conflicts. At the most abstract, and most open, level, the problem of order involves all three conflicts. For a full appreciation of what order involves, including the sacrifices, a totalist view is necessary; that is, every system of freedom must be seen as operating within the system of control, including legal controls, necessary for it, and that both maintenance and change of the status quo require legal controls. Any change, including any legal change, may be evaluated on its own terms or under the criteria of the status quo which it proposes to change. Inasmuch as every system involves both change and continuity, it may be observed that the market economy involves not only "secure" rights but also the opportunity to create change thereby (more or less fortuitously) both destroying and creating others' rights; see Schumpeter (91).

The legal system is a mode of creating both a sense and the reality of order. The politico-legal system is part of the process for working out piecemeal solutions of the conflicts which comprise the problem of order as well as incremental results of the social valuation process; Jerome Frank (35) pp. xix-xx; J. P. Frank (36), p. 409. Thus, a major function of law is social control; Friedman (40), p. 796. For example, the courts perform the role of moral leader; Levi (64), pp. 417, 422. The question, however, which must be worked out is: Law and order on whose terms? With respect to the economy, the legal system is intimately involved with its organization and control, and with its power structure, in part through the property system; Parsons (73), Commons (20), Friedman (40), pp. 788, 796. A key question is: To whose interests does "order" give effect through law? The problem does *not* involve more versus less government but the interests to which the law is to give effect and the changes which are to be made therein. It is through the continuing (re)determination of the interests to which government will help give effect that the problem of order, the normative structure of society, and a sense of coherence, security, and orderliness are worked out. Throughout all this, too, is the problem of "who decides"; Friedman (40), p. 788. It is true both that rules of law function in part to distribute power *and* that the rules are a function of power: The law allocates power *and* is an instrument of power. "The law itself is an instrument of power, and the person who knows it, or controls it, or both, has a weapon of many megatons of force. ... Legal systems ... are clearly used as weapons in struggles for political power" [Friedman (41), pp. 47, 48]. Thus there is conflict both over use of the legal system and between the legal system and the market (between those who predominate in each). The law is an object and means of economic control and the market is an object of legal control. Out of this, order is produced—and inevitable noncompensated losses.

Politics and Self-Government: Legislature and Judiciary

Governance connotes decision-making or choice and involves having to differentiate between analytically equivalent cases on normative grounds (Alpha can do this to Beta but not that). The problem of order is complicated in systems of self-government or politics. The nature and structure of these systems governs the form in which freedom versus control and continuity versus change conflicts arise. Belief in and practice of self-government, or democratic politics, is functionally equivalent to the mutability of rules, that is, legal change through politics. In nondemocratic systems, it is the total legal-political process which makes policy and alters rules. Further, inasmuch as democracy tends to imply "equality" of some sort, for example, of rights, democratic politics is necessarily (and perhaps paradoxically) involved in treating Alpha and Beta unequally due to the dual nature of rights, quite aside from distributive inequalities.

In a system of self-government or politics, law is not the command of a sovereign above the population but is (re-)created in part through more or less majoritarian election of representatives. Consequent to legal change, the compensation requirement becomes instrumented primarily through litigation involving the taking clause of the Fifth Amendment. Such litigation, and the policy process which it engenders, involves the juxtaposition of, and conflict between, legislature and judiciary.

It should be clear that both legislature and judiciary are exercising the power of governance. The differentiation of governance into the two branches[23] is a function of the disaggregation of the power of government through the system of checks and balances. It represents a pluralist politico-legal system. Such a division of power within government implies limits, review (accountability), and ambiguity of authority; see Friedman (40), p. 796. It also implies eternal conflict over jurisdiction, exercise of discretion, and substantive policy. Both branches are sources of substantive rights and legal change of rights. Each has its own evolving institutional ideology.

The institution of judicial review, especially with regard to the "constitutionality" of legislation, is a function of this division of power, at least as it has worked out in this country from the jurisprudential architectonics of John Marshall.

Constitutional law provisions and doctrines (many if not most of which are not explicit in the document, being a result of judicial introspection) acquire an aura of objective reality. Content is ascribed to them as part of the evolution of society and the interaction of the several branches of the politico-legal system (including power struggle, however moderated and channeled by the supplemental institution of political parties). Insofar as they are functional, the provisions and doctrines operate as part of social reality as both determined and determining variables and are meaningful only (for present purposes) in their functioning with regard to the organization and control of the politico-economic system.

Judicial attitudes with regard to reviewing constitutionality are necessarily ambivalent. Their application generally is within the extremes of abrogating any such role, leaving policy fully up to the legislature, and always substituting (or being willing to substitute) its own wisdom for that of the legislature [Ackerman (1a); Large (61), pp. 1062, 1076, 1077]. In taking cases, the issue arises in the form of conflict between narrow and broad conceptions of the police power as the latter is juxtaposed to private (property) rights.[24] There is no ultimately given role for the courts and the legislature vis-à-vis each other; they must and do work out continuing accommodations to each other. Their relationship is necessarily something that is worked out and subject to continuing mutual adjustment; Friedman (40), pp. 797–798, 822. The judiciary's conception of its role—for example, rules of reception vis-à-vis refusal of cases, or, following Ackerman (1a), judicial activism, reformism, or deference—enables and alters the realization of the effective demand for courts which is derived from the demand for rights; Friedman (40), pp. 810, 815. Such roles have complex behavioral consequences. For example, pressure for legislatively adopted systems of compensation increases in response to greater willingness of the courts to permit restrictions on land use; Bosselman (12), pp. 684, 685. In any event, the Fifth Amendment taking clause is, *inter alia*, a mode of grounding legal decisions (choices).

As implied above, the legislature may adopt compensation as a matter of policy.[25] Even without judicially determined (or anticipated) constitutional "necessity" for compensation, the legislature can award compensation (and in magnitudes independent of the scope of actual loss) at its discretion.[26]

Finally, while it is more or less obvious that deep judicial decision-making is obscured by invocation of constitutional (or common law) doctrines, it must be recognized that the hard (controversial) decisions often are left to the courts, both intentionally and otherwise, by the legislature; Ditwiler (26), pp. 672, 675. At the same time, there are serious limits to judicial policy determination as a mode of governance. [The limits imposed by the narrow confines of cases and case law have been discussed by Pound (74); Large (61), p. 1062; and Laitos (59), pp. 429 n. 10, 437, 444, 448.]

The Matrix of Legal Principles

Each principle of common and constitutional law exists within a matrix of correlative and opposing principles. Each principle has at least several significantly rival meanings or interpretations. Each principle has its highest level of meaning within the context of the matrix, or network, formed by all principles with which it interacts. The conflict of the Fifth Amendment just compensation clause with the state police power (through the Fourteenth Amendment due process of law clause) and with federal powers, of eminent domain with police power principles, or of the police power with property rights, however expressed, has meaning ultimately only within the larger matrix formed by their juxtaposition, as well as the juxtaposition of such other constitutional provisions as the commerce power with the Tenth Amendment, the supremacy clause with the Tenth Amendment, and, *inter alia*, the state police power with other provisions of the Fourteenth Amendment. The same is true on the state constitution and common law levels. Economic and general policy conflicts in American society tend to become ultimately expressed in constitutional terms, in part as each side attempts to pre-empt the high ground of argument and rhetoric and in part because it is in constitutional terms that conflict resolution takes place.

Each principle is seemingly total, broad and absolute, yet each requires a definition of terms and confrontation with conflicting principle(s). The matrix of principles forms a conceptual system which helps define and structure problems but which does not automatically solve them. It functions to abet social peace by enabling the articulation in its terms of both sides of particular issues, perhaps especially the assertion of new claims of right. It provides a semantic and conceptual system with which issues are articulated and decisions are phrased. Interests and aims can be expressed in terms of common and constitutional law, in each case often heightening the sense of conflicting "guarantees"; Abraham (1), p. 291. Continuity and change, freedom and control, hierarchy and equality, and Alpha-Beta rights conflicts are resolved and "balanced" within the matrix, each solution being expressed in terms of the superiority of this or that principle.

In all this, the court system, as a norm and decision-producing process, interacts (reinforces and conflicts) with the political system. Common, statute, and constitutional law form a process; a set not of absolute principles or rights but of relative principles or rights each perceived as absolute.

Constitutional law, for example, is "not a fixed body of truth but a mode of social adjustment"; Waterman (109), pp. 933–934. "General legal rules and principles are working hypotheses, needing to be constantly tested by the way in which they work out in application to concrete situations …"; Dewey (25), p. 26. Claims (and findings) of principle and right may function to support certain interests or their rivals. The precise meaning of conservative or liberal with regard to the status quo depends on empirical content; thus "the slogans of the liberalism of one period often become the bulwarks of reaction in a subsequent era"; (*ibid.*). The pattern of meaning formed by the matrix changes. As a mode of the resolution of the problem of order, however, the matrix necessarily incorporates principles supportive of freedom, control, change, continuity, hierarchy, and equality as these come to be constituted in a world of radical indeterminacy, selective perception, and the dual nature of rights. Perhaps needless to say, there is much sophisticated and subtle power play exercised over the principles, the matrix, and the conceptions of society and interests for which, at any point in time, they are symbolic and functional. The myth of absolute and/or fixed legal principles is overwhelmed by the realities of the matrix of which each is a part and by the change which each, and the pattern of the total matrix, undergoes.

The Matrix of Legal Rights

Similarly, each right has meaning as part of a network of rights and interdependencies. Each right has problematical meaning only within the total matrix of rights and their interaction through time. Each right has economic and practical significance only with regard to the rights of others with which it is interdependent.

Persons and groups can form either absolutist or relativist metaphysical views of rights. The approach of absolute rights is generally the analytical or normative equivalent of a continuity-oriented definition of the problem of order. Yet not only are rights in reality relative (as described above) but each absolutist identification of rights tends to specify them differently, thereby requiring choice, which the very notion of absolutism was intended to avoid. Arguments over rights are essentially arguments over continuity versus change (always selectively) or over inconsistent uses. Appeals to rights are claims to certain conduct by others; Tribe *et al.* (105), p. 108.[27] Each argument presumes the object for which it attempts to adduce support. As one unusually perceptive and candid court said, "We cannot start the process of decision by calling such a claim as we have here a 'property right'; whether it is a property right is really the question to be answered."[28]

Among other things, rights protect interests, channel behavior, and enable participation in social decision-making. But each right is relative to other rights (that is, in part, their correlative obligations or duties) and the exercise of other rights as well as to the exercise of governmental conflict resolution. The protection accorded to each is necessarily limited by the protection accorded to conflicting rights and expectations.

Property rights, and indeed all rights, are simultaneously both private and public in nature. They are manifestly private in their assertion or ascription of entitlement and ownership; they are clearly public, first, in their legal generation (definition and assignment) and, second, in their dual and externality-producing nature. Notice how readily the very idea of private property gives rise to conflicting themes: Property may be seen as the right to injure others [J. Smith (94), p. 383], as not the right to injure others,[29] and as the right to be free of injury caused by others; Carmichael (17), p. 749, cf. p. 755. That is, the matrix of rights is highly kaleidoscopic. It is in continual flux due to changes in economic conditions, technology, values, attitudes, problems, and law. Because of such change and also because of the complexities of the problem of order, interdependence in the forms of the dual nature of rights and the reciprocal character of externalities, and radical indeterminacy, rights are contextual, contingent, and problematic in nature.[30] Rights are limited, altered, destroyed, and enhanced in their socioeconomic and legal significance through both the market and the legal system. The creation of a new right for Alpha necessarily constitutes alterations of the circumstances and reach of some Beta's rights. Rights are inevitably ambiguous due to change and the multiplicity of other rights with which they may come in conflict.

There is, then, an ultimate necessity of choice as to who will have what rights and who will be exposed to the exercise of the rights of others and in what way or within what limits, that is, who will have what capacity to act and to inflict gains and losses on others. The cloud of ambiguity is partially lifted in each court case as conflicting claims are weighed and one interest is made to yield to the other. The process of determining compensability is one such mode of creating and destroying rights.[31]

For instance, every person takes his/her "rights" as given, real, substantial and known—until the person confronts a problem. At that time the person learns that there is a difference, and perhaps a significant difference, between what he/she took for granted as his/her "rights" and the complexity of human arrangements arising from the confrontation of right and right or legal principles. The person has discovered radical indeterminacy. What had been taken as objective reality is now seen as "but" a sign of subjective meaning and revealed to have illusory or at best problematic substance; P. I. Berger and Luckmann (10), pp. 2, 35, cf. pp. 22, 24. Granted that all rights are not equally problematical, it is *not* true that "At any moment of time there is a legally sanctioned structure of property rights in existence" [Furubotn and Pejovich (44), p. 1142], if these rights be seen as fully, clearly, and permanently defined.

The matrix of private property is part of the larger matrix of rights which, as has been argued above, must be seen in conjunction with the matrix of legal principles. Contrary to our tendency to reify property rights as absolutes, which *is* part of our reality, is the further reality of the dynamic matrix of property:

> The essence of property, as we actually use the term, is not fixity at all, but fluidity. Property is the end result of a process of competition among inconsistent and contending economic values. Instead of some static and definable quantity, property really is a multitude of existing interests which are constantly interrelating with each other, sometimes in ways that are mutually exclusive. We can talk about a landowner having a property interest in "full enjoyment" of his land, but in reality many of the potential uses (full enjoyment) of one tract are incompatible with full enjoyment of the adjacent tract. It is more accurate to describe property as the value which each owner has left after the inconsistencies between the two competing owners have been resolved. And, of course, even then the situation is not static, because new conflicts are always arising as a result of a change in the neighborhood's character, or in technology, or in public values. These changes will revise once again the permitted and permissible uses which we call property. Property is thus the result of the process of competition.
>
> Once reoriented to this more fluid concept of property as economic value defined by a process of competition, the question of when to compensate a diminution in the value of property resulting from government activity becomes a much less difficult one to formulate. The question now is: to what kind of competition ought existing values be exposed; and, from what kind of competition ought existing values be protected.[32]

Ambiguity of the property right status quo is a function of radical indeterminacy, the dual nature of rights, the reciprocal character of externalities, and legal-economic (including technological and knowledge) change. Further, the ambiguity underscores the role of compensation determination in the process of selectively redetermining rather than merely protecting pre-existing rights.[33]

Property Rights, Regulation, and Taking

From the perspective of normative decision-making, the taking issue is the differentiation of taking from regulation. The treatment accorded the problem is often conclusionary and tautological, as in the proposition that a valid exercise of the police power does not require compensation: Olson (72), pp. 445, 446, 450, 451, 458; Roby (76), pp. 508, 513.[34] The distinction is increasingly seen as illusory; Waite (108), pp. 292, 293. Whether seen as a taking (requiring compensation) or regulation (not requiring compensation), the governmental action at issue operates to diminish rights, opportunities, freedom, and value for one party (parties) and to enhance same for another('s). Thus we read that:

> In a sense, all governmental restrictions on property use deprive the owner of valuable opportunities to profit from property to which he has formal title. As restrictions grow, it quickly becomes difficult, if not impossible from a purely economic standpoint, to distinguish a formal condemnation and seizure of property from the regulatory destruction of valuable use rights; ... Note (115), p. 1018.

> The sharp dichotomy that exists in the law between inverse condemnation, calling for full compensation, and a police power exercise, with no compensation, has always been rather questionable. In many situations, the injury or loss to the individual is exactly the same, and whether he recovers or not depends wholly on how the court characterizes the exercise of governmental power involved; Elias (31), p. 31.

In each case, the distinction seems to be dependent upon the identification of the interest to be protected as a right, although this premise is not understood or at least not often clearly stated. Is regulation a taking or is it a prevention of a private taking? Whether regulation is a prevention of Alpha from harming Beta, or having Alpha return to Beta what Alpha improperly acquired from Beta, or a "sense of fair play translated into adequate law" or the use of government to correct abuses arising from the hitherto otherwise unregulated private economy [Eisenhower (30), pp. 811, 812], or a taking from some Alpha, will depend upon the legal choice of property definitions and assignments. Upholding government action as permissible regulation means that the claimed property right is nonexistent or inconsequential and that some other claimed private or public interest is protected; asserting that the governmental action is a taking requiring compensation means that the claimed right is affirmed—and that some other claimed private or public interest is negated. To say that a compensation award implies that a property right has been abridged is misleading [Kratovil and Harrison (58), p. 612]; the award itself constitutes or connotes abridgment. Both regulation-holdings and takings-holdings may be said to stabilize values in the market, but different values are stabilized depending upon the holding; Lesser (62), pp. 135, 138.

The fact of the matter is that statutory regulation is a mode of protecting interests such that regulation is the analytical equivalent of (common law or court-determined) rights. In this respect, regulation functions in the same manner as holding a governmental action subject to compensation: Each affirms, and negates, claims of interests. Most, if not all, regulation creates rights; Dales (23), p. 492; Samuels and Schmid (87), pp. 102, 103, 105. Regulation is a mode of changing and adjusting rights; Waite (108), p. 284. Although the myth is predominant that newly articulated rights have an antecedent existence, and although there is widespread failure to recognize regulation as a mode of creation and protection of rights— Netherton (70), p. 51—all new protections of interests and solutions to new Alpha-Beta conflicts, whether identified as regulation or rights, involves the more or less creeping abrogation of existing rights. Courts may invent certain easements to extend protection to the "reasonable" interests of property owners [Kratovil and Harrison (58), p. 613]; in such and many other cases, the courts are—and necessarily so—creating rights [Waterman (109), pp. 928, 933; Kratovil and Harrison (58), p. 630] in a manner analytically equivalent to the legislature when the latter is said to "regulate." The irony is that if *regulation* may be said to be a taking requiring compensation, so too may *deregulation*: In each case there are losers. Deregulation is not typically associated with an affirmation of compensation, in part because of selective identification or specification of the status quo. The interests of those protected by regulation are not given the status of rights. That ubiquitous compensation is neither theoretically nor practically possible, as above, is another matter. Regulation as opposed to rights cannot dispose of the compensation question.[35]

The point is, of course, that the matter cannot be fully and conclusively dispositive of the regulation versus taking issue. We desire to infuse human dignity with rights, the idea that individuals have rights not only vis-à-vis each other but also against the state—Murphy (69), p. 303; Buchanan (15). The problem lies in the conflict of the democratic "right" to self-government with the democratic "right" to be protected from a majoritarian will—all quite aside from the ostensibly nondemocratic nature of judicial decision-making. Again, the matter involves inexorable choice, the division of the power of governance, and radical indeterminacy.

The decisions and the commentaries in this field, understandably, are somewhat schizophrenic. [The most recent major work, that of Ackerman (1a) posits two essentially mutually exclusive but coexisting legal analytics.] They posit an absolute takings limitation or an absolute police power, or emphasize that private property rights and public interests (the police power) must somehow be "balanced." They have promulgated a number of tests, criteria, principles, and requirements with which to distinguish compensable takings from noncompensable exercises of the police power.

The tests include: physical invasion, noxious use, diminution of value, conflict mediation versus governmental enterprise, balancing social gains against private losses, maximum total net benefit, private fault vis-a-vis public benefit, and considerations of efficiency and fairness.[36] The use of these tests is essentially selective and arbitrary. Their use in any particular case is a matter of decision, of ultimate pure choice. They are not deducible by deductive logic or by inference from the facts. There is no automatic litmus test by which the tests themselves can be selected for applicability. They are categories (empty boxes) with variable selective contents whose adoption is almost if not wholly subjective. They neither individually nor collectively provide a formula or calculus by which Fifth Amendment takings can be distinguished from unprotected police power actions.[37] Each test represents a relevant, however imprecise, consideration or basis for differentiation but collectively they both permit and require the exercise of choice in their selection and application. The very use of these tests functions to legitimize takings which escape their use while also functioning to obscure the inevitable choice and specificity of application involved. Such is the inexorable existential burden of radical indeterminacy.

There is concern both that overemphasis upon the just compensation requirement may severely limit public action and that a broad and permissive interpretation of the police power may emasculate the protection provided by the compensation requirement.[38] It is no wonder that both courts and commentators find confusion, diversity, and contradictions in the relevant decisions. This situation is due, as argued above, to the necessity of choice which is mandated by the reciprocal character of externalities and the dual nature of rights. Given this necessity of choice, the irony of the matter lies in the impossibility of a complete Lockean policy. Although the compensation requirement is predicated upon conservative values, such a requirement cannot be uniformly conservative due to the inevitability of ubiquitous uncompensated losses arising from the reciprocal character of externalities and the dual nature of rights. Constitutional rhetoric about the integrity of the just compensation requirement and of the police power (and other similar powers) will not obviate this situation. The problem, in fact, is not the protection of property against governmental takings but which mode of change and of sacrifice, and which distribution thereof, is to be given legal sanction.

V THE ROLE OF THE COMPENSATION PRINCIPLE

It will be seen that although the protection of particular property rights is not the function of the compensation principle (except selectively), the requirement does function to protect the *institution* of private property and therefore the basic organization of society.

Service in the Framework of Legal Policy-making

The compensation principle must be seen as one principle within the matrix of principles with which the politico-legal system articulates and seeks solutions to problem-of-order and value-clarification-process conflict.[39] It is one rule in competition with other rules (and its subsidiary rules — the "tests" of taking — are each one rule vis-à-vis other rules). The compensation principle is a vehicle for the introduction into policy analysis and decision-making of certain interest claims. It is one mode of giving effect, however selectively (because of the dual nature of rights and the reciprocal character of externalities), to continuity-oriented considerations. In this regard, it must be clear that the "legalism" of the compensation requirement does not necessarily operate to support the status quo; rather, it is part of the process of restructuring the status quo: Sax (88), pp. 54–58; Friedman (39), p. 168. The use of the compensation principle is one example of the use of legal fictions and principles to permit change without open admission thereof; Friedman (41), pp. 35, 37; (40), pp. 839–840. As will be further seen below, the role of the just compensation requirement, paradoxically, is to tend to legitimize all legal change, compensated or not. In a narrow sense, the compensation requirement is often invoked as a strategic limitation to prevent change. More broadly, however, the requirement is part of the mode of judicial and societal determination of the maximization of net benefits, as it were, not only within extant rights but through changing rights; Sax (88), pp. 48, 61–62. As such it is only one facet of a larger matrix of principles. It is, as Sax (88), pp. 53, 55, 56, cf. Michelman (65), p. 1179, has insisted, a myth to believe that the function of the taking provision of the Fifth Amendment is to maintain and protect existing values; as, he has also argued, its chief role is in problem-solving [Sax (89), pp. 185–186], and it so functions as part of the total matrix of legal principles only in the terms of which the principle has meaning.

Service as a Check on Arbitrary and Tyrannical Power

The availability of the compensation requirement serves to institutionalize the sense and values of procedural fairness; Sax (88), pp. 40–41, 54–57, 58–60, 64; Stoebuck (100), pp. 596ff, cf. 586–587. It does this by enabling the effectuation of the division of power within government,[40] especially through judicial review. It permits the disgruntled to have their day in court without the necessity of more elaborate rules provided in advance; Friedman (40), pp. 835–836. It provides a sense of participation in the legal order. It also reinforces the "independent" role of lawyers' law vis-à-vis statutory and administrative law.

This service of the compensation requirement, however, must not be understood in exaggerated or idealized form. The Fifth Amendment taking provision does in one respect limit governmental authority and power. It limits or checks the unilateral exercise of the powers of governance by the legislature. The courts also unilaterally exercise their powers of governance in these matters. However, the compensation requirement has not been imposed (even selectively) upon their decision-making. Insofar as the compensation requirement serves as a check on arbitrary and tyrannical power, it does so only through the use of governmental power to check other governmental power the exercise of which in its totality remains arbitrary. In so functioning it operates to channel the exercise of arbitrary government power in one direction rather than another, to protect one set of private interests rather than another. While the compensation requirement serves as a check on arbitrary power it is the remaining functions of the compensation requirement which are paramount.

Psychic Balm

Scarcity, as manifest in the dual nature of rights and the reciprocal character of externalities in a radically indeterministic world, implies the reality of conflict and therefore the necessity of choice among inconsistent or disharmonious interests. Decisions must be reached as to which interests, claims, and expectations are to survive and which are to perish. Sacrifice, and redistribution of income and wealth, are inevitable; Michelman (65), pp. 1166, 1208, 1258. Considerations of policy, that is, of expediency modified by public sentiments—J. Smith (94), p. 384—necessarily control; Cormack (21), p. 259. In this process the state is not merely an umpire but a critical factor in the continuing process of reformulating the matrix of rights. The burden of this process is not solely the ubiquitous inevitable noncompensated losses which occur but also the anxiety consequent to the realization of policy consciousness. The pretense of a law which is found and applied is preferred; attitudes of law obeying and law maintaining are elevated over the attitude of law making; Tapp and Kohlberg (103). Yet the reality of legal choice forces its way upon consciousness. Grandiose ideological systems, among other things, function to produce and rationalize systems of sacrifice so to minimize the perceived costs and antagonism thereto; P. L. Berger (9).

All politics, in the broad sense inclusive of common and constitutional law, is at least in part a matter of hurt feelings [Goedecke (46), pp. 10–11]; in such a context, justice is the relating of feelings of injustice to reality (*ibid*), p. 11. The compensation principle serves by its very existence (and our belief in its objective reality) to overcome anxiety over change (and especially what is perceived as legal change) in social affairs.

The primary role of the compensation principle lies not in its use as such but in its very presence. The role of the compensation principle is to serve as a psychic balm in the face of radical indeterminacy. It functions to obscure the necessity of choice, to absorb the reality of loss through reference to high principle, and to soothe the realization of instrumentalism and rationality; Friedman (41), p. 39. Belief in the compensation principle sets minds at rest—Shackle (92), pp. 288, 288–289—creates and reinforces a sense of fairness, and beautifies "what is disagreeable to the sufferers."[41] Even infrequently awarded compensation aborts conflict and anxiety and reinforces the sense of security and legitimacy; Friedman (41), pp. 39, 63. Thus the psychic balm function of the principle in general is infinitely more important than the existence of a coherent and consistent compensation policy. The fact of definite decisions, and the omnipresent availability of the principle, is more important than the content of the decisions, at least within ambiguous limits. It is an open question as to how well the system would work if the truth be known: "The thoroughly liberal society, in short, cannot know what makes it work."[42]

Legitimation

In performing the above functions, especially the psychic balm role, the compensation principle also serves a legitimation function. The compensation principle is part of the process of legal change and its legitimation, in which man seeks congruence between his behavior and his beliefs and attitudes; Holsti (52), p. 15. Decisions are justified by linking them with some rule or law of unquestioned legitimacy: Friedman (39), p. 161; R. Smith (95); legal principles and constitutional clauses are rules by which other rules and decisions are made and legitimized; Friedman (40), p. 795. What is legitimized includes specific substantive legal changes (for example, changes in the differential legal protection accorded to interests or rights), the existing decisional system and structure, and the mode of thought (the legal style of thinking, definition of reality, and normative structure of social reality). Successful legitimation keeps the peace, avoids dissatisfaction, complaint, criticism, and especially insurrection and attack.[43] Conclusionary and tautological declarations and absolutist principles serve the legitimation function, as well as the psychic balm role, often admirably well.[44]

The Fifth Amendment just compensation provision, quite paradoxically, tends to legitimize all legal change (in the sense used here) whether or not compensated.[45] The legal system compensates in some or many cases but in having the compensation provision available it induces the acceptance of legal change without compensation. The loser in a litigated (or lobbied) Alpha-Beta conflict has been given a hearing, has learned that another principle—often one which carries its own readily comprehensible rationale—is superior, and, having lost, can now retire to lick his wounds. However the matrix of rights and of exposures to rights has been changed, the system of law and the property system remain unassailable. The loser has given his cause a good try, within the system, and the system and the substantive decision are legitimized. The ultimate irony is that the compensation principle, ostensibly a check on legal social control, is itself a mode thereof. It is one means through which "most victims are prepared to bear such losses or can be educated to be willing to accept them"; Keeton (55), p. 1347.

Such are the paradoxes of legal social control.

FOOTNOTES

The authors are: Professor of economics, Michigan State University, and assistant professor of economics, University of New Orleans, respectively. The authors are indebted to Jurgen Backhaus, Daniel Bronstein, James Buchanan, Daniel Chappelle, Philip Favero, Leighton Leighty, H. H. Liebhafsky, Daniel Saks, Allan Schmid, Robert Solo, George Stigler, Richard Zerbe, and an anonymous referee for discussions in various forms bearing on this article; to numerous persons in state and federal governments for discussions relating to particular problem areas in their experience; to Jon Wesa, Thomas Kennedy, and Mary Jo Tormey for uncommonly helpful research assistance; and to the members of Professor Samuels's seminars on Political Economy: Institutions and Theory (Winter 1973) and Law and Economics (Summer 1974).

1. " ... nor shall private property be taken for public use without just compensation," U.S. Constitution, Fifth Amendment. All states except North Carolina have a similar clause, some of which read "taken or damaged." (In North Carolina the just compensation requirement has been reached through judicial interpretation of the due process clause of the state constitution.) Compensation is neither inherent nor originally included in the power of eminent domain (the right to take) but has been added as a limitation; see Netherton (70), p. 39, and Stoebuck (100), p. 575. Land was early appropriated for roads without compensation; Sax (88), p. 53.

2. Injunctive relief is an alternative course of action which, if successful, voids the offending action thereby obviating the need for compensation. In recent years, "inverse condemnation" cases have proliferated in which private plaintiffs assert compensable takings by government action typically otherwise unobjectionable.

3. *Dual nature of rights*: For Alpha to have a right is for some Beta to have an exposure to Alpha's right (and the actions and choices enabled thereby) and vice versa. Thus, Alpha-Beta conflicts.

Reciprocal character of externalities: The injury (cost, damage) which the polluter visits upon others has as its reciprocal the injury which pollution control visits upon the former polluter and others. Neither party is the "cause" alone and either party can be exposed to the burden. A policy to promote or require "internalization," say, upon the polluter, actually may mean a change in the patterns of rights, exposures, and adjustments. Compensation is a problem of which interest, among inconsistent interests, to protect and which to inhibit and is part of the process through which rights, loss, and compensation are *jointly* determined; see Samuels (85).

4. The courts on several occasions have been quite candid: "There is no set formula to determine where regulation ends and taking begins"; *Goldblatt v. Town of Hempstead*, 369 U.S. 590, 594 (1962). "No rigid rules can be laid down to distinguish compensable losses from noncompensable losses"; *United States v. Caltex, Inc.*, 344 U.S. 149, 156 (1952). "The amendment does not contain any definite standards of fairness by which the measure of 'just compensation' is to be determined"; *United States v. Cors*, 337 U.S.

325, 332 (1949). "A compensable taking under the federal constitution ... is not capable of precise definition"; *Harris v. United States*, 205 F. 2d 765, 767 (10th Cir. 1953). It is a matter of no surprise, then, that commentators have said such things as the following: "The predominant characteristic of this area of law is a welter of confusing and apparently incompatible results" Sax (88), p. 37 ... the impression that the Court has settled upon no satisfactory rationale for the cases and operates somewhat haphazardly, using any or all of the available, often conflicting theories without developing any clear approach to the constitutional problem" (*ibid.*), p. 46. The court decisions are "often vague, conflicting, and without pattern" Harris (50), p. 636. There is "a crazy-quilt pattern of Supreme Court doctrine," "a haphazard accumulation of rules," "no 'specific constitutional limitations,'" and "floundering and differences among judges and among generations of judges" Dunham (28) pp. 63, 64, 68, 105. There is "judicial schizophrenia" Large (61), p. 1055, n. 60; "lack of uniformity" Sackman (80), pp. 335, 336; "no definite rules or standards" Kratovil and Harrison (58), p. 597; "confusion, uncertainty and diversity of rules and results" Note (110a) p. 162; "highly ambiguous and irreconcilable decisions" Broeder (14), p. 228; decisional results "liberally salted with paradox" Michelman (65), p. 1170; "artificial distinctions without basis other than in semantics" Aloi and Goldberg (2) p. 647; "a judicial maze of inconsistent and arbitrary opinions" Note (112), p. 693; and, *inter alia*, "conceptual confusion, inconsistency, and utter absence of logic ... are part and parcel of eminent domain law" Kanner (54) p. 58.

5. In the absence of rules uniquely dispositive of litigation and with strong elements of pure normative choice in a world of reciprocal externalities and dual rights, it is not surprising, further, that decisions are "often explained in conclusionary terminology, circular reasoning, and empty rhetoric." Decisional results are stated. "Why this result necessarily follows from the legal premise, however, is seldom explained. Often, on the apparent assumption that the connective reasoning is self-evident, the result is merely announced in conclusionary form." On important points, "typical judicial decisions are generally uninformative"; Van Alstyne (106), pp. 2, 29. Courts reach *ex post* determinate results by placing each case in this or that empty box, the decisional language being conclusionary and tautological with regard to either or both the choice and application of rules. Decisions never systematically identify or classify the conflicting interests; rather, they tend to be replete with "hyperbolic images" [Funston (43), p. 281 n. 110; cf. Van Alstyne (106), p. 35]. Principles and tests are often stated in "seemingly inflexible terms"; Van Alstyne (106) p. 34. It has been said that the distinction between compensable and noncompensable government activity "is not altogether precise, and can readily be manipulated to reach divergent results"; (*ibid.*), p. 26. The nature of the phenomenon has been aptly characterized by a perceptive court: "It is possible to manipulate concepts by the selection of a different level of verbalization, that is, a different level of generalization. An entirely different result can be 'logically' forced. ... That kind of analysis is fruitless because the conclusion is dictated by the way one starts the train of reasoning"; *Cromwell v. Ferrier*, 19 N.Y.2d 263 (1967), quoted in Holme (51), p. 255 n. 22. One may question how "fruitless" that process is, however, It *is* descriptively accurate and determinate results *are* reached. (One may not derive an *ought* from an *is* alone, yet *ought* conclusions are derived from *is* premises associated with implicit *ought* premises. So may concepts be associated with decisional results, however arbitrary or conclusionary the procedure.)

On the conclusionary nature of the decisional language, see Kratovil and Harrison (58), pp. 601, 630; Elias (31), p. 31; Costonis (22), p. 1058; Dunham (28), p. 82; Harris (50), p. 667; Holme (51), pp. 255–256n. 22; Sax (88), p. 60; Michelman (65), pp. 1203, 1203 n. 79; and Note (114), p. 1082.

On the tautological nature of the decisional language, see Costonis (22) pp. 1022,

1029 n. 37; Levi (64), p. 405; Olson (72), pp. 445, 446, 450, 457, 458; and Note (114), pp. 1034, 1039 n. 25.

On the failure to identify or classify conflicting interests, see Kratovil and Harrison (58), p. 610 n. 109; Stoebuck (100), p. 604; and Van Alstyne (106), pp. 39 and *passim*.

6. The problem is not unique, of course. In the late nineteenth century, for example, comparing two cases involving the same question, one commentator remarked that "It will not escape observation that the Court of Appeals of New York and the Supreme Court of Pennsylvania reached opposite conclusions on a question relating so vitally to the natural, inalienable, and primordial rights of the citizen.... We have at all events that which is regarded as a fundamental right in New York considered not to be such in Pennsylvania"; Foster (33), p. 55. One does not have to be a complete rule skeptic; Friedman (40), pp. 789; Costonis (22), p. 1025, to appreciate that rules of law are neither precise nor mechanically applied and therefore ambiguous and uncertain. "Many rules of law are so framed as to be totally unpredictable in effect"; Friedman (39), p. 155. Nonetheless, it is striking to read of "the thorniest problem in modern property law,... where to draw the line distinguishing compensable from noncompensable takings..." Note (114), p. 1089, that "coherent principles defining the respective contours of the police power and the takings clause of the fifth amendment have proven... elusive" Note (113), p. 1019 n. 28, and that "the fact is that the law in this area is a hopeless mess and one can find just about any statement for which he is looking if he reads enough cases" [Cal. Law Revision Comm'n, Memorandum 70–29, at 5; quoted in Fadem (32), p. 298, as are several of the above quoted statements and many others]. Thus, speaking of the case decisions, Michelman (65) offers "the hypothesis that decisional rules simply cannot be formulated which will yield other than a partial, imperfect, unsatisfactory solution and still be consonant with judicial action" (*ibid.*), p. 1171; and, of the "tests" of compensability, "that none of the standard criteria yields a sound and self-sufficient rule of decision—that each of them, when attempts are made to erect it into a general principle, is either seriously misguided, ruinously incomplete, or uselessly over-broad" (*ibid.*), p. 1184. Perhaps predictably, Carmichael (17), p. 754, concludes that "the 'taking' question is some metaphysical blend of factors ... "

7. "You can find law for both sides of any proposition on any issue that is going to arise in a condemnation case"; Fadem (32), p. 296. For examples of conflicts see: Sackman (80); Note (11) (overflights), Van Alstyne (106), pp. 14, 18, 21 (aesthetic aims); Kratovil and Harrison (58), p. 639 (platting of future streets); Carmichael (17), p. 763 (regarding "any and all" use); and Stubbs (102), pp. 211–212 (goodwill and profitability).

8. The right to pollute may be seen as the right (say, a private eminent domain right) to take others' rights; J. Smith (94), p. 394. Standardized or adhesion contracts may be seen as a mode of private taking; Goldberg (89). Regulation would be prevention of a private taking; Sax (89), p. 181, n. 64.

9. In re taking a right to impair others' access rights, explicitly stated, see Cormack (21), p. 248 n. 143.

10. Michelman (65), pp. 1178, 1179, 1180; Cormack (21), pp. 224 n. 21, 225 and n. 25, 228, 257, 259; Downs (27), pp. 70, 90, 98; Kottke (56), p. 407; Waite (108), pp. 287 and n. 7; Costonis (22), p. 1070; Note (111), pp. 1444, 1445; and Note (114), pp. 1064 n. 148, 1067, 1068, 1086, 1089.

11. Ackerman (1a) identifies two markedly different but coexisting legal analytics: Scientific Policymaking (and within it the also markedly different Utilitarian and Kantian modes of perception and adjudication) and Ordinary Observation (and Ordinary Adjudication). In addition, he identifies two corresponding different views of property, several different conceptions of judicial role, a multiplicity of conflicting lines of reasoning, and a heterogeneous Conventional View (or paradigmatic concep-

tion of social reality). Ackerman's two analytics have much in common with but are not strictly equivalent to analytical vis-à-vis realist jurisprudence. Ackerman applies the two legal analytics to the taking problem and finds the compensation principle approached and applied differently by various types of judicial roles within each.

12. Note (114), p. 1096.

13. Consider the following examples perception of which is likely to be selective: interests, rights, freedom, coercion, government, progress, growth, development, private, and public; benefits vis-à-vis costs; definition of problems: "Problems, as well as their solutions, are largely subjective. Perception of problem areas determines which property rights questions are relevant as well as which solution among the possible alternative solutions is appropriate. There are few objectively right or wrong property right laws"; Ditwiler (26), p. 663; cf. Arnold and Bromley (4), Miller (66), pp. 148, 162–163; when maximum individual freedom is consistent with the integrity of society [Levi (64), p. 405]; negative regulation vis-à-vis affirmative protection; legitimate expectations; government as intervener vis-à-vis (property) right producer; government largess as a right or a grant; public assistance as compensation for systematic disadvantage; abuse of power; whether sonic booms cause significant injury to persons and/or property; the reach of navigable servitude; "arbitrary" and "unreasonable"; "grievous social injustice," and "serious indignity" (Sax and Hiestand (90), pp. 875, 877, 881–882, 884); the definition of absolute rights and of fee simple absolute; whether a tariff establishes a "legitimate vested interest" (say, with a ten-year phase-out)—Simons (93), p. 70; what government acquires vis-à-vis what an owner loses [Olson (72), pp. 442–443; Ruegsegger (77), p. 336]; change within law vis-à-vis change of existing law; "exigencies" [Large (61), p. 1082]; "destruction by necessity" [Nichols (71), sec. 1.43]; reach of the public trust doctrine or of the life tenant concept, with respect to inter-generational relations [Large (61), pp. 1067ff]; Bosselman, Callies and Banta (13), pp. 24 and passim; Carmichael (17), pp. 759–760; reach of public rights, with respect to diffuse private interests [Sax (89)]; when Alpha's procedures are not reasonably related to Alpha's legitimate intended purposes and therefore violate Beta's rights (that is, when Beta's right is dependent upon the reasonableness of Alpha's procedures) [Dawes v. Philadelphia Gas Co., No. 73–2592 (E.D. Pa., Oct. 5, 1976)]; when regulation is "unduly restrictive"; what is "natural" [Holme (51), p. 268]; new priorities and needs [Carmichael (17), pp. 749, 750]; when progress in an area erodes and renders antiquated certain traditional legal doctrines and rights [United States v. Causby, 328 U.S. 256 (1946)]; Note (111), p. 1431; Note (115), p. 1020; when plausibility for compensation is lent by giving an economic claim a property-sounding name [Kratovil and Harrison (58), pp. 612, 613]; when losses are accidental and unavoidable; when a risk is voluntarily assumed; when "novel" property rights are federally protected by the Fifth Amendment taking provision (ibid.) pp. 632, 645; when zoning is no longer suitable for an area (ibid.) pp. 635–636; when an action represents "bad faith, manifest oppression or gross abuse" [Harris (50), p. 678]; what is the legitimate cost of doing business (in a world of reciprocal externalities) [Holme (51) p. 257]; when rights are "extreme," as in "'extreme rights' cannot be enforced" [Spur Industries, Inc. v. Del E. Webb Development Co., 494 Pac. Rep.2d 700, 707 (1972)]; what "the times dictate" [Haik (49), p. 25]; newly recognized externalities; when the legislature reflects rather than is out of touch with contemporary values; "bad faith or palpably unreasonable exercises of the police power" [Costonis (22), p. 1076]; mala in se vis-à-vis mala prohibita; the reach of "harshness of regulation is no objection" (compare the cases cited in Laitos (59), pp. 436, 436 n. 32); the definition of progress and the relation of pollution thereto; when regulation is "overly stringent," the police power "unfairly used" and "unfairly impinges on property owners," government "overreaches," and regulatory excursions "go too far" [Costonis

(22), pp. 1043, 1046, 1058, 1049, 1054, 1059]; rational relationship of a statute to its regulatory objective; the psychic value of "green open spaces"; market failure; and, *inter alia*, the parties at interest, or whose interest should be considered if not counted.

14. The role of injury is also variously given: "no one can obtain a vested right to injure the public" [Sax (88), p. 39]; "not every injury is legally remediable" [Cormack (21), p. 246]; "damage alone is not enough to require compensation" [Note (114), p. 1087]; "without a taking, damage alone is insufficient to require compensation" [*United States v. Willow River Co.*, 324 U.S. 499, 510 (1945)]; some losses must be considered the inescapable risks of ownership [Downs (27), p. 91]; some losses are accidental and unavoidable [Cormack (21), p. 228]; some risks are voluntarily assumed (*ibid.*), 231 and n. 54; some losses are collateral to assuming the rights of a citizen (*ibid.*), p. 258; and so on.

The nature of property is also variously given: emphasis may be on the physical integrity of the property, its use, or its value [Ackerman (1a) pp. 26 ff, 116 ff and *passim*; Olson (72), pp. 442, 457, 458; Sackman (80), p. 342]; even substantial damage may not be considered a taking so long as the property is not rendered uninhabitable, *or* the owner may be asserted to have freedom from substantial interference and the right to unrestricted use and enjoyment [Note (111), pp. 1440, 1441; Ackerman (1a), pp. 123ff]; the more or less traditional physical invasion test may be seen as outmoded for failing to encompass other types of losses [Roby (76), p. 513]; injury may count only if it is special or concentrated [Kratovil and Harrison (58), pp. 632, 648; Cormack (21), p. 245]; injury may have to be unforeseeable [Kratovil and Harrison (58), p. 648]; injury may have to involve the inability to earn a reasonable return [Waite (108), p. 289]; prevention of the highest and best, or most profitable, use [Lesser (62), p. 150; Harris (50), pp. 677, 679, 681–682]; "reasonable beneficial use" Costonis (22); compare C. J. Berger (7), Harris (50), p. 644); or no (or no reasonable) use (*ibid.*), pp. 636, 645, 677. Either an externality or the control thereof can be perceived as the legally relevant injury.

15. Concerning *de minimis*, see Kratovil and Harrison (58), pp. 626, 640, 648; Rayburn (75a), p. 259; *Dawes v. Philadelphia Gas Co.*, No. 73–2592 (E.D. Pa., Oct. 5, 1976). Concerning *damnum absque injuria*, see Stubbs (102), pp. 209–210; Rumble (78), pp. 300, 305, 310, 311, 314; Kratovil and Harrison (58), p. 611; Sackman (79) pp. 176, 189–191; Cormack (21), p. 237; Large (61), p. 1044 n. 23; Roby (76), p. 509; and Nichols (71), sec. 1.42 (17).

16. *Hadacheck v. Sebastian*, 239 U.S. 394 (1915); Harris (50), p. 640 n. 30; Large (71), pp. 1051–1053, 1064, 1066.

17. Cormack (21), pp. 235, 237; Dunham (28), pp. 81ff; Note (111), p. 1443.

18. For example, see *United States v. Willow River Co.*, 324 U.S. 499 (1945).

19. "The fact speaks for itself." The maxim also refers to the rebuttable presumption that the defendant was negligent because (1) the injury (say, due to a falling flowerpot) required negligence and (2) the instrument causing the injury was in the defendant's exclusive control. That is, the fact speaks for itself until challenged and rebutted.

20. The phrase "at common law," often found in the literature, is misleading. The common law evolved, and what were "rights" at one point may not have been at another; Parsons (73), p. 174; Large (61), p. 1069; Cohan (19), pp. 491, 492–493, 500; Holme (51), pp. 261–262.

21. Transformation from a seigneurial to a market system property and labor market regime required government decisions against traditional property rights, with loss felt by many, especially those who lost what they perceived or regarded as "perfectly legitimate forms of property"; Fox-Genovese (34), p. 228, cf. pp. 220, 245.

22. "...economic institutions are innovated or property rights are revised because

it appears desirable for individuals or groups to undertake the costs of such changes; they hope to capture some profit which is unattainable under the old arrangement" [Davis and North (24), p. 10]. "A set of principles is required for choosing among the various social arrangements which determine this division of advantages and for underwriting an agreement on the proper distributive shares" [Rawls (75), p. 4]. The conflict in legal history is precisely over which interests will secure rights, and thereby distributive advantages. History written or evaluated from the point of view of the conflict winners will be tautologically optimal.

23. The executive is less directly involved in taking cases. Administrative commissions, however, are often involved.

24. Kratovil and Harrison (58), pp. 609–610; Van Alstyne (106), pp. 5–7; Foster (33), pp. 57, 58, 66, 67; Sackman (79), p. 179; Funston (43), pp. 271, 279; Roby (76), p. 508; Dunham (28), pp. 91–92; and Holme (51), pp. 262–263.

25. For examples of a system of compensation perceived as existing outside of the formal system of property rights, see Highway Beautification Act of 1965, 23 U.S.C. sec. 131 (1965) and Uniform Relocation Assistance and Real Property Acquisition Policies Act of 1970, 42 U.S.C. sec. 4601 *et seq.* (1970). See Netherton (70), p. 52; Holme (51), p. 248 n. 4, p. 278 n. 87; and Bosselman (12), pp. 690 ff.

26. Elias (31), pp. 30–32; Harris (50), p. 676; Dunham (28), p. 91; Stubbs (102), pp. 209–211; and Waite (108), p. 286 n. 5. With regard to (a) what the constitution compels compared to what it permits, see Sax and Hiestand (90), p. 922; (b) legislative assertions of rights which should be recognized at common law (*ibid.*), p. 914 n. 181; and (c) constitutional necessity versus legislative dole or charity; Sackman (79), pp. 186, 189.

27. With regard to different attitudes concerning the grounding of rights, and their consequences for which claims and expectations are legitimized, see Ackerman (1a), Michelman (65a).

28. *United States v. Willow River Co.*, 324 U.S. 499, 503 (1945). The question is always "whether the asserted interest is one which the law will protect"; *Batten v. United States*, 306 F.2d 580, 587 (10th Cir.) (1962). Yet conclusionary and tautological statements are typical: "Such legislation does not disturb the owner in the control or use of his property for lawful purposes, nor restrict his right to dispose of it, but is only a declaration by the state that its use by any one, for certain forbidden purposes, is prejudicial to the public interest"; *Mugler v. Kansas*, 123 U.S. 623, 668–669 (1887). In each relevant case, what is lawful and what is forbidden is precisely at issue. The opinion just quoted was by the elder Harlan; for Holmes and the same problem, see *Emery v. Boston Terminal Co.*, 178 Mass. 172, 185, 59 N.E. 763, 765 (1901) and *McAuliffe v. Mayor*, 155 Mass. 216, 220, 29 N.E. 517, 517–518 (1892). See also Cormack (21), p. 252, and Large (61), p. 1039. On the tautology of lawful vis-à-vis forbidden purposes, also see Cohan (19), p. 509.

29. Laitos (59), p. 433; Sax (88), p. 39; Harris (50), p. 641 n. 35; Kramon (57), p. 152.

30. Compare, for example, the Pennsylvania Constitution, Article I, Sec. 9: "the people have a right to clean air, pure water, and to the preservation of the natural, scenic, historic and esthetic values of the environment." See Lantz (60).

31. Radical indeterminacy and other considerations suggest that the formation of rights is a general interdependence process: Rights are a partial function of government (legal) policy which is a partial function of the competition over the use of government by interested parties which is a partial function of the extant total matrix and distribution of rights. Litigation based on certain rights and assertive of other rights is often rights-changing. Innovative claims accepted by courts produce new rights. In other cases, persons acquiesce in assertions of rights by other parties.

32. Sax (88), p. 61. Sax adopts a view close to what Ackerman (1a) calls the Scientific Policymaker's view of property in contrast with that of the Ordinary Observer. Sax also writes:

> ... a view founded on a recognition of the interconnectedness between various uses of seemingly unrelated pieces of property. Once property is seen as an interdependent network of competing uses, rather than as a number of independent and isolated entities, property rights and the law of takings are open for modification. ... Property does not exist in isolation. Particular parcels are tied to one another in complex ways, and property is more accurately described as being inextricably part of a network of relationships that is neither limited to, nor usefully defined by, the property boundaries with which the legal system is accustomed to dealing. Frequently, use of any given parcel of property is at the same time effectively a use of, or a demand upon, property beyond the border of the user (89), pp. 150, 152.

A similar view is held by Michelman (65), p. 1167:

> In a given period, a person enjoys a certain liberty to do as he wills with certain things which he "owns," and a certain flow of income (utility, welfare, good). The practical boundaries of his liberty, and the practical relationships between it and the sum of goods currently flowing to him, are in significant part determined by existing conditions of economic resource employment within his social universe—call it society, community, state.

33. See Samuels (85). In regard to the normative compensation rule requiring an unambiguous definition of status quo rights, see Goldberg (47), p. 568.

34. Even the law of nuisance is not exempt: "Mr. Justice Pitney said that while the legislature might legalize what otherwise would be a public nuisance, it could not 'confer immunity from action for a private nuisance of such a character as to amount in effect to a taking of private property for public use'" [Cormack (21), p. 241, quoting *Richards v. Washington Terminal Co.*, 233 U.S. 546, 553 (1914)] ; cf. Laitos (59), pp. 431, 432. The issue, of course, is whether control of a nuisance or the granting of immunity from action for a private nuisance (also a control) is held to be a taking; both, in fact, are.

35. A subsidiary issue capable of misinterpretation is whether the definition of property rights is or can be so understood as to include perhaps all future exercises of the police power. See Large (61), p. 1080; Van Alstyne (106), p. 17; Haik (49, pp. 24–25; Michelman (65), pp. 1203 n. 79, 1240; Kratovil and Harrison (58), p. 603; Goldberg (47), pp. 566–567; Foster (53), pp. 52, 71, 74, 80; Stoebuck (100), pp. 558, 585, 592; and Note (111), p. 1442. Argument for or against this proposition is of no analytically effective use in disposing of the takings issue, although it often arises in discussions of the issue as if it could be dispositive. In re William Penn's reservation of the power to retake land, with grants larger than they would otherwise have been by 6 percent, as an historical exception to general practice, see Stoebuck (100), pp. 558–559. Absolute inclusion of police power limitations in property right definitions would prevent any holding of a taking: the putative owner cannot have had taken what he/she does not have. Absolute exclusion of police power limitations from property right definitions (the view that all rights claims not hitherto specifically limited are viable and subject to protection) seemingly would mean universal takings and require universal compensation, which is (perhaps a correct conclusion for the wrong reason) theoretically and

practically impossible, as above. The problem applies not only to the police power but also to nuisance, navigable servitude, taxation, and, *inter alia*, monetary controls [Van Alstyne (106), p. 17; Large (61), p. 1071 n. 127; Dunham (28), p. 77; Samuels and Schmid (87), p. 107] ; property rights always can be defined so as to include or exclude the governmental action at issue. The question is part of the still larger and more complex problem of distinguishing "change of law" from "change within existing law"; Van Alstyne (106), p. 68; Michelman (65), p. 1240 n. 126; Carmichael (17), pp. 751, 752; Goldberg (47), pp. 566–567; Stubblebine (101), p. 43. All of the above discussion indicates the impossibility of any conclusive and nonpresumptive differentiation, which is characteristic of the normative legal-political process.

A further issue concerns the identification of the taking party, a problem in some airport zoning and noise cases; Dunham (28), p. 84; Harris (50), pp. 686–691. A more intriguing problem involves cases holding that economic change has produced a taking within an extant zoning ordinance (that is, there has been no change in the law, only a change in the circumstances in which the law applies); Harris (50), pp. 650, 651, 662–663.

36. The tests are adumbrated and critiqued in Sax (88, 89), Michelman (65), pp. 1183ff, 1203ff, 1224ff; Kratovil and Harrison (58); Stoebuck (100); Olson (72), pp. 442ff; and Downs (27), pp. 94ff.

37. Compare the positions taken by such otherwise like-minded justices as Holmes and Brandeis in *Pennsylvania Coal Co. v. Mahon*, 260 U.S. 393 (1922).

38. Kratovil and Harrison (58), p. 610; Cormack (21), p. 233; Van Alstyne (106), p. 68; Dunham (28), pp. 80–81.

39. Rules function to intellectualize conflict resolution; Parsons (73), p. 178.

40. Even without the Fifth Amendment taking provision, we can be confident that it would have been judicially read into another provision, say, the Fifth and Fourteenth Amendments' due process of law clause, or, for that matter, the Ninth Amendment. The existence of the Fifth Amendment taking provision does not suffice to explain the relevant belief system of legislators.

41. *Tyson v. Banton*, 273 U.S. 418, 446 (1927).

42. Attributed to Paul Weaver, in Moynihan (68), p. 59. See Samuels (81), p. 297 n. 80; and (86), p. 207.

43. Friedman (41), p. 52. See *Home Building and Loan Association v. Blaisdell*, 290 U.S. 398 (1934).

44. Birmingham (11), p. 273; Funston (43), p. 281 n. 10; and Note (114), p. 1074.

45. Among the ironies of the taking principle in relation to social control is the fair return on fair value fallacy of *Smyth v. Ames*, 169 U.S. 466 (1898). If fair value is the capitalized monopoly returns of the unregulated utility and no taking is allowed, then the fair return on fair value formula would function to protect and perpetuate the monopoly return. The courts in fact [insofar as they review rate cases as to "confiscation," which review is now less than prior to *Federal Power Commission v. Hope Natural Gas Co.*, 320 U.S. 591 (1944)] preside over the determination of how much expropriation of monopoly profits will be allowed. Indeed, the process may mask the continuation of monopoly returns and amount to ineffectual regulation; Stigler and Friedland (99).

REFERENCES

1. Abraham, Henry J. (Summer 1975) "'Human' Rights vs. 'Property' Rights: A Comment on the 'Double Standard,'" *Political Science Quarterly*, Vol. 90:288–292.

1a. Ackerman, Bruce A. (1977) *Private Property and the Constitution*, New York, Yale University Press.

2. Aloi, F. A., and Goldberg, A. A. (April 1968) "A Reexamination of Value, Goodwill and Business Losses in Eminent Domain," *Cornell Law Review*, Vol. 53: 604.
3. Arnebergh, Roger. (1974) "Recent Developments in the Law of Inverse Condemnation," in *Proceedings*, Southwest Legal Foundation, Institute on Planning, Zoning and Eminent Domain, New York.
4. Arnold, Victor L., and Bromley, Daniel W. (1970) "Social Goals, Problem Perception, and Public Intervention: The Fishery," *San Diego Law Review*, Vol. 7: 469–487.
5. Auerbach, Carl A. (1959) "Law and Social Change in the United States," *University of California at Los Angeles Law Review*, Vol. 6: 516–532.
6. Barrows, Richard L., and Prenguber, Bruce A. (November 1975) "Transfer of Development Rights: An Analysis of a New Land Use Policy Tool," *American Journal of Agricultural Economics*, Vol. 57: 549–557.
7. Berger, Curits J. (1976) "The Accommodation Power in Land Use Controversies: A Reply to Professor Costonis," *Columbia Law Review*, Vol. 76: 799–823.
8. Berger, Lawrence. (May-June 1974) "A Policy Analysis of the Taking Problem," *New York University Law Review*, Vol. 49: 165–226.
9. Berger, Peter L. (1976) *Pyramids of Sacrifice*, Garden City, N.Y., Anchor Books.
10. ———, and Luckmann, Thomas. (1966) *The Social Construction of Reality*, Garden City, N.Y., Anchor Books.
11. Birmingham, Robert L. (1970) "Breach of Contract, Damage Measures, and Economic Efficiency," *Rutgers Law Review*, Vol. 24: 273–292.
12. Bosselman, Fred P. (October 1975) "Property Rights in Land: New Statutory Approaches," *Natural Resources Journal*, Vol. 15: 681–693.
13. ———, Callies, David, and Banta, John (1973) *The Taking Issue*, Washington, D.C., Council on Environmental Quality.
14. Broeder, D. W. (December 1965) "Torts and Just Compensation: Some Personal Reflections," *Hastings Law Journal*, Vol. 17: 217.
15. Buchanan, James M. (1975) *The Limits of Liberty*, Chicago, University of Chicago Press.
16. ———, and Tullock, Gordon. (March 1975) "Polluters' Profits and Political Response: Direct Controls versus Taxes," *American Economic Review*, Vol. 65: 139–147.
17. Carmichael, Donald M. (October 1975) "Fee Simple Absolute as a Variable Research Concept," *Natural Resources Journal*, Vol. 15: 749–764.
18. Coase, R. H. (1960) "The Problem of Social Cost," *Journal of Law and Economics*, Vol. 3: 1–44.
19. Cohan, Edward M. (1970) "Unemployment as a Taking without Just Compensation," *Southern California Law Review*, Vol. 43: 488–515.
20. Commons, John R. (1924) *The Legal Foundations of Capitalism*, New York, Macmillan.
21. Cormack, Joseph M. (1931) "Legal Concepts in Cases of Eminent Domain," *Yale Law Journal*, Vol. 41: 221–261.
22. Costonis, John J. (October 1975) "'Fair' Compensation and the Accommodation Power: Antidotes for the Taking Impasse in Land Use Controversies," *Columbia Law Review*, Vol. 75: 1021–1082.
23. Dales, J. H. (November 1975) "Beyond the Marketplace," *Canadian Journal of Economics*, Vol. 8: 483–503.
24. Davis, Lance E., and North, Douglass C. (1971) *Institutional Change and American Economic Growth*, New York, Cambridge University Press.
25. Dewey, John. (1924) "Logical Method and Law," *Cornell Law Quarterly*, Vol. 10: 17–27.

26. Ditwiler, C. Dirck. (October 1975) "Water Problems and Property Rights—An Economic Perspective," *Natural Resources Journal*, Vol. 15:663–680.

27. Downs, Anthony. (1970) "Uncompensated Nonconstruction Costs Which Urban Highways and Urban Renewal Impose upon Residential Households," in Julius Margolis, ed., *The Analysis of Public Output*, New York, National Bureau of Economic Research.

28. Dunham, Allison. (1962) "Griggs v. Allegheny County in Perspective: Thirty Years of Supreme Court Expropriation Law," in Philip B. Kurland, ed., *The Supreme Court Review: 1962*, Chicago, University of Chicago Press.

29. Ehrlich, J. W. (1959) *Ehrlich's Blackstone*, Vol. 1, New York, Capricorn.

30. Eisenhower, David D. (1949) "The Middle of the Road: A Statement of Faith in America," *American Bar Association Journal*, Vol. 35: 810.

31. Elias, E. A. (1973) "Significant Developments and Trends in Zoning Litigation," in *Proceedings:* 1–46, New York, Southwest Legal Foundation, Institute on Planning, Zoning, and Eminent Domain.

32. Fadem, Jerrold A. (1973) "Trial Tactics to Make the Compensation Just to the Owner," in *Proceedings:* 261–302, New York, Southwest Legal Foundation, Institute on Planning, Zoning, and Eminent Domain.

33. Foster, W. Frederic (December 1895) "The Doctrine of the United States Supreme Court of Property Affected by a Public Interest, and Its Tendencies," *Yale Law Journal*, Vol. 5: 49–82.

34. Fox-Genovese, Elizabeth. (1976) *The Origins of Physiocracy*, Ithaca, N.Y., Cornell University Press.

35. Frank, Jerome. (1963) *Law and the Modern Mind*, New York, Anchor Books.

36. Frank, John P. (1966) "American Legal History; The Hurst Approach," *Journal of Legal Education*, Vol. 18: 395–410.

37. Frank, Lawrence K. (1960) "What Is Social Order?" in J. G. Manis and S. I. Clark, eds., *Man and Society*, New York, Macmillan.

38. Freud, Sigmund. (1962) *Civilization and Its Discontents*, New York, Norton.

39. Friedman, Lawrence M. (Winter 1966) "On Legalistic Reasoning—A Footnote to Weber," *Wisconsin Law Review:* 148–171.

40. ———. (April 1967) "Legal Rules and the Process of Social Change," *Stanford Law Review*, Vol. 19: 786–840.

41. ———. (1969) "On Legal Development," *Rutgers Law Review*, Vol. 24: 11–64.

42. ———. (1973) *A History of American Law*, New York, Simon and Schuster.

43. Funston, Richard. (Summer 1975) "The Double Standard of Constitutional Protection in the Era of the Welfare State," *Political Science Quarterly*, Vol. 90: 261–287.

44. Furubotn, Eirik G., and Pejovich, Svetozar. (December 1972) "Property Rights and Economic Theory: A Survey of Recent Literature," *Journal of Economic Literature*, Vol. 10: 1137–1162.

45. Fusfeld, Daniel R. (December 1974) Book review in *Journal of Economic Issues*, Vol. 8: 903–905.

46. Goedecke, Robert (October 1961) "Feelings, Facts, and Politics," *Ethics*, Vol. 72: 1–11.

47. Goldberg, Victor P. (September 1974) "Public Choice-Property Rights," *Journal of Economic Issues*, Vol. 8: 555–579.

48. ———. (October 1974) "Institutional Change and the Quasi-Invisible Hand," *Journal of Law and Economics*, Vol. 17: 461–492.

49. Haik, Raymond A. (Winter 1974) "Police Power versus Condemnation," *Natural Resources Lawyer*, Vol. 7: 21–26.

50. Harris, Charles E. (Summer 1973) "Environmental Regulations, Zoning, and Withheld Municipal Services: Takings of Property by Multi-Government Action," *Florida Law Review*, Vol. 25: 635–692.
51. Holme, Richard P. (1974) "Billboards and On-Premise Signs: Regulation and Elimination under the Fifth Amendment," in *Proceedings*: 247–292, New York, Southwest Legal Foundation, Institute on Planning, Zoning, and Eminent Domain.
52. Holsti, Ole R. (September-October 1976) "Cognitive Process Approaches to Decision-Making: Foreign Policy Actors Viewed Psychologically," *American Behavioral Scientist*, Vol. 20: 11–32.
53. Horwitz, Morton J. (1977) *The Transformation of American Law, 1780–1860*, Cambridge, Mass., Harvard University Press.
54. Kanner, G. (Fall 1969) "When is 'Property' not 'Property Itself': A Critical Examination of the Bases of Denial of Compensation for Loss of Goodwill in Eminent Domain," *California Western Law Review*, Vol. 6: 57.
55. Keeton, Page. (May 1966) "Products Liability—Some Observations about Allocation of Risks," *Michigan Law Review*, Vol. 64: 1329–1348.
56. Kottke, Frank. (June 1975) "Social Control of Corporate Power: Comment," *Journal of Economic Issues*, Vol. 9: 405–408.
57. Kramon, James M. (January 1971) "Inverse Condemnation and Air Pollution," *Natural Resources Journal*, Vol. 11: 148–161.
58. Kratovil, Robert, and Harrison, Frank J. Jr. (1954) "Eminent Domain—Policy and Concept," *California Law Review*, Vol. 42: 596–652.
59. Laitos, Jan G. (July 1975) "Legal Institutions and Pollution: Some Intersections Between Law and History," *Natural Resources Journal*, Vol. 15: 423–451.
60. Lantz, Delano M. (Winter 1973) "An Analysis of Pennsylvania's New Environmental Rights Amendment and the Gettysburg Tower Case," *Dickinson Law Review*, Vol. 78: 331–364.
61. Large, Donald W. (1973) "This Land Is Whose Land? Changing Concepts of Land as Property," *Wisconsin Law Review*: 1039–1083.
62. Lesser, Joseph. (1973) "The Dilemma of Airport Zoning—The Constitutionality of Police Power Regulation v. the Necessity of Eminent Domain Acquisition," in *Proceedings*: 117–156, New York Southwest Legal Foundation, Institute on Planning, Zoning, and Eminent Domain.
63. Levi, Edward H. (1961) *An Introduction to Legal Reasoning*, Chicago, University of Chicago Press.
64. ———. (Fall 1973) "The Collective Morality of a Maturing Society," *Washington and Lee University Law Review*, Vol. 30: 399–430.
65. Michelman, Frank I. (April 1967) "Property, Utility, and Fairness: Comments on the Ethical Foundations of 'Just Compensation' Law," *Harvard Law Review*, Vol. 80: 1165–1258.
65a. ———. (1973) "In Pursuit of Constitutional Welfare Rights: One View of Rawls' Theory of Justice," *University of Pennsylvania Law Review*, Vol. 121: 962–1019.
66. Miller, Arthur Selwyn. (1976) *The Modern Corporate State*, Westport, Conn., Greenwood Press.
67. Mises, Ludwig von. (1951) *Socialism*, New Haven, Yale University Press.
68. Moynihan, Daniel P. (January 22, 1977) "The Liberals' Dilemma," *The New Republic*, Vol. 176: 57–60.
69. Murphy, Cornelius. (1971) "Ideological Interpretations of Human Rights," *DePaul Law Review*, Vol. 21: 286–306.
70. Netherton, Ross D. (1968) "Implementation of Land Use Policy: Police Power vs.

Eminent Domain," *Land and Water Law Review*, Vol. 3: 33–57.

71. Nichols, P. (1975) *The Law of Eminent Domain*, 3d ed. rev., New York, Matthew Bender.

72. Olson, James M. (Summer 1971) "The Role of 'Fairness' in Establishing a Constitutional Theory of Taking," *Urban Lawyer*, Vol. 3: 440–465.

73. Parsons, Kenneth H. (1962) "The Contribution of Institutional Economics Analysis to Land Problems Research," in Joseph Ackerman *et al.*, eds., *Land Economics Research*, pp. 168–178, Washington, D.C., Resources for the Future.

74. Pound, Roscoe. (1908) "Common Law and Legislation," *Harvard Law Review*, Vol. 21: 383.

75. Rawls, John. (1971) *A Theory of Justice*, Cambridge, Mass., Harvard University Press.

75a. Rayburn, Madison S. (1973) "Legal Rights and Legal Fictions in Condemnation," *Houston Law Review*, Vol. 10: 251–265.

76. Roby, Ronald H. (October 1967) "Police Power in Aid of Condemnation?" *Appraisal Journal*, Vol. 35: 507–517.

77. Ruegsegger, Martin C. (1974) "Fifth Amendment Taking—Inverse Condemnation," *Journal of Air Law and Commerce*, Vol. 40: 332–341.

78. Rumble, H. H. (February 1918) "Limitations on the Use of Property by its Owner," *Virginia Law Review*, Vol. 5: 297–315.

79. Sackman, Julius J. (1973) "Condemnation Blight—A Problem in Compensability and Value," in *Proceedings*: 157–193, New York Southwest Legal Foundation, Institute on Planning, Zoning, and Eminent Domain.

80. ———. (1974) "Access—A Reevaluation," in *Proceedings*: 335–363, New York, Southwest Legal Foundation, Institute on Planning, Zoning, and Eminent Domain.

81. Samuels, Warren J. (1966) *The Classical Theory of Economic Policy*, Cleveland, World.

82. ———. (October 1971) "Interrelations Between Legal and Economic Processes," *Journal of Law and Economics*, Vol. 14: 435–450.

83. ———. (1972) "Welfare Economics, Power and Property," in G. Wunderlich and W. L. Gibson, Jr., eds., *Perspectives of Property*, pp. 61–148, University Park, Institute for Research on Land and Water Resources, Pennsylvania State University, 1972.

84. ———. (February 1974) "The Coase Theorem and the Study of Law and Economics," *Natural Resources Journal*, Vol. 14: 1–33.

85. ———. (November 1974) "An Economic Perspective on the Compensation Problem," *Wayne Law Review*, Vol. 21: 113–134.

86. ———. (1974) *Pareto on Policy*, New York, Elsevier.

87. ——— and Schmid, A. Allan. (Winter 1976) "Polluters' Profit and Political Response: The Dynamics of Rights Creation," *Public Choice*, Vol. 28: 99–105.

88. Sax, Joseph L. (November 1964) "Takings and the Police Power," *Yale Law Journal*, Vol. 74: 36–76.

89. ———. (December 1971) "Takings, Private Property and Public Rights," *Yale Law Journal*, Vol. 81: 149–186.

90. ——— and Hiestand, Fred J. (March 1967) "Slumlordism as a Tort," *Michigan Law Review*, Vol. 65: 869–922.

91. Schumpeter, Joseph A. (1950) *Capitalism, Socialism, and Democracy*, 3d ed., New York, Harper.

92. Shackle, G. L. S. (1967) *The Years of High Theory*, New York, Cambridge University Press.
93. Simons, Henry C. (1948) *Economic Policy for a Free Society*, Chicago, University of Chicago Press.
94. Smith, Jeremiah. (1917) "Reasonable Use of One's Own Property as a Justification for Damage to a Neighbor," *Columbia Law Review*, Vol. 17: 383–403.
95. Smith, Raymond. (April 1974) "The Economic Loss Cases—The Light at the End of the Tunnel?" *Journal of Business Law*: 119–127.
96. Solo, Robert A. (1974) *The Political Authority and the Market System*, Cincinnati, South-Western Publishing Co.
97. Spengler, Joseph J. (July 1948) "The Problem of Order in Economic Affairs," *Southern Economic Journal*, Vol. 15: 1–29.
98. ———. (September 1974) "Was 1922–1972 a Golden Age in the History of Economics?" *Journal of Economic Issues*, Vol. 8: 525–553.
99. Stigler, George J., and Friedland, Claire. (October 1962) "What Can Regulators Regulate? The Case of Electricity," *Journal of Law and Economics*, Vol. 5: 1–16.
100. Stoebuck, William B. (August 1972) "A General Theory of Eminent Domain," *Washington Law Review*, Vol. 47: 553–608.
101. Stubblebine, William Craig. (1972) "On Property Rights and Institutions," in Gordon Tullock, ed., *Explorations in the Theory of Anarchy*, pp. 39–50, Blacksburg, Center for Study of Public Choice, Virginia Polytechnic Institute and State University.
102. Stubbs, Robert C. (1973) "Compensable and Noncompensable Items and How to Handle the Evidence," in *Proceedings*: 209–259, New York, Southwest Legal Foundation, Institute on Planning, Zoning, and Eminent Domain.
103. Tapp, June L., and Kohlberg, Lawrence. (1971) "Developing Senses of Law and Legal Justice," *Journal of Social Issues*, Vol. 27: 65–91.
104. Tribe, Laurence H. (1975) "From Environmental Foundations to Constitutional Structures: Learning from Nature's Future," *Yale Law Journal*, Vol. 84: 545–546.
105. ———*et al.*, eds. (1976) *When Values Conflict*, Cambridge, Mass., Ballinger.
106. Van Alstyne, Arvo. (1971) "Taking or Damaging by Police Power: The Search for Inverse Condemnation Criteria," *Southern California Law Review*, Vol. 44: 1–73.
107. Viner, Jacob. (October 1960) "The Intellectual History of Laissez Faire," *Journal of Law and Economics*, Vol. 3: 45–69.
108. Waite, G. Graham. (September 1966) "Governmental Power and Private Property," *Catholic University Law Review*, Vol. 16: 283–296.
109. Waterman, Sterry R. (October 1972) "Whither the Concept 'Affected with a Public Interest'?" *Vanderbilt Law Review*, Vol. 25: 927–937.
110. Williamson, Oliver E. (1970) "Administrative Decision Making and Pricing: Externality and Compensation Analysis Applied," in Julius Margolis, ed., *The Analysis of Public Output*, pp. 115–138, New York, National Bureau of Economic Research.

Law Review Notes:

110a. Note. (1966) "Just Compensation for the Small Businessman," *Columbia Journal of Law and Social Problems*, Vol. 2: 144.
111. Note. (December 1965) "Airplane Noise, Property Rights, and the Constitution," *Columbia Law Review*, Vol. 65: 1428–1447.
112. Note. (January 1967) "The Unsoundness of California's Noncompensability Rule

as Applied to Business Losses in Condemnation Cases," *Hastings Law Journal*, Vol. 20: 675.

113. Note (1974) "Just Compensation and the Assassin's Bequest: A Utilitarian Approach," *University of Pennsylvania Law Review*, Vol. 122: 1012–1032.

114. Note (1973) "Utility, Fairness and the Takings Clause: Three Perspectives on *Laird v. Nelms*," *Virginia Law Review*, Vol. 59: 1034–1096.

115. Note. (1973) "Takings and the Public Interest in Railroad Reorganization," *Yale Law Journal*, Vol. 82: 1004–1022.

THE DYNAMICS OF
TRADITIONAL RATE
REGULATION

Patrick C. Mann, REGIONAL RESEARCH INSTITUTE,
WEST VIRGINIA UNIVERSITY

A theoretical framework incorporating the dynamic elements in the regulatory process is a prerequisite to understanding public utility regulation. The purpose of this paper is to construct such a framework and to initiate discussion focusing on the dynamic facets of regulation.

Part I focuses on the numerous relationships among regulatory variables with emphasis on the nature of the linkages, direction of causation, and feedback effects. Some of the variable linkages emerge as unilateral while others emerge as bilateral (feedback effect). Most of the bilateral relationships are of an indirect nature, and most of the unilateral relationships involve variables exogenous to the regulatory environment.

Research in Law and Economics, Vol. 1, pp. 195–212.

Part II focuses on a graphical exposition of the regulatory framework. The graphical presentation provides insight into both the cyclical and dynamic elements of the regulatory environment. Basing regulated prices on costs reflecting output observed in a past period generates a cyclical pattern in which price and present average cost are never equal. The nature of returns to scale and price elasticity of demand for the utility service emerge as the critical factors in determining the specific nature of the cyclical patterns.

The absence of a unified theoretical framework for traditional public utility regulation is periodically a target for the critics. A survey of the literature reveals that, to understand public utility regulation, a theoretical framework incorporating the dynamic elements inherent in the regulatory process is a necessary prerequisite. The purpose of this paper is to construct such a framework to provide insight into the regulatory rate-making mechanism and to initiate discussion regarding the development of more sophisticated analyses focusing on the dynamic facets of regulation. The objective here is to examine the intricate environment of traditional rate regulation.

The primary impetus for this paper can be attributed to several sources. Joskow (4) asserts that to understand price regulation and how it affects performance variables, such as price, quality of service, and internal efficiency, one needs to understand the actual environment of price regulation. Structural models of the regulatory interactions are needed that link the public utility with the regulatory agency and other regulatory participants. These models should aid in analyzing changes in the regulatory process and techniques that flow from changes in the regulatory environment. Trebing (9) asserts that new regulatory concepts need to be developed focusing on regulatory interrelationships; these new techniques are a prerequisite to examining how the interrelationships can be employed to maximize the public interest. Specifically, there is a need for new regulatory concepts giving attention to the interrelationship between market structure (entry control) and price-earnings control. Most regulatory agencies have broad controls over these elements but do not seem to know how the elements interact.

Williamson (10) recognizes the variable linkages inherent in the regulatory environment by focusing on the various points at which regulatory control can be exercised. For example, control can be applied to essential variables (earnings and price), performance specification (pricing rules), reactors (technology, personnel, and other inputs), performance checks (internal efficiency audits, expenditure audits, and comparative performance analyses), and firm environment (product and capital markets). The various control categories are linked by variable interrelationships. The control of essential variables (specification of ends) via profit and expenditure constraints on other performance goals cannot be effectively implemented and achieved without performance control (specification of means) in the form of accounting standards, reporting requirements, pricing rules, financial recommendations regarding debt-equity ratios, and so forth. Similarly, control of efficiency cannot be achieved in a vacuum without recognition of the interrelationships across control categories.

Spann (8) argues that regulated prices based on prior accounting costs (observed average cost in a previous period) produce a regulatory effect similar to the classic cobweb model. The traditional regulatory decision rule of setting price (P) equal to previously observed average cost (AC)—P in time period of t_1 is based on AC_{t_0} for output Q_{t_0}—generates a cyclical pattern of regulatory prices. This cobweb pattern involves price changes producing quantity-sold changes which further change average cost, thus leading to further changes in price in the next time period.

Finally, Lerner and Moag (6) argue that the decision-making technology that regulatory commisions employ has been deficient in that it provides no recognition of the systematic effects of public utility behavior and regulatory decisions upon the public utility itself and the regulatory environment. The same authors (7) stress the need to develop information about the functional relationships in the regulatory process; instead of focusing on profit constraints, regulators need to examine how parameters within the regulatory environment (and within the regulated firm) interrelate. These information requirements are essential to the regulators, since rather than monitoring the effects of changes in activities on a singular element such as rate of return, effective regulation must view the effects of changes in activities on all parameters within the regulatory environment. These authors note, for example, that the revenue requirement approach to rate-setting ignores numerous interrelationships; target profit rates have numerous effects on the firm (and regulatory environment) which have feedback effects on actual earnings.

I THE REGULATORY FRAMEWORK

The focus here is on the several relationships among regulatory variables; an attempt is made to note the nature of the linkage, the direction of causation, and possible feedback effects. Some of the variable linkages are hypothesized to be unilateral, while others are presumed to be bilateral. One example of interdependent relationships is the circular association among utility price, service volume, system capacity, and cost of service. Consumer usage is a determinant of system capacity; system capacity influences costs of service; and costs via the rate-setting mechanism affect price which in turn influences consumer use. Although it does not deny the existence of the linkages, traditional rate regulation tends to subordinate the importance of such interdependencies; that is, in many cases regulatory commissions implicitly presume that the price elasticity of demand for utility services is minimal (price has little effect on use levels or time patterns of consumption). In brief, traditional rate regulation tends to ignore the after-effects of a rate change in which the new price, designed to cover historical costs, determines a new output level and thus a new level of system costs.

It should be noted that the dynamic elements examined herein are dynamic only in a comparative statics sense; that is, the interdependence among costs, output, and prices is examined within a traditional regulatory framework. The broader concept of regulation dynamics in the context of market structure and institutions remains outside the scope of this paper. For example, the effect of technological change and innovation on market structure and regulatory form is not within the scope of analysis; Adams and Dirlam (1). By ignoring the broader regulation dynamics, the analysis may suffer from excluding changes in the regulatory interdependencies over time.

We first examine the important variable relationships within the regulatory environment. The average price or rate level (R_1) permitted a public utility essentially can be viewed as a product of interaction between the regulatory agency and utility management. This interaction is influenced by both economic and institutional factors. The critical variables influencing rate levels include the leverage of the regulatory agency (L_r) relative to that of the public utility (L_u), operating costs (C_o), capacity costs (C_i), the rate base valuation method employed (B), and the relationship of actual rate of return (E_a) to permitted earnings (E_p) since the last rate adjustment.[1] The ratio, E_a/E_p, is important since regulators determine an authorized rate of return which reflects an opportunity but not a guarantee. The rate level determination process can be expressed as:

$$R_1 = f(L_r/L_u, C_o, C_i, B, E_a/E_p). \tag{1}$$

This is obviously a simplified expression of the variables associated with utility rate levels. In specific cases, other variables may have significant influence. For example, owing to the recent emergence of consumerism, a critical factor in some rate level determinations is the relative power of user groups. In some regulatory jurisdictions, increased inflation and other factors have changed passive regulatory commission participation into an active review process.

An explanatory note is in order regarding the concepts of regulatory leverage (L_r), utility leverage (L_u), and consumer leverage (L_c). In discussing variable relationships within the regulatory environment, leverage refers to the capacity of a particular group to influence the behavior of other groups. In this sense, the concept of leverage is similar to the concept of power; Dahl (2) defines power as a relationship among groups or individuals in which the behavior of one group is influenced by the behavior of other groups.[2] Thus, utility leverage (L_u) refers to the capacity of utility management to influence regulatory outcomes; consumer leverage (L_c) refers to the power of user groups to influence regulatory outcomes. In both cases, leverage flows from a combination of political and economic factors. Regulatory leverage (L_r) refers to the propensity of regulatory commissions to be influenced by user groups, utility managements, and the like.

The rate structure (R_s) or relationships among rates for user groups essentially can be viewed as a product of interaction among utility managements, and user groups, with occasional input from regulatory agencies. However, historically, the initiative has been taken up by utility managements.[3] The critical variables in the rate structure determination process include the leverage of the utility management (L_u) relative to that of user groups (L_c), the authorized rate level, the price elasticities of demand for utility services (P_e), and the costs of providing the services (C_s). The rate structure determination process can be expressed as:

$$R_s = f(L_u/L_c, R_1, P_e, C_s). \qquad (2)$$

One cannot realistically portray the regulatory process by describing only the rate determination process. The regulatory environment is much more complex. Additional relationships must be examined.

Assuming that the price elasticities of demand for utility services exceed zero, the rate level (expressed in the rate structure) influences quantity demanded of the utility services. This relationship can be expressed as:

$$Q_d = f(R_1). \qquad (3)$$

Equation (3) can be expanded to incorporate the parameters that cause shifts in demand for utility services such as prices of substitutes (P_s) and complements (P_c), income (Y), taste preferences (t), and service promotion (a). With the exception of promotion, the demand parameters are exogenous to the regulatory environment. The generalized demand relationship can be expressed as:

$$Q_d = f(R_1, P_s, P_c, Y, t, a). \qquad (3)$$

Rational rate-setting must incorporate the price-quantity relationship implied by the demand function. The time factor is critical since price elasticities for utility services tend to increase with longer time horizons. That is, longer time periods allow for changes in production processes, in sources of supply, and in appliances.

Quantity demanded and its timing influence capacity requirements (I_s). This relationship can be expressed as:

$$I_s = f(Q_d). \qquad (4)$$

In reality, various dimensions of a utility system are influenced by different types of demands. For example, a water utility's treatment facilities are generally designed to meet maximum day demand, while its distribution plant is designed to meet maximum hour demand. The rate structure, by incorporating elements of peak load pricing, can affect the timing of consumption, capacity requirements, and thus system investment costs. The shift from peak to off-peak use emerges as improvements in utility load factors. A similar effect on unit costs can be achieved by a rate structure designed to attract new consumers whose maximum demands are diverse. This is reflected as increases in utility diversity factors.[4]

The two important cost components—operating and investment costs—are a partial function of output. Operating costs are influenced primarily by volume of service, system capacity, variable input prices (P_i), and technology (T). This relationship can be expressed as:

$$C_o = f(Q_d, I_s, P_i, T). \tag{5}$$

Investment costs are influenced primarily by system capacity, capital input prices (P_k), and technology. This relationship can be expressed as:

$$C_i = f(I_s, P_k, T). \tag{6}$$

A minor cost category—customer costs (billing, metering)—is essentially unaffected by the factors influencing operating and investment costs; customer costs are a function of the total number of customers served by the system.

In reality, the interrelationship of utility system cost and output is complex. First, the behavior of unit costs for a utility system will vary with the time horizon; that is, the unit cost results from increasing service within the constraint of present capacity tend to differ from the cost results from increasing service by expanding system capacity. In brief, cost must be specified as to short-run behavior (with utilization rate changes) or long-run behavior (with scale changes). Second, the behavior of unit costs for a utility varies with the particular system component; for example, traditional economies of scale in production can be offset by diseconomies of consumer dispersion in distribution. Finally, unit cost behavior also varies with the underlying source of system expansion. That is, increases in per capita consumption with its primary effect on production capacity and minimal effect on distribution capacity tend to produce different cost results than either increases in consumer density, which may necessitate some change in distribution capacity, or an enlargement in the system's service area, which usually necessitates major changes in the distribution network. In sum, different unit cost outcomes can occur varying with the specific time horizon, system function, and nature of demand expansion.

Although the prices of inputs are exogenous to the regulatory environment, technology is not. One can hypothesize that production techniques in a regulatory environment are primarily influenced by the innovative activity of utility equipment suppliers (V) from which most technological change in the public utility sector originates, pressure or lack of it from the regulatory agency, anticipated cost savings from the technological change (C_r), and actual earnings. The latter variable is critical in cases of both internal and external financing. This relationship can be expressed as:

$$T = f(V, L_r, C_r, R_a). \tag{7}$$

An interdependency exists in that costs are affected by technology which is, in turn, influenced directly by actual costs and indirectly by cost effects on earnings.

Service promotion (a) is a partial determinant of output; it is itself a partial function of factors such as earnings, regulatory scrutiny, and management policies. This relationship can be expressed as:

$$a = f(R_a, L_r, L_u). \tag{8}$$

Utility earnings influence both technology and service promotion. Earnings (rate of return earned on rate base) are determined by the interaction of rate level and costs, and all the factors that influence and interact with these two variables. This relationship can be expressed as:

$$R_a = f(R_1, C_o, C_i). \tag{9}$$

One element in the regulatory environment has not been mentioned — service quality. Quality has not been overlooked intentionally; it is pervasive and influenced by numerous factors. To simplify, one could assume service quality (q) to be relatively static and thus incorporate it as an element of output. However, price has no relevance unless it incorporates both monetary and quality elements.[5] The quality relationship can be expressed as:

$$q = f(L_u, L_r, L_c, T). \tag{10}$$

Actual quality of service is a product of the relative pressures and activities of utility managements, consumers, and regulators; in turn, quality affects costs and rates. Quality of service is also influenced by technology, and at any point in time, quantity demanded relative to system capacity. The insertion of the latter is recognition that quality of service can deteriorate significantly if the demanded output strains the existing system capacity, which may be affected by such factors as low water pressure or brownouts.

II A GRAPHICAL ANALYSIS

The variable relationships are both unilateral and interdependent. Most of the bilateral relationships are of an indirect nature. Operation and investment costs directly influence utility rates of return or earnings; the effect of actual earnings on cost levels is indirect through an effect on technology.

Similarly, volume of service is directly affected by rate level and structure; its feedback effect on rates is conveyed through an effect on required capacity and system costs. An example of a more direct bilateral relationship is the behavioral effect that flows from the interaction of regulators and utility managements; for instance, in some states, regulators directly influence management policy on matters such as capital structure, while in other states utility managements appear to have "captured" the regulators. Examples of unilateral linkages include the regulatory effect on service quality, the effect of input prices on costs, and the capital supplier effect on

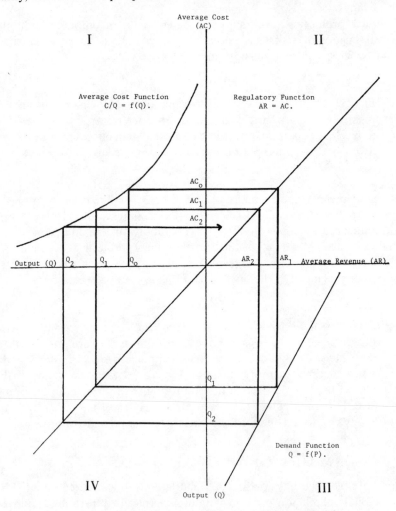

Figure 1. The Regulatory Framework Incorporating
Increasing Returns to Scale.

technology. Most of the unilateral relationships involve variables which can be perceived as exogenous to the regulatory environment.

The numerous variable relationships can be expressed in a simplified graphical form. As shown in Figure 1, the regulatory framework can be perceived diagrammatically in the nature of quadrants.

Quadrant I portrays the long-run average cost function for the utility system—the functional relationship between average costs and output expressed as $C/Q = f(Q)$. The focus is on long-run rather than short-run costs since capacity costs are an important component of total system costs and since regulatory agencies set rates for time periods that may involve changes in system capacity. The average cost function includes both the nodal and network cost components [Dajani (3)] which collectively form the aggregate cost function for the utility system. The nodal component is constituted by the production center (electricity generation, water treatment) in which cost functions are similar to traditional theoretical cost functions. The network component involves the distribution or delivery system in which factors such as consumer density and size of service area, as well as scale, are significant influences.

The curvature of the average cost function is derived from the nature of returns to scale. In Figure 1, the initial assumption is that the public utility experiences increasing returns to scale (declining average costs) over the relevant range of output. The level of the cost function is influenced by both the production function and input prices. The average cost function presumes input prices and technology to be constant; the average cost function includes a normal rate of return (reflecting the opportunity cost of capital) on capital investment. The nature of the average cost function is essentially derived from the utility system's production function. Technology determines the nature of the production function. Parameters affecting technology and thus inducing shifts in the production function include both exogenous variables (innovation by capital equipment suppliers) and endogenous variables (regulatory pressure to adopt new technology). Shifts in the production function can also be attributed to the ability, or inability, of the utility system to achieve maximum productivity within the constraint of a given technology and given system scale. The relative degree of attainment of these x-efficiencies creates cost function differences for utility systems employing the same technology.

The production function—the functional relationship between output and inputs—is not directly incorporated into the graphical portrayal of the regulatory framework. The rationale for its exclusion is that it is reflected in the average cost function for the utility system. To portray the production function for the utility system in a separate quadrant would be redundant.

Quadrant II portrays the traditional regulatory rate-setting mechanism— the revenue requirement approach of setting rates so as to generate revenues to match costs.[6] The regulatory function (average revenue = average cost) bisects the origin of the quadrant at a 45-degree angle. Given the presumption that average costs are employed as the basis for determining the rate level, the specific pricing technique (value of service, incremental costs) influencing rate structure or rate differentials between user groups does not directly affect the regulatory function. If the regulatory commission abandoned traditional average cost pricing for the policy of marginal cost pricing, the system's marginal cost function would be inserted in Quadrant I and the regulatory function in Quadrant II would instead reflect the equation of average revenue and marginal cost.

As Spann (8) so aptly notes, we are not implying that the equality of regulated price and average cost is presumed to be either desirable or efficient. The presumption is only that the regulatory function presented here reflects the reality of traditional regulation. One of the objectives of the framework developed in Figures 1–5 is to show the implications of setting prices equal to historical costs, regardless of whether the cost data reflects average or marginal cost. In traditional regulation, price is set equal to a previously observed average cost rather than average cost at the time at which price is set. The setting of average revenue equal to average cost of an output observed in the past (in the test or representative year) in itself generates a cyclical effect in which present price and present average cost may never be equal. A caveat that needs to be added concerns the several important factors that underlie traditional regulation's reliance on historical costs. These include equity considerations, the allocation of capital costs over time via depreciation and in the context of inflation, more accurate control of excessive earnings. That is, even though serious problems may arise when historical costs deviate from costs actually incurred when the rates are in effect, regulatory commissions have tended to adhere to legal precedents and notions of certainty and simplicity that dictate the use of incurred, rather than anticipated, costs in establishing rates.

Quadrant III portrays the demand function for the utility service—that is, the functional relationship between average revenue (price) and quantity demanded of the service. For purposes of simplicity, we initially presume a singular class of relatively homogeneous users (the complexity of portraying relatively volatile demand functions reflecting peak and off-peak use is eliminated). Given a price elasticity of demand for the service exceeding zero, the average price level influences service volume. Changes in demand parameters, such as income or prices of other goods, produce shifts in the demand function.

Quadrant IV incorporates an analytical device for providing continuity in the exposition of the traditional regulatory framework. Utility output is measured on both axes; the line that bisects the origin at a 45-degree angle reflects the identity of output = output. This device allows for the closure of the model by linking quantity demanded (output) of the utility service with a new level of average cost.

The graphical presentation in Figure 1 indicates the interdependency of regulated prices, output volume, and costs; it also indicates the cyclical pattern that results from basing rates on costs observed in a past period. For example, the initial observed output in time period zero (Q_0) determines an average cost for the same past time period (AC_0). In the traditional regulatory process, AC_0 (generally translated into revenue requirements) becomes the basis for the setting of the regulated price in t_1. The regulated price (AR_1), designed to cover historical average costs, determines a new consumption or output level (Q_1) which in turn, through the production function, determines a new level of unit costs (AC_1). What ensues is another cycle of changes in rates, use of service, and average costs — AR_2, Q_2, AC_2. As demand and cost functions shift over time, the continuous cycling of regulated prices, costs, and so forth will occur as long as regulated prices are based on historical accounting costs. The continuous cycling of regulatory prices is presumed by Spann (8) to be of a converging rather than an explosive nature. The cobweb model may be explosive only if the average cost function is more steeply sloped than the demand function. Given the existing empirical estimates of public utility cost and demand functions, this case does not appear to be very realistic. Thus, for simplicity, one can presume that the cobweb cycles tend to converge rather than to become explosive.

The graphical presentation provides insight into both the cyclical and dynamic elements of the regulatory environment. Basing regulated prices on costs reflecting output observed in a past period generates a cyclical pattern in which price and present average cost may never be equal. As indicated by Figure 1, the critical factors in determining the specific nature of this cyclical pattern are found in Quadrants I and III — that is, the nature of returns to scale and the price elasticity of demand for the utility service. Given the particular combination of cost and demand functions portrayed in Figure 1, the cyclical pattern involves a trend toward decreasing costs, and rates, and increasing output.

If one substitutes in Quadrant I a cost function that reflects decreasing returns to scale over the relevant range of output (Figure 2), the cyclical effect tends to exhibit a tendency toward increasing costs, and rates, and increasing output initially; however, the combination of decreasing returns to scale and some sensitivity of quantity demanded to price changes (price elasticity coefficients exceeding zero) subsequently produces a dampening effect on costs, rates, and output. In brief, the combination of cost and demand functions portrayed in Figure 2 appears to generate a converging cyclical pattern toward increasing costs and output.

Obviously, the specific cyclical effects generated in the regulatory frame-

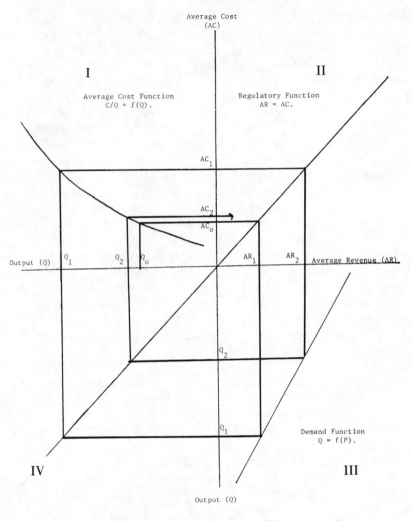

Figure 2. The Regulatory Framework Incorporating
Decreasing Returns to Scale.

work in Quadrants I and II are influenced not only by the nature of returns
to scale but also by the slope of the average cost function (the degree of
economies of scale in the increasing returns to scale case or the extent of
diseconomies of scale in the decreasing returns to scale case), as well as
the initial output (Q_0) employed in the analysis. An exception is the case
where the public utility is confronted by constant returns to scale over the
entire range of output. The framework developed here implies that the cyclical effect is eliminated in the context of constant unit costs. This conclusion

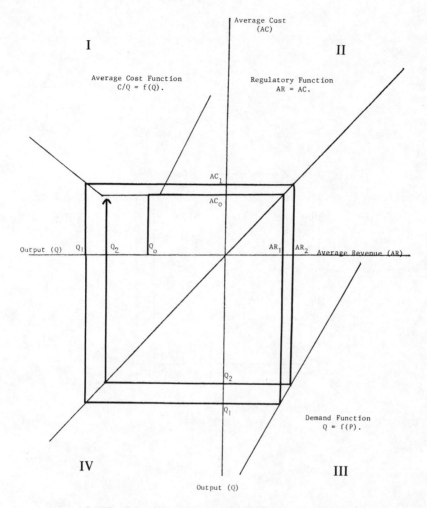

Figure 3. The Regulatory Framework Incorporating a Range
of Constant Returns to Scale.

must be modified if one presumes instead that the utility system experiences constant unit costs over a limited of output. In Figure 3, the analysis shows that even with the initial output (Q_0) being in the constant cost range, there can be a cyclical pattern prior to the eventual result of constant costs, rates, and output.

Changes in the nature of the demand function also affect the cyclical pattern of cost, price, and output. Given increasing returns to scale, the result of inserting a more price-inelastic demand function is a decrease in the volatility of the cyclical pattern. In Figure 4, the regulatory framework

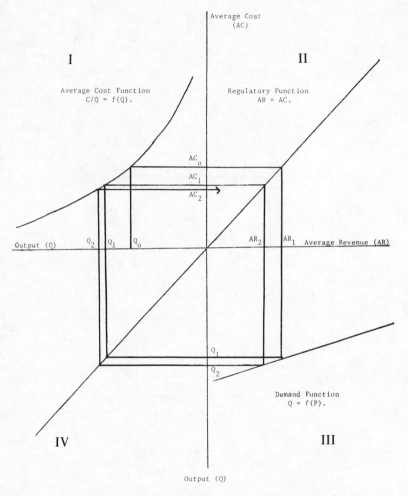

Figure 4. The Regulatory Framework Incorporating
Decreased Price Elasticity of Demand.

incorporates a less price-elastic demand function than that employed in
Figure 1. As compared to Figure 1, the result shows much smaller changes
in the trend toward increasing output and decreasing costs-rates. Although
not portrayed here, the insertion of a perfectly inelastic demand function,
similar to the assumption of constant unit costs, eliminates the cyclical
pattern of changing cost, price, and output. In contrast, again assuming
increasing returns to scale, the result of inserting a more price-elastic demand
function is an increase in the volatility of the cyclical pattern. In Figure 5, the
regulatory framework incorporates a more price-elastic demand function

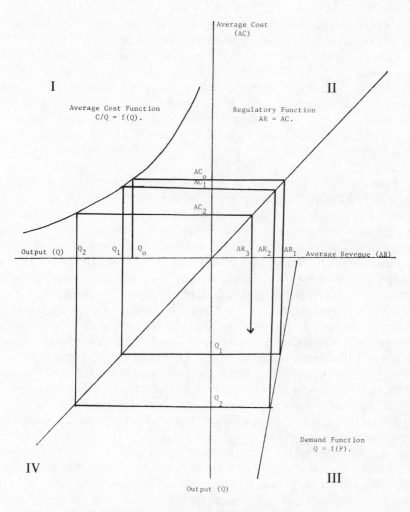

Figure 5. The Regulatory Framework Incorporating Increased
Price Elasticity of Demand.

than that employed in Figure 1. In comparison, the result shows much larger
changes in the trend toward increasing output and decreasing costs-rates.
Although not portrayed here, the insertion of a nearly perfectly elastic
demand results in extreme fluctuations in output, costs, and rates. Again,
the effect of constant returns to scale is to neutralize the effect of changes in
the nature of demand on the cyclical patterns.

The regulatory framework developed herein, and the various sets of
assumptions employed, should be viewed only as a good beginning. The interdependence of prices, output, and costs can be analyzed under various sets of

additional assumptions. For example, one may wish to modify the model to reflect peak-load pricing for a multiproduct firm operating under various returns to scale conditions. One may wish to incorporate the Averch-Johnson effect in the model. One may wish to divide the unit cost function into production and distribution components to allow for diverse cost behavior with expanding scale in the two cost components. Other factors that influence the relationship between usage, capacity, cost of service, and price could be added. In brief, the model's limited number of uses discussed here may represent only a minority of potential uses of such a model.

Parameter changes affecting either the cost function or the demand function can cause a chain reaction of dynamic effects and thus induce changes in the cyclical pattern. Technological innovation, changes in input prices, and changes in system productivity (e.g., increase in x-efficiency) produce modifications in the average cost function. An increase in x-efficiency which produces a change in the level, but not necessarily a change in the shape, of the average cost function, appears to affect the cyclical pattern minimally. Adoption of new cost-saving technology emerges as a more dynamic element, since the curvature of the average cost function may be altered significantly. Shifts in the demand function with little change in the property of elasticity also affect the cyclical pattern minimally. In contrast, shifts in demand with increased or decreased price elasticity emerge as more dynamic elements, possibly creating significant modifications in the cost, rate, and output interrelationship. Finally, changes in regulatory techniques also have effects on the cyclical pattern. For example, if the regulatory commission begins to use "projected" test-year data, rather than historical costs in setting the regulated price, the cyclical pattern would tend to be dampened considerably if the predicted costs approximated the eventual cost outcomes. Of course, for the predicted costs to emerge as equal to the actual outcome, the projections must incorporate the actual cost, rate, and output linkages. This would be true of any rate-setting procedure incorporating expected rather than observed costs. The key to whether these alternative rate-setting techniques (or inflation adjustments) reduce the cyclical nature of regulation is whether the absolute magnitude of the forecasting error (projected costs versus actual costs) is less than the absolute magnitude of the existing error (test-year costs versus actual costs).

III CONCLUSION

There are dynamic elements within the regulatory environment. However, regulators tend to ignore the variable linkages that form the basis for these dynamic elements. Regulated price is generally established on a historical cost basis with little or no recognition of price effects, direct and indirect, on use, costs, and efficiency. However, effective rate regulation cannot be restricted to price or earnings constraints since both are affected by, and in turn influence, numerous other regulatory variables.

The variable linkages pose problems for regulators and for firms in establishing rate levels and rate structures. To prevent excessive earnings and create earnings that attract new capital and compensate existing investors, to minimize price discrimination, and to induce internal technical efficiency, regulatory decision-makers must have knowledge of the dynamic properties of the regulatory process. It is obviously no simple task to quantify the variable linkages, particularly in the context of continuous change in these linkages over time. However, only by the development of empirical information on the several variable linkages can one begin to understand the complexity of rate regulation. To ignore these dynamic elements, as many regulatory commissions appear to do, can only result in defective regulation. By identifying the variables (both exogenous and endogenous) that influence regulatory performance, regulatory decision-makers can induce more satisfactory performance from public utilities. Regulation is imperfect, given its bureaucratic nature and political interference; however, some of the imperfections are a product of the static quality of regulation and thus could be easily eliminated.

The academic regulatory literature has generally focused on several areas of interest: the issue of why regulation occurs and its specific incidence, the issue of choice of regulatory tools, the issue of the effects of regulation on resource allocation, and the issue of why changes in the regulatory process occur. In this paper, the focus has been on what may be described as an additional area of academic concern—the dynamic elements of regulation. It is hoped that the analysis developed here captures the essence of the dynamic properties of traditional rate regulation. Being intellectually satisfying cannot be a sole justification for its exposition; the issue is one of relevance. Upon recognition of regulation dynamics, attempts must be made to quantify the essential functional relationships in the regulatory environment. Only by approximating these functional relationships can contemporary issues be resolved, such as the potential capacity or capital investment savings from the imposition of a peak-load pricing scheme by a public utility.

FOOTNOTES

The author is professor of economics and research associate, Regional Research Institute, West Virginia University.

1. Costs are generally for a test or representative period—e.g., the latest 12 months for which data are available. Adjustments may be made for anticipated system expansion. However, as a result of increased rates of inflation which cause actual costs to deviate

significantly from test-year costs, some commissions are now employing "projected" test-year data allowing firms to predict costs several years into the future; Joskow (4).

2. Some make a technical distinction between the concepts of power and influence. That is, power is of a coercive nature (groups will submit involuntarily to power); influence, in contrast, is more of a pervasive nature (groups will submit voluntarily to influence).

3. Rapid changes in the legal and economic environment in the last decade, such as increases in fuel costs, have modified the regulatory process somewhat and have moved regulatory commissions to a more active role in the determination of rate structures. Part of this change has occurred as user and other interest groups have challenged the validity of rate structures, such as the declining block schedule.

4. A utility's load factor is the ratio of average demand to peak demand. A utility's diversity factor is the ratio of the sum of peak demands for all user groups, regardless of timing, to system peak demand. Similar to utilization rates (the ratio of average demand to designed capacity), load factors can be defined as to time period (daily peaks, annual peaks), system function (production, distribution), and user category (residential, commercial, industrial).

5. Price is a ratio with monetary revenue as the numerator and physical units of a specified quantity and quality as the divisor; Kahn (5).

6. Revenue requirements vary according to ownership forms. The requirements for an investor-owned utility include operation expenses, taxes, depreciation, and allowed earnings. The requirements for a publicly owned utility include operation expenses, taxes or tax equivalents, debt service costs, minor extensions-replacements, and a profit residual that tends to vary significantly across publicly owned firms.

REFERENCES

1. Adams, W., and Dirlam, J.B. (1968) "Market Structure, Regulation, and Dynamic Change," in H. M. Trebing, ed., *Performance under Regulation*, pp. 131–144, East Lansing, Michigan State University, Institute of Public Utilities.
2. Dahl, R. A. (April 1972) "Concept of Power," *Behavioral Science*, Vol. 2: 201–215.
3. Dajani, J. S. (November 1973) "Cost Studies of Urban Public Services," *Land Economics*, Vol. 49: 479–483.
4. Joskow, P. L. (October 1974) "Inflation and Environmental Concern: Structural Change in the Process of Public Utility Price Regulation," *Journal of Law and Economics*, Vol. 17: 291–327.
5. Kahn, A. E. (1970) *The Economics of Regulation.* Vol. I, New York, John Wiley & Sons.
6. Lerner E. M., and Moag, J. S. (August 1968) "Toward an Improved Decision Framework for Public Utility Regulation," *Land Economics*, Vol. 44: 403–409.
7. ———. (1969) "Information Requirements for Regulatory Decisions," in H. M. Trebing and R. Howard, eds., *Rate of Return under Regulation: New Directions and Perspectives.* pp. 195–204, East Lansing, Michigan State University, Institute of Public Utilities.
8. Spann, R.M. (July 1976) "The Regulatory Cobweb: Inflation, Deflation, and Regulatory Lags and the Effects of Alternative Administrative Rules in Public Utilities," *Southern Economic Journal*, Vol. 43: 827–839.
9. Trebing, H. M. (June 1974) "Realism and Relevance in Public Utility Regulation," *Journal of Economic Issues*, Vol. 8: 209–233.
10. Williamson, O. E. (1971) "Administrative Controls and Regulatory Behavior," H. M. Trebing, ed., *Essays on Public Utility Pricing and Regulation*, pp. 411–438, East Lansing, Michigan State University, Institute of Public Utilities.

PRICE DISCRIMINATION AND PEAK-LOAD PRICING SUBJECT TO RATE OF RETURN CONSTRAINT

David L. McNicol, U. S. TREASURY

This paper asks whether the prescriptions that emerge from orthodox peak load pricing models are efficient in the presence of the institutional constraints that characterize public utility regulation. Policies that are "optimal" in an institution free context are, of course, not necessarily "optimal" or even sensible in any particular institutional setting. Nevertheless, in arguing for peak load pricing, economists have generally taken no notice of the crucial institutional features of public utility regulation. The implied assumption is that these institutional considerations have no systematic bearing on the desirability of adopting a policy of peak load pricing. The model developed in this paper suggests that, on the contrary, the conventional prescription—an increase in

Research in Law and Economics, Vol. 1, pp. 213–238.
Copyright © 1979 by JAI Press, Inc.
All rights of reproduction in any form reserved.
ISBN: 0–89232–028–1.

marginal rates during peak periods—is inefficient in the presence of a rate of return constraint.

I INTRODUCTION

The rate schedules of regulated utilities in the United States tend to be "flat." That is, with few exceptions, marginal rates do not vary with daily or seasonal shifts in the level of demand.[1] Viewed in terms of conventional peak-load pricing models, a flat rate schedule seems inefficient, and, on this basis, economists typically hold that regulated firms should be required to move toward a "peaked" structure of marginal rates. In practice, this is often taken to mean that peak-period rates should be increased to the level of long-run marginal cost.

The economists' prescriptions for peak-load pricing are extracted from "institution free" models.[2] What is "optimal" in an institution-free context is not necessarily "optimal" or even sensible in any particular institutional setting. Nevertheless, in arguing for peak-load pricing, economists have generally taken no notice of the institutional arrangements characteristic of rate regulation in the United States. The implied assumption is, apparently, that the institutional features of regulation have no crucial bearing on the feasibility or desirability of adopting a policy of peak-load pricing.

The recent literature on the theory of regulated monopoly is enough to call this assumption into question. For example, it has been shown for simple models of regulated monopoly that the optimal allowed rate of return typically exceeds the competitive rate of return, which runs counter to the conventional wisdom.[3] And the now famous (notorious?) "over-capitalization effect," first pointed out by Averch and Johnson (1), is some-what disquieting, as it suggests that the capacity constraint may not be binding at the peak-period output.

This paper questions the economic efficiency of requiring that regulated utilities adopt some form of peak-load pricing. It is not denied that conventional peak-load pricing models describe an efficient pattern of prices and factor inputs in the absence of institutional constraints. The question raised is, rather, whether imposition of the general policy prescriptions that emerge from these models would promote efficiency within the framework of rate of return regulation.

Pursuit of this question requires a model of regulated monopoly, which, in the present state of the literature, means the Averch and Johnson (A-J) model. The basic A-J model is extended in Section II to incorporate periodic shifts in the level of demand and price discrimination. Subsequent sections then take up various aspects of the optimality of peak-load pricing and, more generally, optimal regulation. Overcapitalization will scarcely be mentioned, and then only as is absolutely necessary.

II A MODEL OF REGULATED MONOPOLY

The regulated firm is assumed to be a monopolist in the product market and a price taker in factor markets, and assumed to face a "peaking" problem. In particular, it is assumed that the relevant period of time (a "year") can be divided into n subintervals of equal length,[4] which are indexed by i. Average revenue in period i is denoted $P_i = D^i(q_i)$, where q_i is output. It is understood that output cannot be stored and that the level of demand varies systematically over the course of the year. The technology available is represented by the production function $q_i = \phi(K_i, L_i)$, where L_i is the quantity of labor employed and K_i is the value of capital (that is, the price of "machines" times the number of machines employed). It is assumed that the value of capital employed cannot be varied during the year, so $K_i = K$, $i = 1, \ldots, n.$[5] Finally, the production function and demand functions are assumed to possess the usual properties.

Regulated utilities typically use two-part tariffs and/or declining block rates, and for this reason it is relevant to include the possibility of price discrimination in the model.[6] The complicated rate structures that occur in practice cannot be simply represented, but the central facts can be captured by dealing with price discrimination of "variable degree." The P_i's are marginal rates and the revenue derived from these rates is denoted

$$\bar{R}(q) = \sum_{i=1}^{n} P_i q_i,$$

where $q = (q_1, \ldots, q_n)$ is the firm's output vector. The total value to consumers of the firm's outputs is:

$$V(q) = \sum_{1}^{n} \int_{0}^{q_i} D^i(\hat{q}_i) d\hat{q}_i, \tag{1}$$

where the $\hat{q}_i$'s are dummy variables of integration, and consumers' surplus is

$$S(q) = V(q) - \bar{R}(q). \tag{2}$$

It is assumed that the firm is permitted to obtain, via block rates and fixed charges, a fraction $\lambda, 0 \leq \lambda \leq 1$, of consumers' surplus. The firm's total revenue is then:

$$R(q) \equiv \bar{R}(q) + \lambda S(q). \tag{3}$$

The regulatory agency is assumed to control the value of λ.

The regulatory agency is also assumed to set the allowed rate of return s, and, having specified s, to require that the inputs and outputs selected by the firm satisfy the regulatory constraint:[7]

$$R(q) - w \sum_{1}^{n} L_i - sK \leq 0. \tag{4}$$

The profit-maximization problem of the regulated firm is then

$$\max_{\left\{\substack{q_i, L_i, K \\ i=1,\dots,n}\right\}} [\text{II}] = R(q) - [rK + w\sum_1^n L_i],\tag{5}$$

subject to:

$$\mathscr{L}(q_i, K) - L_i \le 0, i = 1, \dots, n.\tag{6}$$

and Eq. (3), where $L = \mathscr{L}(q_i, K)$ is the labor requirements function (which is obtained by solving the production function), r is the rental rate, and w is the wage rate. Subscripts will be used to denote the derivatives of $\mathscr{L}$, for example: $\mathscr{L}_1(q_i, K) \equiv \dfrac{\partial \mathscr{L}}{\partial q_i}$.

The profit-maximizing solution could be characterized without further ado, but, since the discussion which follows focuses on prices and outputs, it is useful to put the problem in a different form. There is a set of output vectors which, because of the rate of return constraint, the regulated firm cannot produce at minimum cost.[8] This set is denoted by B. For any particular output vector $\hat{q}$ in B, maximization of profit obviously requires minimization of expenditures on capital and labor subject to the rate of return constraint and, of course, the technological constraints. Solution of this problem yields the "expense" function:

$$E(q,\lambda,s) = rK^*(q_i,\lambda,s) + w\sum_1^n L_i^*(q,\lambda,s), q \in B,\tag{7}$$

where $K^*(\cdot)$ and $L_i^*(\cdot)$, $i = 1, \dots, n$ are, respectively, the expense-minimizing values of capital and labor. Using this expression, the profit-maximization problem can be restated as:

$$\max_{q \in B} = R(q) - E(q,\lambda,s).\tag{8}$$

The first-order conditions for $q_i^*, i = 1, \dots, n$ to maximize profit are of the conventional form:

$$R_i'(q_i^*) - E_i(q^*;\lambda,s) = 0, \quad i = 1, \dots, n,\tag{9}$$

where $q^* = (q_i^*, \dots, q_n^*)$, $R_i'(q_i^*)$ is marginal revenue[9] and $E_i(\cdot) = \dfrac{\partial E}{\partial q_i}$ is marginal expense. It is shown in the Appendix that Eq. (9) reduces to

$$R_i'(q_i^*) - w\mathscr{L}_1(q_i^*K^*) = 0, \quad i = 1, \dots, n\tag{10}$$

where $w\mathscr{L}_1(\cdot)$ is marginal variable expense.

The model specified here has, as would be expected, properties analogous to those of the standard A-J model. First, the model involves overcapitalization:

Proposition 1. If $\mathscr{L}_i = \mathscr{L}(q_i, K)$, $i = 1, \ldots, n$ is strictly convex in K; $\phi(0, L_i) = \phi(K, 0) = 0$, $_i = 1, \ldots, n$; and $s > r$; then for each $q \in B$:

$K^*(q, \lambda, s) > \tilde{K}(q)$, where $\tilde{K}$ is the value of capital required to produce q at minimum cost; \hfill (a)

$L_i^*(q, \lambda, s) \leq \tilde{L}_i(q)$, $i = 1, \ldots, n$, where $\tilde{L}_i$, $i = 1, \ldots, n$ are the values of labor required to produce q at minimum cost. \hfill (b)

The profit-maximizing outputs of the model also exceed the profit-maximizing outputs for the corresponding unregulated monopoly model. Let $\rho_m(\lambda)$ be the rate of return of an unregulated monopoly that discriminates to degree λ and q_{mi}, $i = 1, \ldots, n$, the profit-maximizing outputs. Then:

Proposition 2. For $\rho_m(\lambda) > s > r$ and $0 \leq \lambda \leq 1$, if: (i) there are unique optimal monopoly outputs q_{mi}, $i = 1, \ldots, n$ and profit is positive if these outputs are produced at cost; and (ii) $\mathscr{L}_{22}(q_i, K) > 0, \mathscr{L}_{12}(q_i, K) < 0$, $i = 1, \ldots, n$; then $q_{mi} < q_i^*$, $i = 1, \ldots, n$.

Proofs of Propositions 1 and 2 appear in the Appendix.[10]

III INCENTIVES FOR PEAK-LOAD PRICING

The direct effects of regulation are captured in the model, as it is formulated here, in the expense function. Apart from the choice of factor inputs, and the implications of these choices for expenditures, the model of regulated monopoly "works" in the same way as the corresponding unregulated monopoly model. Now, in the face of periodic variations in the level of demand, an unregulated monopoly will, for the cost conditions usually assumed, be led to set a "peaked" pattern of prices. There is, then, a presumption that the profit-maximizing prices for the model of regulated monopoly will also fall into a "peaked" pattern. But existing utility rate schedules tend to be "flat."

These comments present the question of whether regulation is, in some not readily apparent way, connected with the fact that utilities do not practice peak-load pricing. This issue is of some interest in itself and, as will appear, has a bearing on the desirability of requiring that rate schedules be modified towards some form of peak-load pricing.

It is useful to begin with the fixed coefficient case, which figures so prominently in the literature on peak-load pricing.[11] In particular, assume that the production function is:

$$q_i = \min\left\{\frac{1}{\gamma}K, \frac{1}{\alpha}L_i\right\}, \quad i = 1, \ldots, n. \tag{11}$$

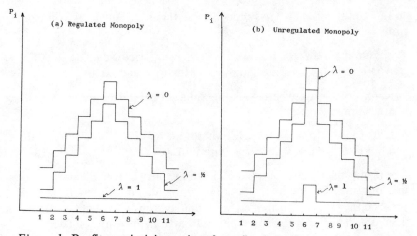

Figure 1. Profit maximizing prices for a fixed coefficient technology.

Suppose, further, that the year is divided into eleven periods and assume that:

$$P_i = A_i(a - bq_i), i = 1, \dots, n, \tag{12}$$

and that:

$$A_i = \begin{cases} i, i = 1, \dots, 6 \\ 12 - i, i = 7, \dots, 11. \end{cases} \tag{13}$$

Given these assumptions, the profit-maximizing prices are:

$$P_i^* = \left(\frac{1}{2 - \lambda}\right)\left[(1 - \lambda)aA_i + \omega\alpha\right], i = 1, \dots, 11. \tag{14}$$

A derivation of these expressions is presented in the Appendix.

The left-hand side of Figure 1 shows the values of the profit-maximizing prices for three values of λ. The right side of the figure presents, for the sake of comparison, the profit-maximizing prices for the corresponding unregulated monopoly model.

The rates shown in Figure 1 have two features which appeared in earlier analyses of peak-load pricing subject to rate of return constraint. First, for any given degree of price discrimination, the two models yield the same price for off-peak periods. Second, the profit-maximizing peak period price for regulated monopoly is less than that for unregulated monopoly. Taking these two points together, it might be said that regulation leads to a "flatter" rate structure. However, aside from its vagueness, this statement rests on the equality of off-peak rates in the two models, which is an artifact of the assumption of a fixed coefficient technology. Proposition 1 implies that, in general, regulation leads to lower rates in both peak and off-peak periods.

The novel and, for present purposes, most important features of Figure 1 lie in the changes produced by increases in the degree of price discrimination. In both the regulated and the unregulated models, an increase in λ reduces both peak and off-peak rates, but the effect on the peak price is more pronounced for regulated monopoly. Given the fixed coefficient technology, the perfectly discriminating unregulated monopoly would set a single price for all off-peak periods, but a higher price, equal to long-run marginal cost, in the peak period. Under these conditions, however, the regulated monopoly model gives the same price for both peak and off-peak periods; that is, a perfectly flat rate schedule.

While this feature of the regulated monopoly model does not lend itself to a simple, intuitive explanation, it can to some extent be understood as a consequence of the rate of return constraint. Still assuming a fixed coefficient technology, in the unregulated case peak-period output determines capacity. In particular, if q_p is peak-period output, the capital required is $K = \gamma q_p$. This is *not* the case for the regulated monopoly model. It follows directly from results presented in the Appendix that the expense-minimizing quantities of labor are $L_i^* = \alpha q_i$, $i = 1, \ldots, n$. Then the smallest value of capital which can be employed while satisfying the constraint, denoted K^*, is described by:

$$R(q) - \left[sK^* + w\sum_1^n \alpha q_i \right] = 0, \quad q \in B; \tag{15}$$

which implies:

$$K^* = \frac{1}{\rho}\left[R(q) - w\sum_1^n \alpha q_i \right] 0, \quad q \in B. \tag{16}$$

The argument which led to Eq. (15) implies that K^* *exceeds* the value of capital required to produce the peak-period output (cf. Appendix, Fig. 4). That is, the capacity constraint is *not* binding at the peak-period output in the regulated monopoly model. Furthermore, as Eq. (16) indicates, the capital employed by the regulated monopoly depends directly on total revenue. Thus, an expansion of output in any period — peak or off-peak — requires that capital expenditures change at the rate $r/s(R_i' - w\alpha)$ even though additional capital is not technologically required to produce the additional output. In this sense, there is nothing special about the peak period in the model of regulated monopoly. Profit maximization requires balancing marginal revenue for each period against marginal expenditures on labor and capital. Given a fixed coefficient technology and perfect price discrimination, this happens to lead to a flat rate schedule.

In the general case, the profit-maximizing outputs and, given the demand functions, the profit-maximizing prices are described by the first-order conditions, Eq. (10). For $\lambda = 1$ these become:

$$P_i^* = w\,\mathscr{L}_1(q_1^*, K^*), \quad i = 1, \ldots, n. \tag{17}$$

Completely fortuitous cases aside, then, it is clear that profit maximization leads to a completely flat rate structure only if $\lambda = 1$ and short-run marginal expense is constant. The latter condition is satisfied for a fixed coefficient technology and can also be satisfied if capital and labor are substitutes only over a limited range.

The rate schedules used by electric and gas utilities in the United States are not, of course, perfectly discriminatory, but they can be described as very thoroughly discriminatory.[12] It is also generally held that there is little or no possibility of short-run substitution of variable inputs for capital in the utility industries. If so, the profit-maximizing rate structure, computed without regard to the costs of administering a system of peak/off-peak differentials, might be quite "flat." Consideration of administrative costs would, of course, lead to an even "flatter" rate schedule. The least that can be claimed on the basis of this discussion is that the model of regulated monopoly permits, without unduly strained interpretations, a "flat" rate schedule. In contrast, given the usual assumptions on cost and demand, a "flat" rate structure is completely anomalous when viewed in terms of a model of unregulated monopoly.

IV THE OPTIMALITY OF PEAK-LOAD PRICING

The logic of conventional peak-load pricing models turns on the distinction between short and long-run costs and the assumption that, in some sense, peak output determines capacity. Economic efficiency then requires that peak users pay long-run marginal costs, while off-peak users pay only short-run marginal costs which, for the cost structures usually assumed, yields a "peaked" pattern of rates.[13] As existing rate schedules tend to be flat, argument along this line leads to the suggestion that regulated firms be required to adopt some form of peak-load pricing. But what if the firm holds more capital than is required to produce the peak-period output or if output in the peak period is less than that required by marginal cost pricing? It would seem, then, that price in peak periods (and perhaps off-peak periods as well) should be decreased rather than increased. These possibilities at least raise the question of whether it is economically efficient to impose peak-load pricing policies on regulated utilities.

Concrete proposals for peak-load pricing assume a variety of different forms. In some cases only seasonal rate differentials are considered, while the more ambitious proposals are for time-of-day rates. None of the possibilities can be represented exactly in a simple model, but their spirit can be captured by introducing a zero*th* period and assuming that price in this period, denoted P_0, is directly set by the regulatory agency. It is relevant to regard P_0 as price in the peak period, although the analysis does not assume that peak demand occurs in period zero. The question asked is this: does economic efficiency require setting P_0 at a higher level than the firm would adopt if it could set price in all periods, subject to the rate of return constraint?

The criterion typically used to answer questions of this sort is, for the model considered here:

$$W = (1 - \lambda)S(q) + \Pi(q), \tag{18}$$

where $\Pi(q) \equiv R(q) - E(q, \lambda, s, P_0)$ is the firm's profit. It should be noted that Eq. (18) is not a distributional standard but is, instead, a partial equilibrium form of the Pareto efficiency criterion. In particular, at an "optimum," consumers' surplus retained by consumers cannot be increased without reducing profit and, conversely, profit cannot be increased without reducing consumers' surplus retained by consumers.

The agency is assumed to control s and λ as well as P_0 but, for the moment, attention is limited to changes in P_0 for given values of s and λ. The question posed above requires a comparison of the value of P_0 that maximizes W with the value of P_0 that maximizes profit. This can be accomplished by evaluating dW/dP_0 at the profit-maximizing vector of prices. If, at these prices, $dW/dP_0 > 0$, then an increase in P_0 is warranted. But, if $dW/dP_0 \leq 0$ at the profit-maximizing prices, then P_0 should be left at the level selected by the firm or reduced.

The profit-maximizing outputs for periods $i = 1, \ldots, n$ are described by Eq. (10). Using these relationships, dW/dP_0 simplifies to:

$$\frac{dW}{dP_0} = (1 - \lambda)\left[\sum_1^n S_i' \frac{dq_i^*}{dP_0} + S_0' \frac{dq_0}{dP_0}\right] + (R_0' - E_0)\frac{dq_0}{dP_0}, \tag{19}$$

where $S_i' = \dfrac{\partial S(q)}{\partial q_i}$, $i = 0, \ldots, n$. Let P_0^* be the profit-maximizing price in period 0 and denote the vector of profit-maximizing prices by P^*. At P_0^*, $R_0' - E_0' = 0$, so:

$$\left(\frac{dW}{dP_0}\right)_{P*} = (1 - \lambda)\left[\sum_1^n S_i' \frac{dq_i^*}{dP_0} + S_0' \frac{dq_0}{dP_0}\right]. \tag{20}$$

Since $S_i' > 0$ and $dq_0/dP_0 < 0$, the sign of $\left(\dfrac{dW}{dP_0}\right)_{P*}$ turns on the signs of the rates of change of off-peak outputs with respect to the peak-period price.

It is shown in the Appendix that the profit-maximizing outputs in the fixed coefficient case are:

$$q_i^* = \frac{a A_i - W \alpha}{b A_i (2 - \lambda)}, \quad i = 1, \ldots, n. \tag{21}$$

Then, for this case, $dq_i^*/dP_0 = \dot{0}, i = 1, \ldots, n$, and:

$$\left(\frac{dW}{dP_0}\right)_{P*} = (1 - \lambda) S_0' \frac{dq_0}{dP_0}. \tag{22}$$

Since $dq_0/dP_0 < 0$, Eq. (22) implies that $(dW/dP_0)_{P*} < 0$ for $0 \leq \lambda < 1$, in the fixed coefficient case. Thus, the appropriate policy would not be to force an increase in the peak-period price but, on the contrary, to force a decrease.

Extension of this analysis to a general production function requires no work for the case of perfect price discrimination. If $\lambda = 1$, maximization of profit and maximization of W are equivalent, so the profit-maximizing peak-period price is also the welfare-maximizing price. Consequently, under perfect price discrimination, efficiency does not require a change in the peak-period price from its profit-maximizing level even if the rate schedule is perfectly "flat."

For the case in which price discrimination is less than perfect, the signs of the changes in the off-peak outputs with respect to a change in the peak-period price must be determined to extract a conclusion from Eq. (20). The Appendix provides a proof of the following:

Proposition 3. If the conditions of Proposition 2 are satisfied, then
$$dq_i^*/dP_0 < 0, i = 1, \ldots, n, \quad \text{for } P_0 > P_0^*.$$
That is, an increase in the peak-period price above the profit-maximizing level P_0^* leads to a reduction in output in the off-peak periods. Now, increasing P_0 about P_0^* clearly reduces profit and Proposition 3 implies that such an increase would also reduce consumers' surplus retained by consumers. Consequently, even under imperfect price discrimination, it is inefficient to force the peak-period price above its profit-maximizing level. On the contrary, the appropriate policy is to force a decrease.

Figure 2 provides a way of pointing to the factors that lie behind this conclusion. Marginal revenue is positive at P_0^*, so an increase in P_0 from this level leads to a decrease in revenue. In fact both revenue and marginal profit decrease and, as a consequence, the expense-minimizing value of capital for any vector of off-peak outputs decreases. At given off-peak outputs, then, the capital-labor ratio is lower and hence the marginal productivity of labor is lower. Forcing an increase in P_0 from P_0^* then causes the marginal expense curve in each period, at given outputs in the other periods, to shift upward, as shown in Figure 2. The usual logic of profit maximization then leads to a decrease in the profit-maximizing output. This is clearly the case whether marginal expense is increasing, as shown in Figure 2, or decreasing.

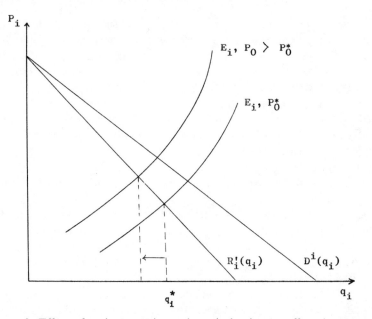

Figure 2. Effect of an increase in peak period price on off peak outputs.

V OPTIMAL VALUES OF THE INSTRUMENTS

The results of this discussion do not deny that conventional peak-load pricing models describe the efficient pattern of prices and inputs in the absence of institutional constraints. They do, however, indicate that policies extracted from these models are not necessarily efficient—or even an improvement—when applied to firms subject to rate of return regulation.

The general features of the model considered here flow from two broad assumptions. First, and this can hardly be challenged, it is assumed that regulatory agencies have only specific and fairly well-defined powers. Second, while the legal powers of the agencies may be sufficient to enforce cost minimization and marginal cost pricing, it is assumed that, in practice, regulatory agencies do not have the information they need to do so.[14] If these assumptions are granted, the policy problem is to describe the optimal use of the powers actually available to the regulatory agency.

In the model considered here, the agency is assumed to control s, λ, and P_0. Formally, then, the policy problem is:

$$\max_{\{s, \lambda, P\}} [W] = (1 - \lambda)S[q^*(s, \lambda, P_0)] + \Pi[q^*(s, \lambda, P_0)]. \qquad (23)$$

If perfect price discrimination is possible, the optimal solution to this problem is obvious: the agency should "require" perfect price discrimination and set the allowed rate of return high enough so that the rate of return constraint is not binding. The resulting pattern of prices and inputs would be that described by conventional marginal cost-pricing models, and any distributional issues could be "tidied up" with lump sum taxes and transfers.

Perfect price discrimination, of course, is presumably not a practical possibility and, even if it were, perfect price discrimination would probably be precluded by political constraints. Political and legal constraints may well also fix upper and/or lower limits on the allowed rate of return. Given that such constraints exist, there is a problem of describing the values of λ and s that maximize "welfare" (that is, W).

An analysis of this problem, reported in the appendix, leads to the following conclusions:

Proposition 4. If the conditions of Proposition 2 are satisfied and $r < s < \rho_m(\lambda)$, then the value λ^* that maximizes W is less than unity.

Proposition 5. If the conditions of Proposition 2 are satisfied and $0 \leqq \lambda < 1$, then $s^* < \rho_m(\lambda)$, where s^* is the value of the allowed rate of return that maximizes W.

The first of these propositions, in effect, states that if s is "sufficiently low," then perfect price discrimination is not optimal. Proposition 5 states that the optimal allowed rate of return is less than the monopoly rate of return. While neither of these propositions is surprising, both point to qualifications on the policy prescriptions that emerge from conventional models.

Coase (7) provides a survey of suggestions made by himself and others for the use of multipart tariffs to deal with some of the problems of efficiency presented by increasing returns industries. The analysis that leads to this prescription turns on two propositions: (1) that the fixed portions of a multipart tariff do not affect consumption decisions and hence are nondistortional; (2) a perfectly discriminatory monopoly will be led to set prices equal to marginal cost. Proposition 4 challenges neither of these points, but indicates that if there are limits on the allowed rate of return, something less than perfect price discrimination is efficient. That is, taking rate of return regulation and limitations on the allowed rate of return as given, there is a limit on the extent to which price discrimination promotes efficiency.

It is usually held that regulated firms should, taking the proper account of risk, be allowed to earn the competitive rate of return, or perhaps a bit more as an incentive for efficiency. Proposition 5 does not speak directly to this position. However, it has been shown for the single period case that the optimal allowed rate of return can exceed the competitive rate of return by a large margin [Klevorick (10)]; and, furthermore, the optimal allowed rate of return may exceed the competitive rate of return even if average cost is decreasing; [Bailey (3), McNicol (12)]. If these results also hold for the multiperiod case, and it seems virtually certain that they do, the optimal allowed rate of return will typically exceed the competitive rate of return.

The preceding section provides another, more dramatic example of the difference between optimal policies in a model of regulated monopoly and the policies suggested by conventional analyses. For the conditions usually assumed, conventional marginal cost-pricing models imply that a "peaked" pattern of prices is required for efficiency, which provides the theoretical rationale for suggestions that regulated firms be required to adopt some form of peak-load pricing. In contrast, the theory of regulated monopoly implies that it is inefficient to force an increase in the peak-period price beyond the level that maximizes profit. On the contrary, if price discrimination is less than profit, consideration of efficiency argues for a reduction in the peak-period price.

VI CONCLUDING COMMENTS

The upshot of this discussion is that "institutions matter" in the formal analysis of regulatory policy. While, considered in isolation, this statement is perhaps a platitude, it takes on force in terms of the results that have been obtained. Existing "flat" rate schedules probably are inefficient in the sense that, in the absence of institutional constraints, better rate schedules could be devised. However, imposition of the remedies suggested by conventional marginal peak-load pricing models on regulated firms may not be an improvement. On the contrary, considerations of economic efficiency might argue for a reduction rather than an increase in peak-period rates.

This analysis can at least be jabbed with its own petard. Why assume that the regulatory agency controls only the degree of price discrimination? Why not, instead, assume that the agency exercises detailed control over what markets can be distinguished and rate structures? And why assume that the agency directly sets only the peak-period price? It would perhaps be possible to find satisfactory answers to such questions in terms of existing institutional arrangements; but the answers would, then, call those arrangements into question. That is appropriate. The burden of this discussion is that what can be achieved by regulation and the optimal policies for regulation depend crucially on the instruments actually available to regulatory agencies.

APPENDIX

This Appendix presents in this order: a proof of Proposition 1; a derivation of Eq. (10) and a proof of Proposition 2; a development of the fixed coefficient case; a proof of Proposition 3; and proofs of Propositions 4 and 5. Unless otherwise indicated, the notation and assumptions used in the text are maintained.

Proof of Proposition 1

Proof of Proposition 1 is a matter of developing a theory of cost and production subject to rate of return constraint.[15] This task involves an examination of the expenditure associated with different input combinations and a comparison of the costs incurred by regulated and unregulated monopoly in producing given outputs. For the sake of clarity, then, the expenditures required to purchase arbitrary input combinations must be distinguished from the minimized value of expenditures in the two models.

Expenditures for a given input combination are denoted by $\mathscr{E}$. By definition:

$$\mathscr{E} = rK + w \sum_{1}^{n} L_i; \tag{24}$$

and, if excess labor is not employed:

$$\mathscr{E} = rK + w \sum_{1}^{n} w\mathscr{L}(q_i, K). \tag{25}$$

The minimized value of $\mathscr{E}$ in the absence of a rate of return constraint will be referred to as "cost" and denoted C. The minimized value of expenditures in the presence of the rate of return constraint will be called "expense" and denoted by E.

The cost-minimization problem for the multiperiod case presented in the text can be stated as:

$$\min_{\{K\}} [\mathscr{E}] = rK + w \sum_{1}^{n} \mathscr{L}(q_i, K). \tag{26}$$

The cost-minimizing value of capital, denoted $\tilde{K}$, is described by:

$$\frac{\partial \mathscr{E}}{\partial \tilde{K}} = r + w \sum_{1}^{n} \mathscr{L}_2(q_i, \tilde{K}) = 0, \tag{27}$$

and second-order conditions. The corresponding cost-minimizing values of labor are $\tilde{L}_i = \mathscr{L}(q_i, K), i = 1, \ldots, n$; and the cost function is:

$$C = C(q) = r\tilde{K}(q) + w \sum_{1}^{n} \mathscr{L}[q, \tilde{K}(q)]. \tag{28}$$

Marginal cost is denoted $C_i' \equiv \partial C/\partial q_i, i = 1, \ldots, n$.

Profit maximization obviously requires that given outputs be produced at cost *if it is feasible to do so*. But if the rate of return ρ obtained by producing q at cost exceeds the allowed rate of return s, the rate of return constraint precludes producing q *at cost*. Define:

$$B = \{q \mid s < \rho \equiv [R(q) - w\,\mathscr{L}(q_i, \tilde{K})]/\tilde{K}\}. \tag{29}$$

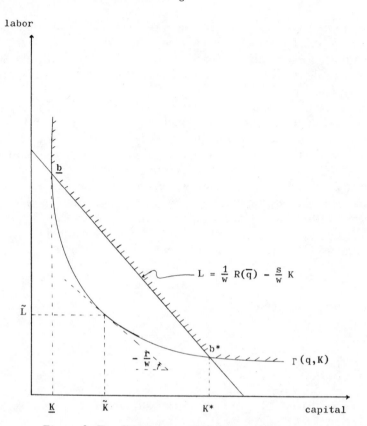

Figure 3. Feasible input combinations for $\bar{q} \in B$.

Output vectors in B, which are of principal relevance to the theory of regulated monopoly, cannot be produced at cost.

Figure 3 describes the feasible combinations of capital and labor for an output vector $\bar{q} \in B$. The total quantity of labor required to produce $\bar{q}$ is $L \equiv \sum_{1}^{n} \mathscr{L}(q_i, K)$. Assuming that this amount of labor is distributed among periods in the required manner, the technological constraint can be written as:

$$L \geq \Gamma(q, K) \equiv \sum_{1}^{n} \mathscr{L}(q_i, K). \tag{30}$$

$\Gamma(q, K)$ will be referred to as the "aggregate labor requirements function." The combinations of labor and capital which satisfy the rate of return constraint (4) are described by:

$$L \geq (1/w)R(q) - (s/w)K. \tag{31}$$

The problem is to compute the values of labor and capital that minimize expenditure subject to the constraints (30) and (31). The Kuhn-Tucker conditions are typically used in the literature to characterize the solution to this problem. However, the argument which follows is perhaps both simpler and more informative.

Only boundary points of the feasible set need be considered, as expenditure is obviously not minimized at any interior point. It is assumed that $\bar{q} \in B$, so the combination $[\tilde{K}, \tilde{L}]$ that minimizes cost is infeasible. However, assuming that $\Gamma(q,K)$ is strictly convex in K,[16] feasible movements along the "isoquant" toward K reduce expenditure. In particular, at any value of capital less than $\underline{K}$, expenditure is reduced by increasing K; and at any value of capital greater than K^*, expenditure is reduced by reducing K. Therefore, the values of labor and capital that minimize expenditure subject to the constraint must lie on the segment of the boundary of the feasible set labeled $\underline{b}b^*$ in Figure 3. Along this segment of the boundary:

$$R(q) - [sK + wL] = 0 ; \tag{32}$$

which, on rearrangement, gives:

$$\mathscr{E} = R(q) - (s - \acute{r})K . \tag{33}$$

Then, if $s > r$, along this segment of the boundary $\dfrac{\partial \mathscr{E}}{\partial K} = -(s - r) < 0$.

It follows that $[K^*, L^*]$ minimizes expenditure subject to the constraints. This completes the proof of Proposition 1.

Loosely speaking, the preceding argument implies that the rate of return constraint is itself an implicit description of the expense-minimizing derived demand for capital. To make this point more precisely, define:

$$\psi = R(q) - [sK + w\Gamma(q,K)], \quad q \in B. \tag{34}$$

The rate of return constraint holds with strict equality at the expense-minimizing input combination and labor is not wasted. Hence, $\psi(q,K^*) = 0$. It is also clear from Figure 3 that $\psi(q,\underline{K}) = 0$. That is, for given q, there are two values of capital which solve $\psi = 0$. But, by Proposition 1, it is the larger of these which minimizes expenditure subject to the rate of return constraint.

It is possible to solve $\psi = 0$ for the expense-minimizing derived demand for capital $K^* = K^*(q,\lambda,s)$ and $K^*(\cdot)$ is continuous and has continuous first derivatives, if $\dfrac{\partial \Psi}{\partial K} = -(s + w\Gamma_2) \neq 0$. The first-order condition for cost minimization (27) requires that $r + w\Gamma_2(q,\tilde{K}) = 0$. By Proposition 1, $K^* > \tilde{K}$. Now, $\mathscr{L}_2 < 0$[17] and is assumed to increase with K, which implies that $\Gamma_2 < 0$ and increases with K. Therefore:

$$r + w\Gamma_2(q, K^*) > 0, \quad q \in B; \tag{35}$$

and, since $s > r$:

$$s + w\Gamma_2(q, K^*) > 0, \quad q \in B. \tag{36}$$

Hence, the required condition is satisfied. However, the condition fails at limit points of B if $s = r$.

The upshot of this discussion is that $\psi(q, K^*) = 0$ and that expense is minimized by the larger of the two values of K that solve $\psi = 0$, providing a complete description of the expense-minimizing value of capital. Eq. (34) can then be used to establish the comparative statics properties of the expense-minimizing derived demands for capital and labor.[18]

The expense function is:

$$\begin{aligned} E = E[q, \lambda, s] &= rK^*[q, \lambda, s] \\ &+ w \sum_{i=1}^{n} \mathscr{L}[q_i, K^*(q, \lambda, s)], \quad q \in B. \end{aligned} \tag{37}$$

When $E(\cdot)$ or $K^*(\cdot)$ are used in what follows, it is understood that they are evaluated at an output vector in B and that s exceeds r.

Derivation of Eq. (10) and Proof of Proposition 2

It is convenient to derive Eq. (10) before presenting a proof of Proposition 2. Note, first, that:

$$E_i = [r + w\Gamma_2(q, K^*)]\frac{\partial K^*}{\partial q_i} + w\mathscr{L}_1(q_i, K^*). \tag{38}$$

Eq. (34) for $\psi = 0$ can be differentiated to give:

$$\frac{\partial K^*}{\partial q_i} = \frac{R_i'(q_i) - w\mathscr{L}_1(q_i, K^*)}{s + w\Gamma_2(q_i, K^*)}. \tag{39}$$

Substitution of Eq. (39) into Eq. (38) yields on simplification:

$$E_i = \theta R_i'(q_i) + (1 - \theta)w\mathscr{L}_{q_1}(q_i, K^*). \tag{40}$$

where:

$$\theta \equiv \frac{r + w\Gamma_2(q_i, K^*)}{s + w\Gamma_2(q_i, K^*)}. \tag{41}$$

Using this expression to eliminate E_i in the first-order conditions (9) gives:

$$(1 - \theta)[R_i'(q_i^*) - w\mathscr{L}_1(q_i, K^*)] = 0, \quad i = 1, \ldots, n. \tag{42}$$

It is clear from Eq. (35) and Eq. (36) that $0 < \theta < 1$, so Eq. (42) can be divided by $1 - \theta \neq 0$ to give Eq. (10).

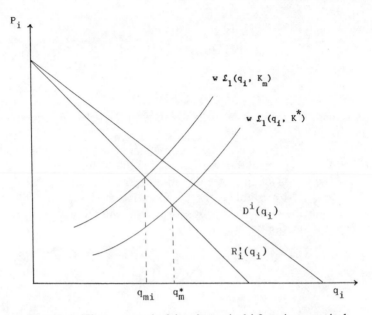

Figure 4. The output decision in period i for given capital.

Proof of Proposition 2 requires a comparison of the profit-maximizing outputs for the regulated monopoly model with those of the corresponding unregulated monopoly model. The profit-maximization problem for the unregulated model is:

$$\max_{\{q\}} \ [\Pi] = R(q) - \left[rK(q) + w\sum_{1}^{n}\mathscr{L}(q_i, K) \right];$$

(43)

and the first-order conditions for q_{mi}, $i = 1, \dots, n$ to maximize profit are:

$$R'_i(q_{mi}) - \left[(r + w\sum_{1}^{n}\mathscr{L}_2)\frac{\partial \tilde{K}}{\partial q_{mi}} + w\mathscr{L}_1 \right] = 0, \quad i = 1, \dots, n.$$

(44)

In view of the first-order conditions for cost minimization, Eq. (44) reduces to:

$$R'_i(q_{mi}) - w\mathscr{L}_1(q_{mi}, K_m) = 0, \quad i = 1, \dots, n.$$

(45)

where K_m is the cost-minimizing value of capital for the output vector $q_m \equiv (q_{m1}, \dots, q_{mn})$.[19]

Figure 4 shows graphs of $w\mathscr{L}_1(q_i, K)$ for K and K*. Whether $w\mathscr{L}_1(\cdot)$ is increasing in q_i, as is assumed in Figure 4, or decreasing in q_i, it is clear from Eq. (10) and Eq. (45) that $q_i^* > q_{mi}$ if an increase in K shifts the graph of $w\mathscr{L}_1(\cdot)$ to the right. Proof of Proposition 4 then requires: (1) identification of the conditions under which an increase in K shifts the graph of $w\mathscr{L}_1(\cdot)$ to the right; and (2) demonstration that $K^* > K_m$.

Assume that $q^* \in B$ and note that[20] $w \mathscr{L}_1(q_i, K) = [\phi_{L_i}(K, L_i)]^{-1}$, where $\phi_{L_i} \equiv \dfrac{\partial \phi(K, L_i)}{\partial L_i}$. Assume further that $K^* > K_m$. Then $w \mathscr{L}_1(q_i, K^*)$ $< w \mathscr{L}_1(q_i, K_m)$ if and only if:

$$\mathscr{L}_{12}(q_i, K) = -\frac{1}{\phi_L^2}\left[\frac{\partial \phi_L}{\partial K}\right]_{q_i} < 0. \tag{46}$$

The crucial condition, then, is that the marginal productivity of labor increases with increases in capital along an isoquant. It is assumed in what follows that $\mathscr{L}_{12} < 0$.

Given this assumption, the issue comes down to whether K^* exceeds K_m. Differentiate Eq. (34) for $\psi = 0$ and solve to obtain:

$$\frac{dK^*}{ds} = \left[\frac{R_i' - w \mathscr{L}_1}{s + w\Gamma_2(q, K^*)}\right]\frac{dq^*}{ds} - \left[\frac{K^*}{s + w\Gamma_2(q, K^*)}\right]. \tag{47}$$

Since $R_i'(q_i^*) - w \mathscr{L}_i(q_i^*, K^*) = 0$, and $s + w\Gamma_2 > 0$, Eq. (47) implies $\dfrac{dK^*}{ds} < 0$. As s is assumed to be less than the monopoly rate of return, it follows that $q_i^* > q_{mi}$, $i = 1, \ldots, n$.

A verification of the assumption that $q^* \in B$ can be constructed along the following lines. Note that any limit point $\bar{q}$ of B is produced at cost and consider:

$$d\Pi = \sum_1^n \{R_i'(\bar{q}_i) - C_i'(\bar{q})\} d\bar{q}_i. \tag{48}$$

The monopoly output vector q_m is assumed to be unique and an interior point of B. Therefore, $d\Pi$ is not identically zero and there is at least one $\bar{q}_k > q_{mk}$. It is feasible to choose $d\bar{q}_i = 0$, $i \neq k$ and:[21]

$$d\bar{q}_k = \left[\frac{R_k'(\bar{q}_k) - C_k'(\bar{q})}{s + w\Gamma_2(\bar{q}, K)}\right]dK. \tag{49}$$

Since $\bar{q}_k > q_{mk}$ and q_m is assumed to be unique, $R_k'(\bar{q}_k) - C_k'(\bar{q}) < 0$. Then profit can be increased by choosing $dK > 0$ and $d\bar{q}_k < 0$. Therefore, if $s > r$, and q^* is a unique maximum to the regulated monopoly problem, then $q^* \in B$.

The Fixed Coefficient Case

Figure 5 shows the set of feasible input combinations assuming a fixed coefficient technology; see Eq. (11). The *cost*-minimizing value of capital is $\tilde{K} = \gamma q_p$, where q_p is the largest of $\bar{q}_1, \ldots, \bar{q}_n$. The *cost*-minimizing values of labor are $\tilde{L}_i = \alpha \bar{q}_i$, $i = 1, \ldots, n$, so, given cost minimization, the total

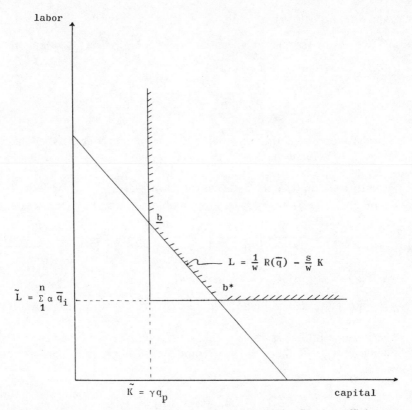

Figure 5. Feasible input combination for $\bar{q} \in B$ in the fixed coefficient case.

amount of labor employed is $\tilde{L} = \alpha \sum\limits_{i=1}^{n} \bar{q}_i$. From this point, the argument proceeds as in the proof of Proposition 1. The expense-minimizing value of capital is K^* and the expense-minimizing values of labor are $L_i^* = \alpha\bar{q}_i$, $i = 1,\ldots,n$.

Inserting the expense-minimizing values of labor in (34), and solving for $\psi = 0$, the expense-minimizing value of capital is:

$$K^* = \frac{1}{s}\left[R(q) - \alpha w \sum_{i=1}^{n} q_i \right]. \tag{50}$$

Note that $K^* > \gamma q_p$ (cf. Figure 5). Substituting Eq. (50) in the definition of expenditure and simplifying:

$$E = \frac{r}{s}R(q) + (1 - r/s)\alpha w \sum_{1}^{n} q_i. \tag{51}$$

Using this expression for cost, the first-order conditions (9) simplify to:

$$R_i'(q_i^*) - w\alpha = 0, \quad i = 1, \ldots, n. \tag{52}$$

Note that $R_i' = \lambda S_i' + \bar{R}_i'$, $i = 1, \ldots, n$, and that $S_i' = P_i - \bar{R}_i'$, where $\bar{R}_i'$ is marginal revenue as conventionally defined. Given the average revenue functions assumed in the text, Eq. (52) can be solved for:

$$q_i^* = \frac{aA_i - w\alpha}{bA_i(2 - \lambda)}, \quad i = 1, \ldots, n. \tag{53}$$

Substitution of these values in the average revenue functions then yields the profit-maximizing prices; see Eq. (14).

The "shifting peak" case identified by Houthakker (8) and Steiner (19) cannot occur in the regulated model because expense minimization leads to excess capacity. A shifting peak is, however, a possibility in the unregulated model. It was assumed in constructing Figure 1 that the levels of demand, and the values of r and w, are such that there is a firm peak in period 6. Given this assumption, the profit maximization problem is:

$$\max_{\{q\}} [\Pi] = R(q) - \left[r\gamma q_6 + w\alpha \sum_{i \neq 6} q_i \right]; \tag{54}$$

and the first-order conditions are:

$$R_6'(q_6^*) - [r\gamma + w\alpha] = 0, \text{ and} \tag{55}$$

$$R_i'(q_i^*) - w\alpha = 0, \quad i \neq 6. \tag{56}$$

Solution of Eqs. (55) and (56) for the assumed average revenue functions gives the prices for the regulated case shown in Figure 1.

Proof of Proposition 3

It is assumed for the purpose of this section that the agency sets the peak-period price P_0. The expense-minimizing value of capital and the profit-maximizing outputs for periods $1, \ldots, n$ then depend on P_0 as well as on s. On this understanding, Eq. (10) can be differentiated to give, on rearrangement:

$$\frac{dq_i^*}{dP_0} = \left[\frac{w\mathscr{L}_{12}}{R_i' - w\mathscr{L}_{11}} \right] \frac{dK^*}{dP_0}, \quad i = 1, \ldots, n. \tag{57}$$

Adding the assumption that $\mathscr{L}_{11} > 0$, the bracketed term in this expression is positive.[22] Differentiate Eq. (34) for $\psi = 0$ with respect to P_0 to obtain:

$$(R_0' - w\mathscr{L}_1)\frac{dq_0}{dP_0} + \sum_1^n (R_i' - w\mathscr{L}_1)\frac{dq_i^*}{dP_0} - (s + w\Gamma_2)\frac{dK^*}{dP_0} = 0. \tag{58}$$

The first-order conditions (10) imply that the second term in this expression is zero; therefore:

$$\frac{dK^*}{dP_0} = \left[\frac{R'_0 - w\mathscr{L}_1}{s + w\Gamma_2}\right]\frac{dq_0}{dP_0}. \tag{59}$$

Denote the profit-maximizing peak-period price by P_0^*. Assuming that the profit-maximization problem (for $i = 0, i, \ldots, n$) has a unique solution:

$$R'_0(q_0) - w\mathscr{L}_1[q_0, K^*(q, \lambda, s, P_0)] > 0, P_0 > P_0^*. \tag{60}$$

It follows that $dK^*/dP_0 < 0$ for $P_0 > P_0^*$ and then, from Eq. (57), that $dq_i^*/dP_0 < 0$, $i = 1, \ldots, n$ for $P_0 > P_0^*$.[23] This completes the proof of Proposition 3.

It was stated in the text that increasing the peak-period price from P_0^* causes the marginal expense curve for each period to shift upward. This assertion can be demonstrated as follows. Let $q \in B$ be a vector of off-peak outputs and partially differentiate Eq. (40) with respect to P_0 to obtain:

$$\left(\frac{\partial E_i}{\partial P_0}\right)_q = (1 - \theta)w\mathscr{L}_{12}\left(\frac{\partial K^*}{\partial P_0}\right)_q - w\mathscr{L}_1\left(\frac{\partial \theta}{\partial P_0}\right)_q. \tag{61}$$

Using Eq. (34) for $\psi = 0$:

$$\left(\frac{\partial K}{\partial P_0}\right)_q = \left[\frac{R'_0 - w\mathscr{L}_1}{s + w\Gamma_2}\right]\frac{dq_0}{dP_0}; \tag{62}$$

and, by the argument used above, $(\partial K/\partial P_0)_q < 0$ for $P_0 > P_0^*$. Differentiation of Eq. (41) yields, on rearrangement:

$$\left(\frac{\partial \theta}{\partial P_0}\right)_q = (1 - \theta)\left(\frac{w\mathscr{L}_2}{s + w\Gamma_2}\right)\left(\frac{\partial K^*}{\partial P_0}\right)_q; \tag{63}$$

which implies that $(\partial\theta/\partial P_0)_q < 0$ for $P_0 > P_0^*$. It then follows from Eq. (61) that $(\partial E/\partial P_0)_q > 0$ for $P_0 > P_0^*$.

Proofs of Propositions 4 and 5

It is convenient to begin by establishing the signs of $\partial q_i^*/\partial\lambda$ and $\partial q_i^*/\partial s$, $i = 1, \ldots, n$. Differentiate Eq. (10) to obtain:

$$\frac{\partial q_i^*}{\partial\lambda} = -\frac{1}{H_i}\left(S'_i - w\mathscr{L}_{12}\frac{dK^*}{d\lambda}\right), \quad i = 1, \ldots, n; \tag{64}$$

$$\frac{\partial q_i^*}{\partial s} = \frac{1}{H_i}\left(w\mathscr{L}_{12}\frac{dK^*}{ds}\right), \quad i = 1, \ldots, n; \tag{65}$$

where $H_i \equiv R''_i - w\mathscr{L}_{11} < 0$, $i = 1, \ldots, n$. It was shown above that $dK^*/ds < 0$ and a similar computation yields $dK^*/d\lambda > 0$. Eqs. (64) and (65), respectively, then imply $\partial q_i^*/\partial\lambda > 0$ and $\partial q_i^*/\partial s < 0$, $i = 1, \ldots, n$.

The first-order condition for $\lambda^*, 0 \le \lambda^* \le 1$ to maximize W reduces to:

$$\frac{\partial W}{\partial \lambda^*} = (1 - \lambda^*) \sum_1^n s_i' \frac{\partial q_i^*}{\partial \lambda^*} - \left(\frac{\partial E}{\partial \lambda^*}\right)_q , \rho_m > s > r. \qquad (66)$$

Note that:

$$\left(\frac{\partial E}{\partial \lambda}\right)_q = (r + w\Gamma_2)\frac{\partial K^*}{\partial \lambda}. \qquad (67)$$

Partial differentiation of Eq. (34) for $\psi = 0$ gives:

$$\frac{\partial K^*}{\partial \lambda} = \frac{S}{s + w\Gamma_2}; \qquad (68)$$

and, substituting this expression in (67):

$$\left(\frac{\partial E}{\partial \lambda}\right)_q = \theta S > 0. \qquad (69)$$

Eq. (66) then implies that $(\partial W / \partial \lambda)_{\lambda = 1} < 0$, which establishes Proposition 4. The first-order condition for s* to maximize W for given λ reduces to:

$$\frac{\partial W}{\partial s^*} = \sum_1^n p_i^* \frac{\partial q_i^*}{\partial s} - \frac{dE}{ds} = 0. \qquad (70)$$

Note that:

$$\frac{dE}{ds} = (r \pm w\Gamma_2)\left(\frac{\partial K^*}{\partial s}\right)_q + w \sum_1^n \mathscr{L}_1(q_i, K^*)\frac{\partial q_i^*}{\partial s}. \qquad (71)$$

For $s = \rho_m(\lambda)$, the unregulated monopoly solution is feasible and profit is accordingly maximized by producing q_{mi}, $i = 1, \dots, n$, at minimum cost. Then $K^* = K_m, r + w\Gamma_2(q_{mi}, K_m) = 0$, and $\mathscr{L}_1(q_{mi}, K_m) = C_i'(q_m)$, and Eq. (70) becomes:

$$\left(\frac{\partial W}{\partial s}\right)_{s = \rho_m} = \sum_1^n \{P_i - C_i'\}\left(\frac{\partial q_i^*}{\partial s}\right)_{s = \rho_m}. \qquad (72)$$

If $\lambda < 1$, then $P_i - C_i'(q_m) > 0$, $i = 1, \dots, n$, so $\left(\dfrac{\partial W}{\partial s}\right)_{s = \rho_m} < 0$. This proves Proposition 5.

FOOTNOTES

This work was done while the author was at the University of Pennsylvania and in no way reflects the policy of the U.S. Treasury.

Preparation of this paper was partially supported by a grant from the National Science Foundation through the University of Pennsylvania National Center for

Energy Management and Power and by a grant from the University of California, Los Angeles, Conference on Public Utilities, sponsored by the American Telephone and Telegraph Company. I had the benefit of comments on an early draft by members of the Industrial Organization Workshop of the University of Pennsylvania Department of Economics.

1. Shepherd (17) presents data on the rate schedule of electric utilities in the United States.

2. Theoretical models of peak-load pricing originated with Boiteux (5). For subsequent developments, see Steiner (19), Williamson (21), Brown and Johnson (6), Pressman (16), and Panzar (15). There is also an extensive literature on applications of peak-load pricing models to public utility regulation. References to this literature can be found in Kahn (9).

3. See Klevorick (10), Sheshinski (18), and Bailey (3).

4. Williamson (21) shows how periods of different lengths can be handled.

5. An explicit capacity constraint does not appear in the model; but, if it is assumed that capital and labor can be substituted only over a limited range, then there is a maximum output for each value of capital.

6. Regulatory agencies prohibit "undue" price discrimination. However, this is simply a limitation on the markets that can be distinguished rather than a prohibition on price discrimination, in the economic sense of that term. Oi (14) shows that under certain conditions perfect price discrimination can be achieved by the use of two-part tariffs.

7. Rate-making rests on a determination of the "legal cost of service." This is the sum of "justified expenditures" (cost of goods sold, overhead, depreciation, and all or part of expenditures on promotional activities and R&D) and a "fair" return to the capital employed. Although the statement passes by several problems, it is roughly correct to say that revenue is required to be no greater than the legal cost of service. Regulatory agencies also typically have the authority to exclude "unproductive" capital from the rate base and to restrict particular prices.

8. This set is described for the single period case in Zajac (22) and, in a different way, in McNicol (11).

9. But not marginal revenue as conventionally defined; cf. Eq. (3).

10. The conditions of Proposition 2 are not satisfied in the fixed coefficient case. In particular, the labor requirements function is not differentiable at the cost-minimizing input combination and, away from the "corner," $\mathcal{L}_{12} = 0$. It is worth noting that Wellisz (20) and Bailey (2) assume a fixed coefficient technology and assume (in different ways) that the capacity constraint is binding at the peak-period output. The latter assumption is incorrect if it is viewed, as Wellisz and Bailey seem to, as a consequence of profit maximization. Proposition 1 implies for the fixed coefficient case that it is optimal to hold more capital than is physically required to produce the peak period output.

11. A fixed coefficient technology is explicitly or implicitly assumed by, among others, Steiner (19), Williamson (21), Wellisz (20), Bailey (2), and Bailey and White (4). The assumption of a fixed coefficient technology, however, is often not made explicit. For example, Bailey (2) and Bailey and White (4) assume that operating cost is independent of the quantity of capital employed, which is the case only for a fixed coefficient technology.

12. Electric utilities in the United States typically distinguish residential, commercial, and industrial users. Residential users are typically charged on the basis of block rates. Industrial, and often large commercial users, are usually billed on the basis of two-part tariffs, both parts of which may be block rates.

13. Bailey and White (4) discuss cases in which "inverted" rate structures may arise.

14. This point is developed in McNicol and Phillips (13).

15. The argument of this and the following section is an extension to the multi-period case of the approach developed in McNicol (11).

16. Formally, the assumption is that $\mathscr{L}_{22}(q_i, K) > 0$.

17. Totally differentiate the production function and set $dq_i = 0$ to obtain $dL_i/dK \equiv \mathscr{L}_2 = -\phi_k/\phi_{L_i} < 0$.

18. $\psi(q, K^*) = 0$ is one of the first-order conditions for expense minimization and the structure of the problem is such that the formulas for the derivatives of the expense-minimizing derived demand for capital can be obtained using only this relationship.

19. It may be worth noting that the step between Eq. (44) and Eq. (45) reflects nothing more than the equality of short and long-run marginal cost at a long-run profit maximizing equilibrium.

20. Totally differentiate the production function and set $dK = 0$ to obtain $dL_i/dq_i \equiv \mathscr{L}_1 = 1/\phi_{L_i}$.

21. Note that if $s = r$, at a limit point of B, cost is minimized so $w\mathscr{L}_1(\bar{q}_k K) = C'_k(\bar{q})$.

22. Differentiate $\mathscr{L}_1 = 1/\phi_{L_i}$ to obtain $\mathscr{L}_{11} = -(1/\phi_{L_i})^3 \phi_{L_i L_i}$. The crucial assumption then is $\phi_{L_i L_i} < 0$.

23. Note that dq_0/dP_0 is simply the slope of the peak-period demand function.

REFERENCES

1. Averch, H. and Johnson, L. (December 1962) "Behavior of the Firm under Regulatory Constraint," *American Economic Review*, Vol. 52: 1053–1069.

2. Bailey, E. (July/August 1972) "Peak Load Pricing under Regulatory Constraint," *Journal of Political Economy*, Vol. 80: 662–679.

3. ———. (1973) *The Economics of Regulatory Constraint*, Lexington, Mass., D.C. Heath.

4. Bailey, E. and White, L. (Spring 1974) "Reversals in Peak and Offpeak Prices," *Bell Journal of Economics and Management Sciences*, Vol. 5: 75–92.

5. Boiteux, M. (August 1949) "La tarification des demands en point: Application de la theorie de la vente au coût marginal," *Revue générale de l' électricité*, Vol. 58 (August 1949), translated as "Peak Load Pricing," *Journal of Business*, Vol. 33: 157–179 (April 1960).

6. Brown, G. and Johnson, M. (March 1969) "Public Utility Pricing and Output under Risk," *American Economic Review*, Vol. 59: 119–128.

7. Coase, R. (Spring 1970) "The Theory of Public Utility Pricing and its Application," *Bell Journal of Economics and Management Science*, Vol. 1: 113–128.

8. Houthakker, H. (March 1951) "Electricity Tariffs in Theory and Practice," *Economic Journal*, Vol. 61: 1–25.

9. Kahn, A. (1971) *The Economies of Regulation*, 2 vols., New York, John Wiley and Sons.

10. Klevorick A. (Spring 1971) "The 'Optimal' Fair Rate of Return," *Bell Journal of Economics and Management Science*, Vol. 2: 112–153.

11. McNicol, D. (Autumn 1973) "The Comparative Statics Properties of the Theory of the Regulated Firm," *Bell Journal of Economics and Management Science*, Vol. 4: 428–452.

12. ———. (October 1974) "The Effect of a Change in the Allowed Rate of Return on Productive Efficiency in the Averch-Johnson Model," Discussion Paper No. 288, University of Pennsylvania Department of Economics.

13. ———, and Phillips, A. (July 1975) "Theoretical Models of Rate Regulation: A

Survey and Critique," Discussion Paper No. 77, University of Pennsylvania, Fels Center of Government.

14. Oi, W. (February 1971) "A Disneyland Dilemma: Two Part Tariffs for a Mickey Mouse Monopoly," *Quarterly Journal of Economics*, Vol. 85: 77–96.

15. Panzar, J. (Autumn 1976) "A Neoclassical Approach to Peak Load Pricing," *Bell Journal of Economics*, Vol. 7: 521–530.

16. Pressman, L. (Autumn 1970) "A Mathematical Formulation of the Peak Load Pricing," *Bell Journal of Economics*, Vol. 1:304–326.

17. Shepherd, W. (July 1976) "Marginal Cost Pricing in American Utilities," *Southern Journal of Economics*, Vol. 23: 58–70.

18. Sheshinski, E. (March 1971) "Welfare Aspects of a Regulatory Constraint: Note," *American Economic Review*, Vol. 61: 175–178.

19. Steiner, P. (November 1957) "Peak Loads and Efficient Pricing," *Quarterly Journal of Economics*, Vol. 71: 585–610.

20. Wellisz, S. (February 1963) "Regulation of Natural Gas Pipeline Companies: An Economic Analysis," *Journal Political Economy* Vol. 71: 30–43.

21. Williamson, O. (September 1966) "Peak Load Pricing and Optimal Capacity under Indivisibility Constraints," *American Economic Review*, Vol. 56: 810–827.

22. Zajac, E. (March 1970) "A Geometric Treatment of Averch-Johnson's Behavior of the Firm Model," *American Economic Review*, Vol. 60: 117–125.

INDEX

239

OTHER ANNUAL SERIES OF INTEREST FROM JAI PRESS INC.

Consulting Editor for Economics: Paul Uselding, University of Illinois

ADVANCES IN APPLIED MICRO-ECONOMICS
Series Editor: V. Kerry Smith, Resources for the Future,
Washington, D.C.

ADVANCES IN ECONOMETRICS
Series Editors: R. L. Basmann, Texas A & M University, and George F.
Rhodes, Colorado State University

ADVANCES IN ECONOMIC THEORY
Series Editor: David Levhari, The Hebrew University

ADVANCES IN THE ECONOMICS OF ENERGY AND RESOURCES
Series Editor: Robert S. Pindyck, Sloan School of Management,
Massachusetts Institute of Technology

APPLICATIONS OF MANAGEMENT SCIENCE
Series Editor: Randall L. Schultz, Krannert Graduate School of
Management, Purdue University

RESEARCH IN AGRICULTURAL ECONOMICS
Series Editor: Earl O. Heady, Director, The Center for Agricultural and
Rural Development, Iowa State University

RESEARCH IN CORPORATE SOCIAL PERFORMANCE AND POLICY
Series Editor: Lee E. Preston, School of Management and Center for
Policy Studies, State University of New York, Buffalo

RESEARCH IN ECONOMIC ANTHROPOLOGY
Series Editor: George Dalton, Northwestern University

RESEARCH IN ECONOMIC HISTORY
Series Editor: Paul Uselding, University of Illinois

RESEARCH IN EXPERIMENTAL ECONOMICS
Series Editor: Vernon L. Smith, College of Business and Public
Administration, University of Arizona

RESEARCH IN FINANCE
Series Editor: Haim Levy, School of Business, The Hebrew University

RESEARCH IN HEALTH ECONOMICS
Series Editor: Richard M. Scheffler, University of North Carolina,
Chapel Hill and the Institute of Medicine, National Academy of
Sciences

RESEARCH IN HUMAN CAPITAL AND DEVELOPMENT
Series Editor: Ismail Sirageldin, The Johns Hopkins University

RESEARCH IN INTERNATIONAL BUSINESS AND FINANCE
Series Editor: Robert G. Hawkins, Graduate School of Business
Administration, New York University

RESEARCH IN LABOR ECONOMICS
Series Editor: Ronald G. Ehrenberg, School of Industrial and Labor
Relations, Cornell University

RESEARCH IN LAW AND ECONOMICS
Series Editor: Richard O. Zerbe, Jr., SMT Program, University of
Washington

RESEARCH IN MARKETING
Series Editor: Jagdish N. Sheth, University of Illinois

RESEARCH IN ORGANIZATIONAL BEHAVIOR
Series Editors: Barry M. Staw, Graduate School of Management,
Northwestern University, and Larry L. Cummings, Graduate School of
Business, University of Wisconsin

RESEARCH IN PHILOSOPHY AND TECHNOLOGY
Series Editor: Paul T. Durbin, Center for the Culture of Biomedicine and
Science, University of Delaware

RESEARCH IN POLITICAL ECONOMY
Series Editor: Paul Zarembka, State University of New York, Buffalo

RESEARCH IN POPULATION ECONOMICS
Series Editors: Julian L. Simon, University of Illinois, and Julie DaVanzo,
The Rand Corporation

RESEARCH IN PUBLIC POLICY AND MANAGEMENT
Series Editors: Colin C. Blaydon, Institute of Policy Studies and Public
Affairs, Duke University, and Steven Gilford, Chicago

ALL VOLUMES IN THESE ANNUAL SERIES ARE AVAILABLE
AT INSTITUTIONAL AND INDIVIDUAL SUBSCRIPTION RATES.
PLEASE WRITE FOR DETAILED BROCHURES ON EACH SERIES

A 10 percent discount will be granted on all institutional standing orders placed directly
with the publisher. Standing orders will be filled automatically upon publication and will
continue until cancelled. Please indicate which volume Standing Order is to begin with.

◢Ⴝi **JAI PRESS INC.**
P.O. Box 1285
165 West Putnam Avenue
Greenwich, Connecticut 06830

(203) 661-7602   Cable Address: JAIPUBL.

Research in Law and Economics

A Research Annual

Series Editor: **Richard O. Zerbe, Jr., SMT Program, University of Washington.**

Volume 2.   **Spring 1980**   **Cloth**   **Ca. 250 pages**   **Institutions: $ 27.50**
ISBN 0-89232-131-8   **Individuals: $ 14.00**

CONTENTS: Economic Analysis of Federal Election Campaign Regulation. *Burton A. Abrams and Russel F. Settle, University of Delaware.* **The Quality of Legal Services: Peer Review, Insurance and Disciplinary Evidence,** *Sidney L. Carrol and Robert J. Gaston, University of Tennessee.* **Price Discrimination in the Municipal Electric Industry,** *Daniel R. Hollas, University of Michigan and Thomas S. Friedland, University of Illinois.* **The Resolution of the Compensation Problem in Society,** *Warren J. Samuels and Nicholas Mercuro, Michigan State University.* **Monopoly Profits and Social Losses,** *Levis A. Kochin, University of Washington.* **The Evaluation of Rules for Making Collective Decisions: A Reply to Kormendi,** *T. Nicholas Tideman, Virginia Polytechnic Institute and State University.* **Tort Liability for Negligent Inspection by Insurers,** *Victor P. Goldberg, University of California - Davis.* **The Economics of Property Rights: A Review of the Evidence,** *Louis De Alessi, University of Miami.* **The Problem of Social Cost in Retrospect,** *Richard O. Zerbe, University of Washington.*

Supplement 1 to Research in Law and Economics

Economics of Nonproprietary Institutions

Editor: **Kenneth W. Clarkson and Donald L. Martin, Law and Economics Center, University of Miami.**

                 September 1979 Cloth   **Ca. 330 pages**   **Institutions: $ 28.50**
ISBN 0-89232-132-6   **Individuals: $ 14.50**
CONTENTS: Series Editor's Preface. Editor's Introduction.
MANAGERIAL CONSTRAINTS. **Managerial Behavior in Nonproprietary Organizations,** *Kenneth W. Clarkson, University of Miami.* **The Economics of Seat Pricing: Rose Bowl vs. Hong Kong,** *Steven Cheung, University of Washington.* **Delivered Comments,** *Ross D. Eckert, University of Southern California and H.E. Frech, University of California - Santa Barbara.* **Discussion.** MUTUAL ORGANIZATIONS. **Health Insurance: Private, Mutuals or Government,** *H.E. Frech, University of California - Santa Barbara.* **The Union as a Nonproprietary Firm,** *Donald Martin, University of Miami.* **Delivered Comments,** *Louis DeAlessi, University of Miami and Walter Oi, University of Rochester.* **Discussion.** CHARITABLE ORGANIZATIONS. **Charity and Nonproprietary Organizations,** *Earl Thompson, University of California - Los Angeles.* **Private Goods, Collective Goods: The Role of the Non-Profit Sector,** *Burton Weisbrod, University of Wisconsin.* **Delivered Comments,** *Mark Pauly, Northwestern University and Armen A. Alchian, University of California - Los Angeles.* **Discussion.**
GOVERNMENTAL ORGANIZATIONS. **Is There a Theory of Public Organizations?,** *C. M. Lindsay.* **Producing Knowledge in Nonproprietary Organizations,** *Roland McKean.* **Delivered Comments,** *Andrew Whinston and James Buchanan.* **Discussion. General Discussion. Index.**

◢Ai   **JAI PRESS INC., P.O. Box 1285, 165 West Putnam Avenue, Greenwich, Connecticut 06830.**

Telephone: 203-661-7602   **Cable Address: JAIPUBL**

Research in Law and Sociology

A Research Annual

Series Editor: **Rita J. Simon, Director, Program in Law and Society, University of Illinois.**

Volume 1. Published 1978 Cloth 334 pages Institutions: $ 27.50
ISBN 0-89232-024-9 Individuals: $ 14.50

CONTENTS: **Foreword,** Rita J. Simon. **The Lessons of Self-Estrangement: On the Methodology of Law and Development,** Robert B. Seidman, Boston University School of Law. **Scholars in the Fun House: A Reply to Professor Seidman,** David M. Trubek and Marc Galanter, University of Wisconsin. **A Reply to Professors Trubek and Galanter,** Robert B. Seidman, Boston University School of Law. **Human Rights Development Theory,** Richard P. Claude and James C. Strouse, University of Maryland. **The First Amendment: Symbolic Import-Ambiguous Prescription,** Rozann Rothman, University of Illinois. **Public Support for Civil Liberties in Israel and the United States,** Rita J. Simon and David Barnum, University of Illinois. **Deterrence, Penal Policy and the Sociology of Law,** Jack P. Gibbs, University of Arizona. **The Political Economy of Smack: Opiates, Capitalism and Law,** William J. Chambliss, University of Delaware. **Ascriptions of Dangerousness: The Eye (and Age, Sex, Education, Location and Politics) of the Beholder,** John Monahan and Glorida L. Hood, University of California - Irvine. **Law and Social Status in Colonial New Haven, 1639-1665,** M.P. Baumgartner, Yale University. **Justice, Values and Social Science: Unexamined Premises,** Edward Seidman, University of Illinois. **Causal Analysis and the Legal Process,** Stuart Nagel and Marian Neef, University of Illinois. **School Desegregation and the Social Science: The Virginia Experience,** Adolph H. Grundman, Metropolitan State College - Denver. **The Use of a Personal Service Assistant in the Treatment of Mental Health Problems: A Proposal and Some Speculations,** R. Kirk Schwitzgebel, Harvard University. **Adoption for Black Children: A Case Study of Expert Discretion,** Jacqueline Macaulay and Stewart Macaulay, University of Wisconsin.
    Guest Editor: **Steven Spitzer, Department of Sociology, University of Northern Iowa, Cedar Falls.**

Volume 2. October 1979 Cloth 345 pages Institutions: $ 27.50
ISBN 0-89232-111-3 Individuals: $ 14.00

CONTENTS: I. LAW IN CAPITALIST SOCIETY. **The Creation of Law,** William J. Chambliss, University of Delaware. **The State, Law and Economic Organization,** Warren J. Samuels, Michigan State University. **The Technocratic Administration of Justice,** Wolf V. Heydebrand, New York University. **The Context Within Which Legal Theory Developed in England During The Nineteenth Century: An Introduction,** David Sugarman, School of Law, University of London. II. SOCIAL THEORY AND THE LAW. **Marx's Theory of Bourgeois Law,** Gary Young, School of Law, University of Wisconsin - Madison. **Ideology and Rationality in Max Weber's Sociology of Law,** Piers Beirne, University of Connecticut. **The Limit of Idealism: Max Weber and the Sociology of Law,** Maureen Cain, Brunel University, England. **The Sociology of Law of Gurvitch and Timasheff: A Critique of Theories If Normative Regulation,** Alan J. Hunt, School of Law, Middlesex Polytechnic, England. III. LAW AND SOCIAL CHANGE. **Notes Towards a Theory of Punishment and Social Change,** Steven Spitzer, University of Northern Iowa. **Public Interest Law: Crisis of Legitimacy or Quest for Legal Order Autonomy,** Shirley Castelnuovo, Northeastern Illinois University. **Access of Latin American Rural Poor to The Public Allocation of Goods and Services,** Joseph R. Thome, University of Wisconsin - Madison.

Advances in Law and Child Development*

Studies in Public Policy

A Research Annual

Series Editor: **Robert L. Sprague, Director, Institute for Child Behavior and Development, University of Illinois.**

The aim of this series is to examine the broad area of law and public policy pertaining to child development. Public policy includes a comprehensive range of governmental activities including legislation at both federal and state levels, litigation in the courts, regulations issued by federal agencies, regulations and guidelines issued by state agencies particularly for the public schools, significant advances in research development areas likely to impinge in the near future on public policy decisions, and important cross-cultural aspects of child development as revealed by public policy decision in other nations. The first volume deals with topics of current interest. The federal government issued regulations concerning research with children a few months ago, and this topic is discussed by three authors with different perspectives. Laws and litigation concerning public schools is an active area as is litigation regarding mental health programs. The final chapters in the volume include a cross-cultural review of laws concerning children and a discussion of how the child develops an understanding first of rules then law.

Volume 1.   **Spring 1980**   **Cloth**   **Ca. 300 pages**   **Institutions: $ 27.50**
ISBN 0-89232-094-X   **Individuals: $ 14.00**

CONTENTS: The Report and Recommendations of the National Commission for the Protection of Human Subjects: Research Involving Children, Barbara Mishkin, National Commission for the Protection of Human Subjects of Biomedical and Behavioral Research. **Policy Guidelines and Peer Review at the National Institute of Mental Health and the National Institute of Child Health and Human Development,** Natalie Reatig, National Institute of Mental Health. **Regulation of Research Involving Children: Origins, Costs and Benefits,** Linda S. Wilson, University of Illinois. **State Statutory and Administrative Regulation of Pupil Placement in Public Schools,** Laura Means Pope Miller, University of California - Los Angeles. **The Right of Minors to Medical Treatment (According to Israeli Law),** Amnon Carmi, Judge in Haifa, Israel. **The Administration of Services to Individuals Who Are Developmentally Disabled: The Impact of Litigation in Illinois,** Arthur Dkystra, Jr., Illinois Department of Mental Health and Developmental Disabilities. **Law and the Child's Evolving Legal Conscience,** Peter Scharf, University of California - Irvine. **Index.**

*Previously advertised as: **Advances in Law and Psychology**

A 10 percent discount will be granted on all institutional standing orders placed directly with the publisher. Standing orders will be filled automatically upon publication and will continue until cancelled. Please indicate which volume Standing Order is to begin with.

◢Ai **JAI PRESS INC., P.O. Box 1285, 165 West Putnam Avenue, Greenwich, Connecticut 06830.**

Telephone: 203-661-7602   **Cable Address: JAIPUBL**

JEI

JOURNAL of ECONOMIC ISSUES

Published by the Association for Evolutionary Economics and Michigan State University

The symposium on the Chicago School which appeared in two issues of the *JEI* has been reprinted with four additional chapters covering a constructive critique.

The Chicago School of Political Economy

paperbound   *537 pp./$8.00*

Available from: Division of Research, 5-J Berkey Hall, Michigan State University, East Lansing, MI 48823.

Contributions from recent issues include:

Philip A. Klein, "American Institutionalism: Premature Death, Permanent Resurrection"; W. Paul Strassmann, "Can Technology Save the Cities of Developing Countries?" Roger M. Troub, "Kenneth Boulding: Economics from a Different Perspective"; Laurence S. Seidman, "Would Tax Shifting Undermine the Tax-Based Incomes Policy?" Gunnar Myrdal, "Institutional Economics"; Robert Solo, "The Neo-Marxist Theory of the State"; Thomas R. De Gregori, "Technology and Economic Dependency"; Ivan C. Johnson, "A Revised Perspective of Keynes's *General Theory*"; and Kenneth Fraundorf, "Competition and Public Policy in the Nursing Home Industry."

Annual membership dues are: $6.00 per year for three years, student; $15.00, individual; and $20.00, library. Add $2.50 per year for subscriptions outside North America. Inquiries to: AFEE/JEI Fiscal Office, 509 Business Administration Building, The Pennsylvania State University, University Park, PA 16802.